REINHOLD NIEBUHR

OUTSTANDING CHRISTIAN THINKERS

Series Editor: Brian Davies OP

The series offers a range of authoritative studies on people who have made an outstanding contribution to Christian thought and understanding. The series will range across the full spectrum of Christian thought to include Catholic and Protestant thinkers, to cover East and West, historical and contemporary figures. By and large, each volume will focus on a single 'thinker', but occasionally the subject may be a movement or a school of thought.

Brian Davies OP, the series editor, is Vice-Regent of Studies at Blackfriars, Oxford where he also teaches philosophy. He is a member of the Theology Faculty of the University of Oxford and tutor in theology at St Benet's Hall, Oxford. He has lectured regularly at the University of Bristol, Fordham University, New York, and the Beda College, Rome. He is Reviews Editor of *New Blackfriars*. His previous publications include: *An Introduction to the Philosophy of Religion* (OUP, 1982); *Thinking about God* (Geoffrey Chapman, 1985); and he was editor of *Language, Meaning and God* (Geoffrey Chapman, 1987).

Existing titles in the series:

Anselm
G.R. Evans

Denys the Areopagite
Andrew Louth

The Apostolic Fathers
Simon Tugwell OP

Yves Congar
Aidan Nichols OP

Reinhold Niebuhr
Kenneth Durkin

Planned titles in the series include:

Bede
Benedicta Ward

Aquinas
Brian Davies OP

Karl Rahner
Willam Dych SJ

John Calvin
John Platt

George Berkeley
David Berman

Teresa of Avila
Rowan Williams

REINHOLD NIEBUHR

Kenneth Durkin

MOREHOUSE PUBLISHING
HARRISBURG, PENNSYLVANIA

Published in North America by
Morehouse Publishing
Harrisburg, Pennsylvania

First published in North America 1990

British Library Cataloguing in Publication Data
Durkin, Kenneth
Reinhold Niebuhr.—(Outstanding christian thinkers)
1. Christian theology.   Niebuhr, Reinhold, 1892–1971
I. Title   II. Series
230'.092'4

ISBN 0–8192–1490–6 (hardback)
0–8192–1489–2 (paperback)

Typeset by Colset Private Limited, Singapore
Printed and bound in Great Britain by
Biddles Ltd, Guildford and King's Lynn

Contents

To B.

I would like to thank the trustees of the Christendom Trust for funding the research which made it possible to write this book.

I would also like to thank Fergus Kerr OP.

Editorial foreword

St Anselm of Canterbury once described himself as someone with faith seeking understanding. In words addressed to God he says 'I long to understand in some degree thy truth, which my heart believes and loves. For I do not seek to understand that I may believe, but I believe in order to understand.'

And this is what Christians have always inevitably said, either explicitly or implicitly. Christianity rests on faith, but it also has content. It teaches and proclaims a distinctive and challenging view of reality. It naturally encourages reflection. It is something to think about, something about which one might even have second thoughts.

But what have the greatest Christian thinkers said? And is it worth saying? Does it engage with modern problems? Does it provide us with a vision to live by? Does it make sense? Can it be preached? Is it believable?

This series originates with questions like these in mind. Written by experts, it aims to provide clear, authoritative and critical accounts of outstanding Christian thinkers from New Testament times to the present. It will range across the full spectrum of Christian thought to include Catholic and Protestant thinkers, thinkers from East and West, thinkers ancient, mediaeval and modern.

The series draws on the best scholarship currently available, so it will interest all with a professional concern for the history of Christian ideas. But contributors will also be writing for general readers who have little or no previous knowledge of the subjects to be dealt with. Volumes to appear should therefore prove helpful at a popular as well as an academic level. For the most part they will be devoted to a single thinker, but occasionally the subject will be a movement or a school of thought.

In this book Kenneth Durkin deals with the thinking of Reinhold Niebuhr, who has been hailed as the greatest of all American theologians. Niebuhr found in Christianity a tool for understanding the history of the world in the twentieth century, but his view and projects differed considerably over time. He started by preparing Christians for the collapse of capitalism and ended by preparing American politicians for their role in a world where capitalism had renewed itself and embarked on massive expansion. Kenneth Durkin traces and reflects on the progression in Niebuhr's thinking. He displays the continuities and changes in what Niebuhr had to say and he examines the relationship between Niebuhr's developing theology and his varying political stances. Taking account of developments since Niebuhr's death, he also provides a critique of Niebuhr's method and an assessment of his importance. The result should aid readers to situate Niebuhr in the contemporary world.

Brian Davies OP

Bibliography

Books by Reinhold Niebuhr

Does Civilization Need Religion? A Study in the Social Resources and Limitations of Religion in Modern Life (New York, 1927).

Leaves From the Notebook of a Tamed Cynic (Chicago, 1929).

The Contribution of Religion to Social Work (New York, 1932).

Moral Man and Immoral Society: A Study in Ethics and Politics (New York, 1932).

Reflections on the End of an Era (New York, 1934).

An Interpretation of Christian Ethics (New York, 1935).

Beyond Tragedy: Essays on the Christian Interpretation of History (New York, 1937).

Christianity and Power Politics (New York, 1940).

The Nature and Destiny of Man: A Christian Interpretation, I: *Human Nature* (New York, 1941).

The Nature and Destiny of Man: A Christian Interpretation, II: *Human Destiny* (New York, 1943).

The Children of Light and the Children of Darkness: A Vindication of Democracy and a Critique of its Traditional Defense (New York, 1944).

Discerning the Signs of the Times: Sermons for Today and Tomorrow (New York, 1946).

Faith and History: A Comparison of Christian and Modern Views of History (New York, 1949).

The Irony of American History (New York, 1952).

Christian Realism and Political Problems (New York, 1953).

The Self and the Dramas of History (New York, 1955).

Love and Justice: Selections from the Shorter Writings of Reinhold Niebuhr, ed. D. B. Robertson (Cleveland and New York, 1957).

Pious and Secular America (New York, 1958).

The Structure of Nations and Empires (New York, 1959).

Essays in Applied Christianity, ed. D. B. Robertson (New York, 1959).

Reinhold Niebuhr on Politics, ed. Harry R. Davis and Robert C. Good (New York, 1960).

Man's Nature and His Communities (New York, 1965).

Faith and Politics, ed. Ronald H. Stone (New York, 1968).

Justice and Mercy, ed. Ursula M. Niebuhr (New York and Toronto, 1974).

Young Reinhold Niebuhr: His Early Writings, ed. William G. Chrystal (St Louis, 1977).

The Essential Reinhold Niebuhr: Selected Essays and Addresses, ed. Robert McAfee Brown (New Haven and London, 1986).

As co-author

A Nation So Conceived (with Alan Heimart) (New York, 1963).

The Democratic Experience: Past and Prospects (with Paul E. Sigmund) (New York, 1969).

A complete list of Reinhold Niebuhr's published works is contained in: D. B. Robertson (ed.), *Reinhold Niebuhr's Works: A Bibliography* (revised edition, New York, 1983).

This bibliography also contains a comprehensive list of book-length critical studies, and a sample of articles and dissertations about Reinhold Niebuhr.

A selection of books about Reinhold Niebuhr's life and works

June Bingham, *Courage to Change: An Introduction to the Life and Thought of Reinhold Niebuhr* (New York, 1961). Written by an admiring friend. There are no source references and it has difficulty with Niebuhr's theology.

Ernest F. Dibble, *Young Prophet Niebuhr: Reinhold Niebuhr's Early Search for Social Justice* (New York, 1983). Based on a Ph.D dissertation.

Richard Wightman Fox, *Reinhold Niebuhr: A Biography* (New York, 1985). Assiduously researched.

Gordon Harland, *The Thought of Reinhold Niebuhr* (New York, 1960).

Hans Hofmann, *The Theology of Reinhold Niebuhr* (New York, 1956).

Paul Merkley, *Reinhold Niebuhr: A Political Account* (Montreal and London, 1975). Attempts to ground the politics in the theology, and sets both in the context of Niebuhr's life.

T. Minnema, *The Social Ethics of Reinhold Niebuhr: A Structural Analysis* (Kampen, 1958). This book, and Harland's and Hofmann's, are attempts to create a systematic theology out of Niebuhr's unsystematic theology.

Ronald H. Stone, *Reinhold Niebuhr: Prophet to Politicians* (Nashville, 1972). Suggests a method of improving and updating Niebuhr's Christian Realism.

Collections of critical essays

Charles W. Kegley and Robert W. Bretall (eds), *Reinhold Niebuhr: His Religious, Social, and Political Thought* (New York, 1956). Niebuhr has written an introduction to the volume and a response to the criticisms.

Harold R. Landon (ed.), *Reinhold Niebuhr: A Prophetic Voice in Our Time* (Greenwich, Conn., 1962).

Journal of Religion 54 (1974) (Chicago) devotes the entire October issue to essays on Reinhold Niebuhr. It was later edited by Nathan A. Scott and published as *The Legacy of Reinhold Niebuhr* (Chicago, 1975).

Books which contain lengthy discussions of Reinhold Niebuhr's life and/or thought

Dennis P. McCann, *Christian Realism and Liberation Theology* (New York, 1982). Explores Niebuhr's 'mythical method' and compares it to Liberation Theology's use of biblical theology.

Donald B. Meyer, *The Protestant Search for Political Realism* (Berkeley and Los Angeles, 1960). Places Niebuhr's life in its historical context.

Michael Novak, *The Spirit of Democratic Capitalism* (New York, 1982). Argues that Niebuhr would support Novak's contention that capital requires less political restraint in order to accumulate in the private sphere.

Judith Plaskow, *Sex, Sin and Grace: Women's Experience and the Theologies of Reinhold Niebuhr and Paul Tillich* (New York, 1983). Exposes Niebuhr's patriarchal ideology.

Charles C. West, *Communism and the Theologians* (London, 1958). More ammunition for the Cold War.

Other books either cited in the text or of related interest

Selig Adler, *The Uncertain Giant: 1921–1941* (London, 1965).

John Agnew, *The United States in the World-Economy* (Cambridge, 1987).

Sydney E. Ahlstrom, *A Religious History of the American People* (New Haven and London, 1972).

Gustaf Aulén, *Christus Victor: A Historical Study of the Three Main Types of the Idea of the Atonement* (ET; London, 1931).

Paul A. Baran and Paul M. Sweezy, *Monopoly Capital: An Essay on the American Economic and Social Order* (New York, 1966).

Eberhard Bethge, *Dietrich Bonhoeffer: Theologian, Christian, Contemporary* (ET; London, 1970).

David Brody, *Workers in Industrial America: Essays on the Twentieth Century Struggle* (New York, 1980).

Daniel Chirot, *Social Change in the Twentieth Century* (New York, 1977).

Oscar Cullmann, *The Christology of the New Testament* (ET; London, 1959).

Foster Rhea Dulles, *America's Rise to World Power 1898–1954* (New York, 1954).

Frederick Engels, *Anti-Dühring* (Moscow, 1954).

Ludwig A. Feuerbach, *The Essence of Christianity* (London, 1854).

Sidney Fine, *Laissez Faire and the General-Welfare State: A Study of Conflict in American Thought 1865–1901* (Chicago, 1956).

Stanley Hauerwas, *The Peaceable Kingdom* (Notre Dame, 1983).

Stanley Hauerwas, *Against the Nations: War and Survival in a Liberal Society* (Minneapolis, 1985).

William James, *Varieties of Religious Experience* (New York, 1902).

Walter Kasper, *Jesus the Christ* (ET; New York and London, 1976).

Charles W. Kegley and Robert W. Bretall, *The Theology of Paul Tillich* (New York, 1952).

Søren Kierkegaard, *The Sickness Unto Death* (ET; Walter Lowrie, Princeton, 1941).

Peter King, *Modern World Affairs* (London, 1984).

Thomas S. Kuhn, *The Structure of Scientific Revolutions* (Chicago, 1962).

Walter LaFeber, *America, Russia, and the Cold War 1945–1975* (New York, 1976).

William E. Leuchtenburg, *The Perils of Prosperity 1914–1932* (Chicago, 1958).

C. T. McIntire (ed.) *God, History, and Historians: Modern Christian Views of History* (New York, 1977).

D. C. Macintosh (ed.), *Religious Realism* (New York, 1931).

David McLellan, *Marxism and Religion: A Description and Assessment of the Marxist Critique of Christianity* (London, 1987).

John Macquarrie, *Principles of Christian Theology* (London, 1966).

Shailer Mathews, *The Social Teaching of Jesus* (New York, 1897).

Shailer Mathews, *Jesus on Social Institutions* (New York, 1928).

H. Richard Niebuhr, *The Kingdom of God in America* (Chicago, 1937).

Wolfhart Pannenberg, *Jesus, God and Man* (ET; London, 1970).

Gerhard von Rad, *Old Testament Theology* (2 vols) (ET; London, 1962).

Karl Rahner, *Theological Investigations* 5 (ET; London, 1966).

Walter Rauschenbusch, *Christianity and the Social Crisis* (New York, 1907).

Walter Rauschenbusch, *Christianizing the Social Order* (New York, 1912).

Walter Rauschenbusch, *A Theology for the Social Gospel* (New York, 1917).

Richard Rovere, *The American Establishment* (New York, 1962).

Gordon Rupp, *Christologies and Cultures: Towards a Typology of Religious Worldviews* (New York, 1974).

Harvard Sitkoff (ed.), *Fifty Years Later: The New Deal Evaluated* (New York, 1985).

Newman Smyth, *Christian Ethics* (New York, 1892).

John W. Spanier, *American Foreign Policy Since World War II* (New York, 1980).

Pierre Teilhard de Chardin, *The Future of Man* (ET; London, 1964).

Denys Turner, *Marxism and Christianity* (Oxford, 1983).

Immanuel Wallerstein, *The Modern World-System* (New York, 1974).

Immanuel Wallerstein, *The Modern World-System II* (New York, 1980).

Immanuel Wallerstein, *The Capitalist World Economy* (Cambridge, 1979).

Immanuel Wallerstein, *Historical Capitalism* (London, 1983).

Immanuel Wallerstein, *The Politics of the World Economy* (Cambridge, 1984).

Max Weber, *The Protestant Ethic and the Spirit of Capitalism* (ET; London, 1930).

Robert H. Zieger, *American Workers, American Unions, 1920–1985* (Baltimore and London, 1986).

Abbreviations

1

Limitations of Liberalism

Gustav Niebuhr was seventeen years old when he ran away from his father's farm in Hardissen bei Lage in northwest Germany. He arrived in New York in 1881 and went on to Freeport, Illinois, where he took a job as a farmhand. His boss was a German immigrant called William Hummermeier, and he had married Gustav's cousin, Karoline Luttmann. Although Hummermeier was like a second father Gustav soon left the farm to experience life in the city of Chicago. He found work in a sewing machine factory, but within two years he was pleading with Hummermeier to take him back. He brought some city ways back to these tranquil surroundings and used to shock Karoline with the industrial language he had picked up.

Then one Sunday in the spring of 1883, after a forceful sermon at the Salem Evangelical Church, he quit the abrasive language and announced that he wanted to enter the ministry. Hummermeier sent him to Eden Theological Seminary and paid the fees, and Gustav was ordained in 1885 at the age of twenty-two. He was sent to New Orleans for a brief period, and then he was moved to northern California to assist Edward Jacob Hosto, a second generation German immigrant. Gustav took over the church in San Francisco which Hosto had built up, and Hosto worked in a new mission in the foothills of Mount Shasta. Gustav needed a woman to help him with the parish, and Hosto's daughter Lydia left Mount Shasta and they were married. Lydia was seventeen years old.

They had two children while still in San Francisco, Hulda and Walter. Karl Paul Reinhold was born after they had moved to

Wright City in Missouri, in 1892. Two years later their fourth child, Helmut Richard, was born. The family then moved on again, this time to St Charles, Missouri, and eight years later on to Lincoln, Illinois in 1902.

Reinhold was ten when he told his father that he intended to enter the ministry, and his father responded with Greek lessons every Saturday morning. In addition, all the children were introduced to the rudiments of Harnack's theology. His first school was Elmhurst which was a small denominational college for ministers' sons. After four years he moved to Eden Theological Seminary, but during his graduation year his father went into a coma and died at the age of fifty. This was just a few years before insulin injections were discovered. Despite the emotional upset Reinhold managed to graduate and enter Yale Divinity School.

During vacations Reinhold took charge of the Sunday services in Lincoln. He received a BD in 1914 and an MA in 1915, and desiring 'relevance rather than scholarship' he decided against pursuing an academic career and entered the active ministry. He was sent to Bethel Evangelical in Detroit, a church with about 65 members. He took his widowed mother to live with him and to help him run the parish.

LIBERAL PROTESTANTISM

The prevailing ethos in the academic institutions of the Protestant religion in America towards the end of the nineteenth century and in the early years of the twentieth century could be described as 'liberal'. In America today there is confusion about the meaning of the word. In the 1988 presidential campaign the conservative Republican George Bush attacked the Democratic candidate Michael Dukakis for being a 'liberal', and Dukakis spent most of his campaign trying to shield himself from these accusations. The implications were that he was soft on criminals, weak on the drugs issue, and so on. But towards the end of the campaign he took the word on the offensive with him. Sure he was a liberal, just like Roosevelt (FDR) was a liberal, and Truman was a liberal, and Kennedy was a liberal!

Originally the term 'liberal' as applied to Protestantism in America covered a variety of Christian responses to developing scientific and historical criticism. Beginning with his father through to graduating from Yale, Niebuhr was educated in the liberal

Protestant tradition and he set out to apply these values in Detroit. Niebuhr's work cannot therefore be understood without some knowledge of this background.

The movement began in Europe with F. D. Schleiermacher (1768–1838) who described the basic religious experience and consequently the basis of theology as the 'feeling of absolute dependence'. Albrecht Ritschl (1822–89) stressed the importance of historical criticism by attempting to base Christianity on the historical record of the New Testament where Jesus is conceived as the archetypal illustration of human supremacy over nature. Another influential figure was Adolf von Harnack (1851–1930) whom Gustav Niebuhr admired. These theologians were leading exponents of a movement which possessed a number of defining characteristics. American liberalism shared the European characteristics but with different emphases.

Liberal Protestantism assumed that all religions are expressions of an essential feature of human nature and therefore Christianity is merely one religion among others. It is, however, regarded as the highest possible form of religion. Second, the myths and miracles of the scriptures were subject to radical historical criticism. They were 'demythologized' and 'desupernaturalized'. Third, the theology was influenced by contemporary philosophical thought. Fourth, the movement attempted to distinguish between the religion of Jesus and the religion about Jesus with the implication that 'true' Christianity consisted of reproducing the religion of Jesus. Fifth, it tended to emphasize the timeless 'essence' of Christianity rather than the historical uniqueness of the central events. Finally, it tended to regard sin as ignorance due to the lack of knowledge.

In America, Yale Divinity School and Chicago Divinity School became prominent centres of liberal Protestantism around the turn of the century. At Yale there were three important Congregationalist liberals, William R. Harper, Frank Porter, and Benjamin Bacon. The latter two, along with the Canadian Baptist D. C. Macintosh, were noted by Niebuhr as the theologians who had most impressed him. At Chicago the leading light was Charles Clayton Morrison. He founded the journal *Christian Century* (1908) which published many of Niebuhr's articles.

The spirit of the movement was one of generosity and tolerance towards divergent opinions and a desire for intellectual liberty. Liberal theologians wished to liberate theology from the obscurantism and creedal bondage of Christian orthodoxy. It answered to a number of names such as the 'New Theology' or 'Progressive

3

Orthodoxy' or 'Modernism'. The emphasis was upon human freedom and a natural human capacity for altruistic action. As in Europe, sin was considered to be ignorance, poor education, and poor social conditions in general. It was a social concept with a social cure. Moral education, improved living standards, and a strong emphasis on ethical preaching would eventually overcome most of the evils caused by sin. Traditional church dogma and the sacraments were passed over lightly. There was great interest in the reunion of Christendom whose divisions were considered to be scandalous, but this did not extend to the Catholic Church. The Reformation was a liberation movement freeing Christianity from an ecclesiastical feudal tyranny. The biological evolutionary process was thought of as ultimately benefiting the human race. This led to great optimism about the future of the human enterprise. The apparent success of the democratic form of government coupled with scientific and technological advances created the impression that Christianity meant knowingly participating in the building of the Kingdom of God on earth. This also tended to coincide with the belief that the American nation had been elected to play a leading role in the realization of this Kingdom.

The Old Testament was interpreted as the growing awareness of the Jewish people and the main aim of New Testament scholarship was to clarify the religion of Jesus. There were widely diverging views about interpreting the divinity of Jesus, and the interpretation of the Pauline corpus often proved difficult. God's activity in the world, his immanence, was emphasized rather than his transcendence. Horace Bushnell (1802–76), the creative and influential New England Puritan theologian, argued that natural and supernatural were consubstantial and observable in all forms of being. The supernatural and the spiritual tended to be identified, and the spiritual was considered to be equivalent to consciousness. Thus the intellectual side of humanity was emphasized. Bushnell's *Christian Nurture* (1847, revised 1861) is the classic expression of the power of education in the formation of the Christian personality.

There were three general divisions in liberal Protestantism corresponding to the three emphases of the ethical, experiential, and philosophical dimensions. The group which tended to stress the importance of ethics held that ethical conduct is the supreme and sufficient religious act. Foremost among these was Walter Rauschenbusch. The group which concentrated on the experiential dimension in the tradition of Schleiermacher and William James was represented by Bushnell and Newman Smyth. The third group was more interested in metaphysics and the philosophy of religion, represented by Josiah Royce, D. C. Macintosh, and Henry Nelson Wieman.

On attitudes towards the scriptures, the creeds, and the Church, there were two types of approach which cut across these divisions. Liberals were either 'Evangelical' or 'Modernistic'. Evangelical liberals held on to traditional beliefs and scriptural interpretations except where modern knowledge required adjustments to be made. Biblical study remained a central feature, and historical study of Christian doctrine was also emphasized. The term 'Progressive Orthodoxy' was chosen by the Andover Seminary for its manifesto title of 1884. The movement was represented by such people as W. N. Clark, W. A. Brown, and Walter Rauschenbusch. This approach was more widely supported than the more radical European type modernistic and relativistic approach which considered the Bible to be one religious document among many and the Christian faith as one religion among many. The Chicago Divinity School provided the best examples of this approach in Shailer Mathews, Shirley J. Case, and Wieman.

Sydney E. Ahlstrom neatly summarizes what had caused the theological response known as liberal Protestantism in America:

The intellectual challenge with which liberal theologians grappled was awe-inspiring in its magnitude. From every sector the problems converged: the Enlightenment's triumphant confidence in science and in nature's law, the multiform romantic heresy that religion was essentially feeling or poetic exaltation, that nature was a cathedral and communing in it a sacrament; the disruption of the Creation story and the biblical time scale; the evolutionary transformation of the old notion that the world's orderliness bespoke God's benevolent design; the historical criticism of the bible, the relativisation of the Church and its teachings, the denial of human freedom and moral responsibility, and even the abolition of those eternal standards by which right and wrong, the false and the true were to be judged. All this had to be faced, moreover, in the new urban jungles of the Gilded Age, where Americans seemed to be chiefly bent on getting and spending and laying waste their powers. Never in the history of Christianity, it would seem, was a weak and disunited Christian regiment drawn into battle against so formidable an alliance, under such unfavourable conditions of climate and weather, and with so little information on the position and intent of the opposition.[1]

Within liberal Protestantism there was a subordinate element known as the Social Gospel movement. The impetus for this movement was the social conditions associated with industrialism, and the theological influences were European. Ritschl's concept of the Kingdom of God as the ideal community at the end of time establishing a basis for ethical activity was one predominant influence. For him the moral vocation was the development of the autonomous personality in dedicated service to the whole. Another important influence was the English Christian Socialism of F. D. Maurice and Charles Kingsley. Their theology, combined with practical activities such as the founding of colleges for the working classes, and the setting up of workers' co-operatives, provided an obvious inspiration to the American predilection for practical results.

Apart from having to attack social practices which led to serious social dislocations, the Social Gospellers had to attack the general feeling of contempt for poverty which was often encouraged by the Puritan ethic. In the most extreme cases it was considered sinful to be poor. Henry Ward Beecher, for example, even though he had raised money in his pulpit for guns to arm the anti-slavery movement, in 1870 said: 'Looking comprehensively through city and town and village and country, the general truth will stand, that no man in this land suffers from poverty unless it be more than his fault—*unless it be his sin.* . . .'[2] William Graham Sumner, the Broad Church Episcopal minister of Morristown, New Jersey, developed Herbert Spencer's Social Darwinism in such a way as to give the Puritan ethic scientific respectability.

Josiah Strong (1847–1916) became the first leading figure of the Social Gospel movement. He was a Congregationalist, and a great organizer of social concerns. His *Our Country: Its Possible Future and Its Present Crisis* became the most influential Social Gospel book of the nineteenth century. But Walter Rauschenbusch is the man who is normally presented as typifying the movement. He spent eleven years in the ministry of a German Baptist congregation in the proximity of New York's Hell's Kitchen, a centre for drop-outs and social misfits. He fought for playgrounds and housing, and he gathered a group of like-minded disciples into the Brotherhood of the Kingdom between 1893 and 1915. Rauschenbusch insisted that religion and ethics are one and inseparable. The whole Social Gospel

6

message is expounded in his book: *Christianity and the Social Crisis* (1907). His *Christianizing the Social Order* (1912) calls for a reform of capitalism. In Philadelphia, in 1908, 33 denominations brought the Federal Council of Churches of Christ in America into existence thus institutionalizing the Social Gospel movement. This first conference was a debate on 'The Church and modern industry'. It was a movement striving to convert those people who attended church into social concern. However, most American Protestants felt that the Social Gospel and the Federal Council were dangerous. The movement was dubbed 'the praying wing of Progressivism'.

DETROIT 1915—28

Niebuhr spent thirteen years at Bethel Evangelical Church. The church had been founded three years before his arrival for the German immigrant community. The liturgy was conducted in the German language until 1919 when it became the first congregation in the Michigan District to discontinue the practice.

In addition to the normal duties of the ministry Niebuhr became very active in public life in connection with both civic duties and Social Gospel work. For example, he was the chairman of the Mayor's Committee on Racial Relations set up to alleviate post-war racial tensions in the city. The vice-chairman was a Jew called Fred Butzell. Niebuhr later wrote of him: 'Fred Butzell's capacity for magnanimity and social shrewdness was so impressive that it began my long love affair with the Jewish people'.[3]

In the Social Gospel movement Niebuhr became friendly with leading activists such as Sherwood Eddy, Kirby Page, and Will Scarlett. Eddy and Page were founder members of The Fellowship for a Christian Social Order (FCSO) in New York in 1921. By 1926 Niebuhr was the chairman of this organization. Annual conference discussions covered such topics as economic and industrial relations, international relations, race relations, and family relations. In 1928 this movement dissolved itself into the Fellowship of Reconciliation (FOR). Niebuhr had already become the chairman of the FOR in 1923. This body was not a Social Gospel inspiration. It had been founded in 1917 by Henry T. Hodgkin, an English Quaker, as a communion of American ministers who had abandoned their pulpits because of American entry into the Great War.

Niebuhr became involved with the FOR largely as a result of a

visit he made to the German Ruhr in 1923. It was one of Sherwood
Eddy's annual ventures into Europe, and Niebuhr had been invited.
He wrote in his diary:

> The Ruhr cities are the closest thing to hell I have ever seen. I
> never knew that you could see hatred with the naked eye, but
> in the Rhur one is under the illusion that this is possible. The
> atmosphere is charged with it. The streets are filled with
> French soldiers . . . French officers race their automobiles
> wildly through the streets with sirens blowing shrilly. If you
> can gain the confidence of the Germans so that they will talk
> they will tell you horrible tales of atrocities, deportations, sex
> crimes, etc. . . . This is as good a time as any to make up my
> mind that I am done with the war business. (LNTC, p. 68)

Apart from international relations and pacifism, Niebuhr was
involved in the struggle for industrial justice. Two years after
visiting the Ruhr Niebuhr paid a visit to hell on his own doorstep.
He wrote in his diary:

> We went through one of the big automobile factories today.
> So artificial is life that these factories are like a strange world
> to me though I have lived close to them for many years. The
> foundry interested me particularly. The heat was terrific. The
> men seemed weary. Here manual labour is a drudgery and toil
> is slavery. The men cannot possibly find any satisfaction in
> their work. They simply work to make a living. Their sweat
> and their dull pain are part of the price paid for the fine cars
> we all run. And most of us run the cars without knowing what
> price is being paid for them. . . . Beside the brutal facts of
> modern industrial life, how futile are all our homiletical
> spoutings! (LNTC, pp. 99–100)

Detroit was the centre of the American automobile industry, and
since this industry was one of the two main enterprises responsible
for the prosperity of the 1920s Niebuhr was in a favourable position
to analyse social factors which would have repercussions
throughout the nation and ultimately the world. Shortly before he
had arrived in the city Henry Ford had installed the first moving
assembly line initiating what the historian William E. Leuchtenburg
termed 'The Second Industrial Revolution', and what modern
sociologists term the 'Fordist' principles of production. Niebuhr
attacked Ford in the pages of *The Christian Century* complaining

8

about the hypocrisy involved in justifying production practices which were essentially unjust.

In 1926 Niebuhr had been one of the founding members of the 'Emergency Committee for Strikers' Relief'. The group decided that relief could only be given to striking workers if the same relief was also given to those workers who would not join the strike. Niebuhr considered this to be naïve generosity which would be of more assistance to employers rather than the workers it was supposed to be helping.

During that same year the American Federation of Labor held its annual conference in Detroit. The consequences of this event created a lasting impression in Niebuhr's mind. 'The incident', he said later, 'vividly portrayed the irrelevance of the mild moralistic idealism, which I had identified with the Christian Faith, to the power realities of our modern technical society.'[4] The AFL was a combination of craft unions unsuited to organizing the workforces of mass production of the type found in Detroit. Nevertheless their intention had been to organize the automobile industry. It was a standard practice of the AFL to encourage the local churches where the annual conference was being held to invite union leaders to address the evening service or a church club. James Myers, the secretary in 1926, submitted a list of prospective labour speakers to the secretary of the Detroit Council of Churches in preparation for the October convention of the AFL. On 13 September, eighteen of Detroit's 200 Protestant ministers met to plan the event. Niebuhr was of course the chairman of the Industrial Relations Commision of the Detroit Council, and he reported that five of the 200 ministers had requested a labour speaker. The city's employers had suggested to ministers that September should be devoted to 'educational work in the pulpits' to prepare congregations for these union speakers. A Detroit newspaper published a cartoon depicting a labouring man in a pulpit clutching a stink bomb. The Board of Commerce wrote an open letter to the press suggesting that if the planned exchange were to take place it would turn Detroit into a closed shop.

Of the five ministers who originally invited speakers three were over-ruled by their church boards. Only Bethel Evangelical and the First Unitarian supported their ministers. In addition the YMCA had cancelled their invitation to a prominent labour leader, William Green. They had been engaged on a fund-raising drive and had received substantial amounts from non-union employers such as Henry Ford, Fisher Bodies, and S. S. Kresge. In the end James

Myers intervened personally and managed to acquire eight pulpits for his speakers by some friendly persuasion.

DOES CIVILIZATION NEED RELIGION?

The Great War and the international tensions which followed it, the 'second industrial revolution', the racial tensions consequent upon the massive immigration of labour into Detroit, and Max Weber's work on the relationship between the Reformation and capitalism,[5] all combined to encourage Niebuhr to reconsider his religious beliefs and practices particularly in relation to his 'liberal' education and the strategies recommended by the Social Gospel. These problems surface in some 40 articles Niebuhr wrote for various journals, and in the pages of his diary, extracts of which were published in 1929 as *Leaves From the Notebook of a Tamed Cynic*. His articles were mainly published in *The Christian Century*, *The World Tomorrow*, and *The Atlantic Monthly*.

The dilemma facing Niebuhr as a Christian minister in an industrial city is expressed in the article he wrote for *Christian Century* in December 1922 entitled 'The Church and the middle class'. It is difficult, he argued, for ministers to take effective action towards social justice when the victims of injustice are not associated with the Christian congregation and when those who benefit most from those injustices are the ones whose money pays the minister's wages and the church's bills.

Towards the end of his Detroit pastorate he gathered together his thoughts and published them in 1928 as: *Does Civilization Need Religion?*[6] Although Niebuhr himself considered *Moral Man and Immoral Society* to be his first major book the former is important because it introduces most of the themes which were to occupy the rest of his life. *Moral Man* is an exposition of one of the themes making its appearance in *Does Civilization Need Religion?*.

Critics of Niebuhr often present him as a man who was constantly changing his mind on important issues. They tend to stress such things as his changes of mind over the question of violence; or his political shift to the left embracing Marxism, and then, after begrudging acceptance of Roosevelt's New Deal policies, shifting again towards the right; or they fasten on to what appears to be his sudden reappraisal of classical theology. This, coupled with his modesty regarding his standing as a theologian, and the randomness and spontaneity of his journalism, tends to create a general

10

impression that these vacillations were the consequence of his failure to provide a coherent and systematic centre to his thought.

However, a careful analysis of Niebuhr's work reveals that the central theme is the importance of establishing an adequate system of coherence, or principle of interpretation, for understanding life and experience. Niebuhr hoped to devise a theological method which would be applicable regardless of the historical setting. He considered that a systematic theology would be too rigid and incapable of incorporating new experience and knowledge. Establishing this framework could only be achieved by recognizing, first of all, that all systems of knowledge and value are, when fully analysed, 'ultra-rational'. In *Does Civilization* Niebuhr stresses the point that all frameworks of coherence which situate the human being in the world are 'ultra-rational'. To put it in its simplest terms, every system of meaning is bounded by mystery. Therefore a true system of meaning must acknowledge within itself the existence of mystery.

The corollary of stating that every system of meaning is bounded by mystery is, for Niebuhr, to say that all human beings are either explicitly or implicitly religious and if they do not express religious adherence overtly then it will express itself in other areas of life and will not be recognized for what it is. Had Niebuhr been formulating his ideas after T. S. Kuhn's *The Structure of Scientific Revolutions* (1962) he would possibly have made use of the term 'paradigm' to characterize the 'ultra-rational framework' as the basic ground or context of interpretation of life's experiences.

The central theme of Niebuhr's theology is closely related to another theme which runs through all his work, and that is the inadequacies of the liberal Protestant tradition. The liberal Protestant religion was a failure, he argued, because not only did it fail to provide an adequate 'ultra-rational' framework, it was also partly to blame for the serious situation confronting modern civilization. That serious situation was the existence of a great mass of exploited workers who were either oblivious of, or hostile towards, religion. On the one hand liberal Protestantism was the ideology of the bourgeois class which had conjured up the industrial working class to fill its factories, and on the other hand it had exposed the working classes to the influence of Marxism. This latter ideology had borrowed elements from classic Christianity which were lacking in the liberal Protestant framework. Since liberal Protestantism had partly caused the problem it did not possess the resources required to solve it.

11

The liberal Protestant religion is therefore, Niebuhr concludes, both ethically and metaphysically (i.e. philosophically) inadequate. It espoused the simple ethic of Jesus with no real knowledge of the brutal social realities of life. It provided an ethic for intra-group relationships but it failed to acknowledge that the ethical problem of society also consisted of inter-group relationships. In short, liberal Protestantism failed to provide religious resources capable of coping with the existence of class war in modern society, and it failed to provide a suitable framework from which to understand collective behaviour at the national and international level.

Another way of describing the religious crisis is to call it 'secularization'. By this Niebuhr means that it is not simply a question of the gradual displacement of the religious paradigm for a positivistic paradigm. This is basically a middle-class conception, discovering that the metaphysical framework of religion, that is its ability to act as a system of knowledge about reality, has become redundant. Secularization is a reality in the sense that a whole class of people has appeared in modern society which is 'almost universally inimical to religion' (DCNR?, p. 2).

This class of people is indifferent or even hostile to religion because industrial relations which govern the lives of these people appear unethical. It is a naked power struggle. They are hostile because they perceive the ethical impotence of religion in regard to the day-to-day affairs of their lives. Furthermore they regard religion as something belonging to the privileged classes. Thus, for the working classes religion is ethical impotence and for the educated classes religion is 'metaphysical maladjustment'.

In the long run religion must be able to impress the mind of modern man with the essential plausibility and scientific respectability of its fundamental affirmations. But the scientific respectability of religious affirmations will not avail if the life which issues from them will not help to solve man's urgent social problems. If modern churches continue to prefer their intellectual to their ethical problems, they will merely succeed in maintaining a vestige of religion in those classes which are not sensitive enough to feel and not unfortunate enough to suffer from the moral limitations of modern society. An unethical civilization will inevitably destroy the vitality of the religion of the victims and the sincerity and moral prestige of the religion of the beneficiaries of its unethical inequalities. (DCNR?, pp. 16, 17)

Niebuhr is therefore saying that the theological reconstruction brought about in response to the development of the modern sciences, while necessary, failed to include an adequate ethical reconstruction capable of dealing with developing social relations associated with the mode of production.

> In the present situation it is more necessary to inquire if and how the peculiar attitudes and the unique life which proceeds from a religious interpretation of the universe may be made to serve the needs of men in modern civilization. (DCNR?, p. 12)

At best liberal religion is capable of inspiring moral goodwill because it values the individual human personality, but modern industry has mechanized social relations to such an extent that moral goodwill is incapable of creating harmony when the complex social relations aggravate the vices that make life inhuman. This brings the Social Gospel movement itself into the area of Niebuhr's critique in the sense that its ethic is informed by the liberal worldview. Essentially it is involved in the same hypocrisy in that it adheres to a worldview that justifies a high appreciation of personality but at the same time fails to develop an ethic which guarantees the worth of personality in society. This prompts Niebuhr to ask the question: 'Is religion the sublimation of man's will to live or can it really qualify the will of the individual and restrain expansive desires?' (DCNR?, p. 32). Is religion necessarily an ideological weapon of the ruling class or can it be harnessed by the exploited class to alleviate exploitation?

Although Niebuhr is threatening to be radical he has not had the time nor the opportunity for overhauling the theological basis of the liberal worldview. He is still trying to pour new wine into old wineskins. This is clear when he relates the words of Paul: 'In Christ there is neither Jew nor Greek, neither bond nor free' to the central tenet of liberal ethics, the 'high evaluation of personality' (DCNR?, p. 37) and the belief that all 'men' are 'brothers because they are all children of God', instead of indicating that the Christian ideal is a classless society. When Niebuhr says: 'The religious interpretation of the world is essentially an insistence that the ideal is real and that the real can be understood only in the light of the ideal' (DCNR?, p. 46), he is referring to religion's projection of the family as the model for the ethical relationships which should govern humanity as a whole.

The races and groups of mankind are obviously not living as a family; but they ought to. And as the necessity becomes more urgent the truth of the ideal becomes more real. (DCNR?, p. 46)

Niebuhr has not realized some of the limitations imposed upon an ethic by this projection. Within this framework the ethical task becomes one of devising ways in which the classes of society can live harmoniously without bringing into question the whole basis of class division. While religion functions to 'subject every moral value to comparison with a more perfect moral ideal' (DCNR?, p. 51), it is still locked into the liberal worldview if the perfect moral ideal is a harmony of classes instead of the abolition of classes. But Niebuhr allows for this possibility:

Of course the absolute perfection of God is itself conditioned by the imperfect human insight which conceives it. (DCNR?, p. 51)

The answer to this objection is really only a vague repetition:

Yet in its highest form religion does inculcate a wholesome spirit of humility which gives the soul no peace in any virtue while higher virtue is attainable. (DCNR?, p. 51)

Niebuhr claims that religion 'is the courageous logic which makes the ethical struggle consistent with world facts' (DCNR?, p. 50), and this is the nearest Niebuhr comes to establishing the need for what he will later refer to as the positive validation of the Christian faith. For now his recommendation of the religious worldview rests on negative validation. Only by analysing the inadequacies of possible alternatives can the value of the religious worldview be affirmed.

The two alternative ethical systems to be considered are characterized as 'Stoic' and 'absolute determinist'. Essentially Niebuhr is referring to the liberal conception of the autonomy of ethics (the belief in the separation of ethics from religion), and the Marxist ethic which is related to a deterministic view of the world in the sense that the logic of history inevitably leads to the proletariat gaining ownership of the means of production.

The secular ethic of modern civilization issues in a prudential morality which does not go beyond the encouragement of altruism within the social group.

That is precisely what Stoicism did. It is just this pride in partial achievement which complicates the moral problem of

> modern life: for our ethical difficulties are created by the very tendency of reasonable ethics to make life within groups moral and never to aspire to the moral redemption of inter-group relations. Humility is therefore a spiritual grace which has value not only for its own sake but for its influence upon social problems. (DCNR?, p. 55)

Such an ethical system will eventually lead to despair because collective forces are greater than the restraining factors of a prudential ethic. A liberal ethic without religion (an 'irreligious ethical idealism') lacks the essential spirit of humility. It therefore bases itself on illusions about human nature, and when reality punctures these illusions it leads to despair.

Niebuhr finds that the Marxist ethical system is more consistent than the 'Stoic' type in that it has little confidence in the moral integrity of human nature and can find no moral meaning in existence as a whole. But this consistency leads to the absurdity of desiring social reconstruction in the interests of the one class and ruthless conflict becomes the only method of achieving this. Thus modern life is characterized as a tension between an ethic which fails to acknowledge that its system does not cater for the real social situation where personality is not valued and an ethic which does not theoretically value the personality because it interprets modern life as a ruthless struggle between two social groups.

The conclusion is that neither ethical system is a suitable basis for social reconstruction. Religious resources are needed to provide the overall framework which finds value in the personality and creates the requisite spiritual grace to avoid the pitfall of pride in partial achievement. But how can religion become a social resource if the predominant form of the religion is aligned with those social forces whose interest lies in preserving the status quo?

The answer to this question involves a digression on the evolution of the liberal Protestant religion. Whereas the religion sees itself as an attempt to return to the religion of Jesus it is actually a complex of 'many streams of thought'. Building on Weber's 'Protestant ethic' thesis Niebuhr finally concludes that the liberal Church is a composite of Roman imperialism, Greek sophistication, Nordic tribalism and individuality, and the prudential ethics of industrial civilization. Therefore to harness the resources of the religion is a complex operation:

> If the modern church is to become an instrument of social redemption, it must learn how to divorce itself from the moral

temper of its age even while it tries to accommodate itself to the intellectual needs of a generation. (DCNR?, p. 73)

Only by divorcing itself from the moral temper of prudential ethics will religion operate in accordance with its purpose:

The function of religion is to nerve men for an ethical achievement when it promises no immediate returns. (DCNR?, p. 74)

Religion must serve as a moral absolute capable of discovering and amending the limitations of prudential morality. 'It serves the world best when it maintains a high disdain for the world's values' (DCNR?, p. 71).

In order to release the ethical wisdom of Christianity from its predominant expression as liberal Protestantism it requires 'astute intelligence'. 'Astute intelligence' is essentially the knowledge that the 'unethical character of group action is determined as much by the partial virtues as by the vices of individuals' (DCNR?, p. 133). Modern ethics fails to understand that collective action is not the sum of individual action and imperialism is not the sum of individual imperialistic tendencies.

Niebuhr's exposition of 'astute intelligence' prefigures much that is to appear later in *Moral Man*. Here, in *Does Civilization*, there is a discussion on the State as the most unethical of all groups because it is able to command unqualified loyalty. The virtue of self-sacrifice is transmuted in this collective into unethical power. The virtue of democracy is transmuted into the unethical activity of imperialism because it endows patriotism with a higher moral sanction. In this context, too, Niebuhr introduces reflections on American foreign policy by criticizing its isolationism:

The relation of America to the rest of the world is a perfect example of the moral peril in the new intricacies of modern civilization. (DCNR?, p. 137)

The exercise of 'astute intelligence' also involves recognition of the elements of truth in the Marxist analysis.

Economic determinists [Niebuhr's terminology for Marxists] show a superior discernment in recognizing that in a civilization which is forced to organize its economic life across national boundaries the conflict of interest between classes does become more significant than the conflict between states. (DCNR?, p. 145)

But the same intelligence also involves the assumption that Marxist dreams for world unification are unrealizable because the middle classes 'will never be annihilated even by the most ruthless class conflict' (DCNR?, p. 146).

> A society of nations is impossible without those ultra-rational attitudes which either instinct or religion must create and which in the case of this final venture is beyond the resources of natural instincts—except in the event of a threat from some other planetary community. (DCNR?, p. 153)

In short, the religious imagination must be capable of providing a metaphysical framework which is in turn capable of inspiring ethical activity which works towards the creation of a world community, a world society of nations. The two problems with this are, first, that Niebuhr has previously characterized the world in terms of class divisions being of more consequence than national boundaries. Second, Niebuhr himself admits that the 'religious imagination and astute intelligence' (DCNR?, p. 139) that are necessary for the solution of the problem 'are incompatible with each other. . . . The necessary partnership and the inevitable conflict between the religio-moral and the rational forces is obvious in both the political and the economic problems of the present age' (DCNR?, p. 140). However, a few pages further on and Niebuhr has forgotten about their incompatibility. The anarchic desires of nations, he writes, 'can be subdued only by the most astute intelligence united with a high moral passion' (DCNR?, p. 161). 'High moral passion' of course depends on the metaphysical acceptability of the religious framework.

The cause of these confusions and contradictions is the tension between Niebuhr's desire to be radical without developing what is meant by the 'ultra-rational framework'. In the end he settles for a fairly benign conclusion which does not match the depth of some of the analysis found in *Does Civilization*. He writes:

> If religion cannot transform society, it must find its social function in criticizing present realities from some ideal perspective and in presenting the ideal without corruption, so that it may sharpen the conscience and strengthen the faith of each generation. (DCNR?, p. 163)

And politically he advocates the benign policies of the British labour movement where 'a gradual transfer of political power and social privilege to the ranks of the workers is being made with much less peril of social convulsion than in any nation of the continent' (DCNR?, p. 149).

The final chapter of *Does Civilization* (apart from the conclusion which reiterates the arguments of the book) is an attempt to clarify what is meant by the 'ultra-rational framework'. This theme becomes a constant feature of Niebuhr's work and it can be summarized as the attempt to reverse the trend observed by Auguste Comte in his 'Law of Three Stages'. Comte taught that modern civilization had developed through three major stages roughly corresponding to the theological, philosophical, and scientific. At the beginning of *Does Civilization* Niebuhr wrote:

> The various sciences can momentarily afford to indulge in their various determinisms because the prestige of metaphysics as a coordinator of the sciences has been destroyed for the time being. Each science is therefore able to disavow the authority of metaphysics and work upon the basis of its own metaphysical assumptions, which are usually unreflective and generally deterministic. But the bulk of new knowledge which has momentarily destroyed the authority of any unifying perspective must in time be mastered by philosophical thought. (DCNR?, pp. 10, 11)

Niebuhr's thesis is that modern civilization lacks a unifying perspective and that 'biblical religion' is the most adequate source for this unifying perspective. This is, of course, developed in later works. In the present book Niebuhr expresses the theme as follows:

> What is needed is a philosophy and a religion which will do justice both to the purpose and to the frustration which purpose meets in the inertia of the concrete world, both to the ideal which fashions the real and to the real which defeats the ideal, both to the essential harmony and to the inevitable conflict in the cosmos and in the soul. (DCNR?, p. 209)

The 'frustrations of purpose' such as the anarchic nature of international politics, the exploitative nature of industrial organization, and the triumph of the positivistic framework for situating humanity in the world, all lead to a despair of outraged conscience and a cynicism of disillusioned intelligence. If religion is to survive these onslaughts, argues Niebuhr, it will not do so in its liberal Protestant form, a religion which is 'reduced to restraining the petty vices of a small minority which profess it' (DCNR?, p. 192). Niebuhr had been trained for a parish armed with an out-of-date

18

religion. It was still 'crowing about its victories over the ethical and religious prejudices of the Middle Ages' (DCNR?, p. 206) when the practical needs of the present demanded an ethic which is not individualistic and a religion which is not optimistic. Niebuhr's brother, H. Richard Niebuhr, summed up the liberal Protestant religion of his seminary days as 'A God without wrath brought men without sin into a kingdom without judgement through the ministrations of a Christ without a Cross'.[7]

Finally it is interesting to look at two contrasting estimates of Niebuhr's first book. Although Paul Merkley in *Reinhold Niebuhr: A Political Account* (1975) has produced a valuable and informative book, and although he correctly argues that Niebuhr's politics were firmly grounded in his theological worldview, nevertheless the comments on *Does Civilization* are particularly inept. It is difficult to accept that when Merkley says 'It is the only one of his [Niebuhr's] books which reads like the product of a working clergyman. . . . It shows us a man trying to make sense of his experience with church people', he is actually referring to *Does Civilization* and not *Leaves*.

A more sensible appraisal is to be found in Ronald H. Stone's *Reinhold Niebuhr: Prophet to Politicians* (1972). Stone writes:

> The rest of his [Niebuhr's] career was, in a sense, the elaboration of issues raised in Detroit as he saw piety and moral idealism cloak the brutalities of an expanding industrial order.

Stone notes that Niebuhr 'avoided a decisive break with liberalism' and concludes:

> It is not as thoroughly realistic as his mature writings, nor does it reflect the mastery of political theory which occurred later.[8]

Perhaps the main fault of Niebuhr's first book is the familiar one of attempting too much. Niebuhr wants to solve all the problems of modern civilization in 200 pages. It must be remembered, however, that Niebuhr's congregation had grown to over 800 members, and that he had been granted the time to write the book through the generosity of his friend Sherwood Eddy who had paid for an assistant minister. When Niebuhr was writing the book he would not have known whether such an opportunity would appear again. Stone is correct: practically all the major themes Niebuhr developed throughout his life's work are present in this first book, and his subsequent works can be seen as illuminating first one and then another facet of this book.

The critique of liberal Protestantism runs through all his works but always with the intention of utilizing its positive contributions. The necessity for providing a unifying perspective for life and experience based on religion becomes the primary subject of the two volumes of *The Nature and Destiny of Man*; the importance of reassessing the ethic of Jesus becomes the main subject of *An Interpretation of Christian Ethics*; the theme of collective interactions utilizing moral virtues for immoral collective ends becomes the main theme of *Moral Man and Immoral Society*; the necessity of incorporating the 'astute intelligence' of Marxist social analysis into a religious worldview is dealt with in *Reflections on the End of an Era*; and the two themes of the possibilities and limitations of a world community, and the role of American foreign policy, both seen in a theological light, are dealt with in detail in Niebuhr's works of the 1950s and 1960s.

NOTES

1 Sydney E. Ahlstrom, *A Religious History of the American People* (New Haven and London, 1972), p. 774.
2 *Ibid.*, p. 789.
3 Reinhold Niebuhr, *Man's Nature and his Communities* (New York, 1965), p. 12.
4 Charles W. Kegley and Robert W. Bretall (eds), *Reinhold Niebuhr: His Religious, Social, and Political Thought* (New York, 1956), pp. 5, 6.
5 *The Protestant Ethic and the Spirit of Capitalism* by Max Weber was a strong influence on Niebuhr's thought. He read the 1920 revised edition in the original German. The work was first published in 1904.
6 Niebuhr had found more time to write when his friend Sherwood Eddy paid the wages of an assistant at Bethel Evangelical.
7 H. Richard Niebuhr, *The Kingdom of God in America* (New York, 1937), p. 193.
8 Ronald H. Stone, *Reinhold Niebuhr: Prophet to Politicians* (Nashville, 1972), p. 44.

2

Communism and Christianity

In the 1920s Reinhold Niebuhr had been at the centre of the industrial expansion which had initiated the national prosperity of that decade. Shortly before his arrival in Detroit Henry Ford had revolutionized the mode of production in a way that kept workers at their posts and walking was transformed into an unproductive human activity. Soon after Niebuhr arrived in New York, the commercial centre of that prosperity, the raging bull market crashed and announced the onset of the Great Depression.

Niebuhr had been offered a job at Union Theological Seminary by the President of Union, Henry Sloane Coffin, in 1928. He first became acquainted with Coffin in 1923 at a Student Volunteer Convention in Detroit in 1923. But Sherwood Eddy's persuasive style had also been operating behind the scenes because he paid Niebuhr's salary for three years until a permanent opening became available. This opening occurred through the death of Professor Gaylord White. Niebuhr's initial impact at Union can be gauged by the knowledge that Yale also offered him a full professorship before the permanent vacancy became available.

Niebuhr's work during the 1930s must be seen in the context of the Great Depression and the New Deal on the domestic scene, and American isolationism ànd the growth of European fascism on the national and international scene.

THE GREAT DEPRESSION

By the end of the 1920s the 'invisible hand' which manages self-interest in the capitalist mode of production was experiencing difficulties with a rapidly expanding economy. Coolidge's deflationary policies had withdrawn government funds from the economy, retail sales were down in 1927, and the housing market had stabilized in 1926, all signs that the boom of the 1920s was faltering. But the volume of sales on the New York Stock Exchange had risen from 236 million shares in 1923 to 1,125 million in 1928. The frequent saying that 'everyone was in the market' indicated the high level of interest there was in this form of activity. 'In the 1920s', writes William E. Leuchtenburg, 'clerks and bootblacks talked knowingly of American Can or Cities Service and bought five shares "on margin".'[1] Capitalism had become popular and, as October 1987 has shown, it has a way of dealing with this popularity. From early September to 13 November 1929 industrial stocks had their value cut in half. By July 1932 they had dipped from a high of 452 to 58. US Steel had dropped from $262 per share to $22, General Motors from $73 to $8.

The Great Depression was under way. In those three years the total national income had sunk to $41.7 billion from $87.4 billion. Almost 70,000 businesses had gone into liquidation, and 5,000 banks collapsed. In 1930 there were 4,000,000 people unemployed, in 1931 the figure had doubled, and by 1932 12,000,000 people, 25 per cent of the workforce, were out of work. It has been estimated that there were 28,000,000 with no income. Hundreds of thousands lost their homes and their farms; there were 1,000,000 hobos, there were bread lines and hunger riots. People built houses out of tar-paper and sheets of tin and sited them on urban garbage dumps.

President Hoover expanded the government role in managing economic affairs to protect the system and to assist its recovery, but he was fearful lest his efforts led to openings for the left-wing political forces. Hoover tried to control the business cycle, but failed. He had relied too heavily on the private sector to alleviate the problems. By 1932 the general mood of the people was that they would accept a greater role for central government to deal with the crisis.

Left-wing radicals had been forecasting the demise of the capitalist system and the previously hidden internal contradictions of the system were now laid bare for all to witness. The next stage of the theory was the bit where all the exploited and suffering masses rise up against their oppressors. The Communist Party became active among the unemployed, blacks, students, unorganized and unskilled workers, farmers, and intellectuals, helping to prepare them for their social role. The largest organization on the left, the Socialist Party, was led by Norman Thomas, the former Presbyterian minister. This party offered a large-scale programme to deal with the crisis, but it favoured non-violent revolution. The party advocated extensive public ownership and democratic control of basic industries.

However, those who had most to lose from the collapse of the system were also aware of the script and a system of repression developed which involved industrialists, private police forces, politicians, and state and local law enforcement officials, often backed up by federal agencies. Conservatives frequently called for the suppression of agitation and disorder. The military and the police were given special anti-riot training. They were taught how to disrupt meetings, break strikes, and suppress demonstrations of the unemployed and farmers. The most dramatic suppression was in Washington during the summer of 1932. Twenty thousand unemployed war veterans had descended on the capital to persuade Roosevelt to bring forward the payment of a bonus promised for 1945. General Douglas MacArthur and the US army forced them out of the city. The military forces and the police remained loyal to the established institutions.

NIEBUHR AND THE LEFT

Despite the numerous articles Niebuhr had written in the 1920s, his extensive travels in Europe, his pastoral ministry in the industrial city of Detroit, and the competent book he had written on the problems of modern civilization, he had been very apprehensive about coping with his new job at Union.

Looking back from the 1950s he wrote:

> This was a hazardous venture [teaching at Union], since my reading in the parish had been rather undisciplined and I had no scholarly competence in my field, not to speak of the total field of Christian theology. My practical interests, and the devoting of every weekend to college preaching prevented any rapid acquisition of competence in my ostensible speciality. It

was therefore a full decade before I could stand before a class and answer the searching questions of the students at the end of a lecture without the sense of being a fraud who pretended to a larger and more comprehensive knowledge than I possessed. Meanwhile the pressure of academic discipline and my companionship with the distinguished members of the Union faculty did serve to introduce me to the main outlines of biblical faith and to the classical texts of Christian theology.[2]

From 1928 Niebuhr became associated with the Socialist Party. His name is included in a list of members of the faculty at Union who supported Norman Thomas in the presidential election of that year. In the weeks following the election Thomas realized that his campaign would need a broader appeal if he were to stand any chance of making the White House. He therefore sought to establish a new party by approaching the League for Industrial Democracy. Niebuhr was a member of this organization but it contained many who were not Socialist Party members. The discussions between the two groups led to the formation of the League for Independent Political Action in December 1928. Niebuhr was a member of this group from its inception.

In 1930 Niebuhr visited Russia with Sherwood Eddy and a group of American church ministers. Eddy had been to Russia on a number of previous occasions and in 1934 he published two books, *The Challenge of Russia* and *Russia Today*. He had also lived in India for fifteen years, and he had travelled and taught in China. Niebuhr was very impressed with the Russian people and their efforts to build a socialist society. He produced five articles for *The Christian Century*.[3]

In 1931 Niebuhr was instrumental in forming the Fellowship of Socialist Christians. It was based on the principle that the Christian ethic was most adequately expressed and applied in society in socialist terms. It pledged support for the rights of the exploited and the disinherited. It raised funds by levying an income tax on its members. Practical activities included assisting with the organization of labour in parishes, and helping to organize farming co-operatives.

In the summer of 1930 he accepted the Socialist Party nomination for the state senate ticket from the city's Nineteenth District. The Union directors did not approve of this venture. Niebuhr came third in the election with 1,480 votes. The Democratic candidate won with 20,271 votes, and the Republican was second with 10,947 votes.

Niebuhr received 190 fewer votes than the previous Socialist candidate two years earlier.

In May of the following year he became engaged to Ursula Keppel-Compton, a Union postgraduate student from England. She was an Anglican, and an Oxford divinity graduate. They were married on 22 December 1931 at Winchester Cathedral. Ursula was to become a decisive influence in Niebuhr's life and thought.

SOCIAL JUSTICE AND PHILANTHROPY

Niebuhr's second book was a publication of the Forbes Lectures he had delivered at the New York School of Social Work in 1930. It was given the title *The Contribution of Religion to Social Work* and published in 1932. It investigates the religious basis of ethical social activity. It takes the line that charity and philanthropy help to solve immediate problems, but this type of social activity presupposes a given social order and never analyses the underlying causes of social inequalities.

In the introduction to Niebuhr's final book, *Man's Nature and His Communities* (1966), he mentioned some 'revisions' he had made during a lifetime's work. He admitted that he had become increasingly impressed with certain aspects of the Jewish and Catholic faiths, in particular their awareness of the social substance of human existence. In his early work, however, Niebuhr acknowledged this aspect of the Catholic faith. Although he never wavered from completely accepting the necessity of the Protestant Reformation he wistfully remarked that it was inevitable that the Reformation should destroy some of the finest fruits of the mediaeval social spirit. In its attack on sacramentalism, the centre of what was considered to be the cause of externalism (the hypocritical outward demonstration of faith), it had failed to appreciate the virtues of a sacramental conception of the Church in relation to the problems of society. A sacramental Church possessed a feeling for both the Church and the State as a social organism which the more individual types of religious expression lacked. Protestant individualism had found it difficult to preserve what was best of the mediaeval tradition, and in its insistence on justification by faith apart from works it had fostered the attitude that social work was a hypocritical desire for the 'filthy rags of righteousness'. The insistence of Luther that love should be a spontaneous expression and should not be under the guidance or coercion of an institution encouraged the development of philanthropic individuals but it was not conducive to the emergence of a general system of charitable concern. It tended to be haphazard and sporadic. Furthermore, Luther's exhortation (1525) that peasants who had appealed to the gospel for support in their cause for justice should be killed like mad dogs, and that any who died attacking peasants were assured of heaven, provided evidence of blindness to social problems and the weakness and class character of this type of religion. Calvinism too has never been able to overcome the tendency to regard poverty as the consequence of laziness, and to consider it as a punishment inflicted by a righteous God because of sin.

By contrast, argues Niebuhr, the Catholic church during the Reformation developed charities in forms which laid the foundations for modern institutional charities.

> The highest development of its institutional program occurred in France where two great leaders, Francis of Sales and Vincent de Paul, particularly the latter, placed the hospitals under the administration of the sisters of charity; organized sons of charity; created institutions for foundlings, and, in general, exploited the social resource of religion for philanthropic ends. A man like Vincent is a good type of the combination of mystic and man of affairs which Catholic piety so frequently produces. . . . Whatever the weaknesses of institutional charity from the perspective of the total ethical and social problems of a society, it is difficult to escape the conclusion that the superiority of Catholicism over Protestantism in this field of religious activity represents a real virtue of Catholicism—its sense of responsibility for the social realities and the high type of ethical insight developed by the monastic movement. (CRSW, pp. 11, 15)

The brief survey of religious attitudes towards social responsibilities leads Niebuhr to postulate the principle that it is the duty of the Church to pioneer in the field of social work by discovering new social obligations. Once injustice has been located the duties should become the concern of society as a whole.

The real problem confronting Niebuhr addressing a group of future social workers who are to cushion some of the disastrous effects of the recession is: how can a religion which is based on a conception of absolute perfection, and which therefore convicts every present actuality of inadequacy in comparison to this perfection, so often and so easily accept the social situation in which it stands? Why should liberal Christianity seem so divorced from reality?

Niebuhr provided four possible reasons to explain this incongruous fact of Christian life. First, while a sense of the absolute should convict every actuality of imperfection, very often the perfection is conceived so far above the possible that it merely encourages a pessimistic attitude. The present world is so corrupt because of the Fall that no social activity can redeem the situation. Second, the Christian doctrine of humility and self-sacrifice was used as a weapon to stifle the resistance of the dispossessed and the underprivileged. Attempts by these groups to assert their rights were considered to be expressions of selfishness. Christ was held up as an example of non-resistance in the face of extreme provocation. The lower social orders were encouraged to be like Christ by not resisting the unjust situation in which life had inadvertently placed them. Third, the Christian religion has a sense of natural determinism which breeds acceptance of a given social order. The world is under the providence of God, and it is governed by his wisdom and power. It was the Father of Jesus who gave Pilate his power. Niebuhr cites Paul's exhortation to obey civil authority (Rom 13:1–2). Fourth, the Christian religion is largely concerned with ethical attitudes and motives which belong to individual behaviour in small social spheres. Consequently, it finds great difficulty in translating this ethical concern to an entire social organization. Christian ethics do not easily translate into an understanding of group ethics and group nature. It is therefore lacking in its basis for a concept of justice because justice must be a careful calculation of conflicting rights and competing responsibilities.

Following these general considerations concerning the social inadequacy of the Protestant religion, all of which would receive much fuller treatment in Niebuhr's subsequent works, he next focuses on the reasons for the acuteness of the problem in America. In all other industrialized countries, he points out, there are State provisions for the weaker social groups such as the unemployed and the old. But in America, which is informed by the liberal creed, the religious dimension of which is the predominant form of Protantism, religious philanthropy is considered sufficient to meet the needs of social deprivation. However, philanthropy is only capable of providing for the needs created by sudden emergencies or catastrophes, and can only attach itself to those people who are

most obviously in distress. It cannot cope with the social dislocations which accompany such a rapid industrialization as that
experienced in America.

> America alone of all industrial nations has failed to learn the
> lesson that voluntary charity is insufficient to establish justice
> or to alleviate actual human suffering when society deals with
> a basic problem of distribution of wealth. Charity flows only
> where human need is vividly displayed and where it is
> recognized in intimate contact . . . [I]t cannot do justice to
> social needs which arise out of the maladjustments of a
> mechanical civilization and are obscured amidst the imper-
> sonal relationships of an urban civilization . . . [It] results
> merely in monumental hypocrisies and tempts selfish people to
> regard themselves as unselfish. (CRSW, p. 28)

The Protestant Church is a middle-class institution, and these
classes are naïve in outlook and oblivious of the deeper social
problems. It is inevitable that their religious institution should be
tainted with their social conservatism and their complacency. The
middle classes have failed to realize that religious benevolence
involves far more than philanthropy. Jesus was critical of the
benevolence of the rich because philanthropy is a combination of
pity and power in the same act.

How then, asks Niebuhr, is it possible for religious benevolence to
become more than mere philanthropy? To answer this question he
embarks on a careful analysis of the nature of the Christian religion
and both its positive and its negative social consequences. The most
important feature of religion is the framework or paradigm it
provides for the ordering of life. This is Niebuhr's central theme
throughout his work. In later works the constituent elements of this
framework will be isolated and analysed but here Niebuhr is content
to describe the paradigm as an 'ultra-rational affirmation'. The
clarification of meaning which Niebuhr offers does not fully
support all that he wishes to express with the phrase. Niebuhr draws
on the conversion experience in the individual life to illustrate the
point. This is probably drawn from the work of William James who
wrote:

> To be converted, to be regenerated, to receive grace, to
> experience religion, to gain an assurance, are so many phrases
> which denote the process, gradual or sudden, by which a self
> hitherto divided, and consciously wrong, inferior or unhappy,

28

becomes unified and consciously right, superior and happy, in consequence of its firmer hold upon religious realities.[4]

Niebuhr argues that in the case of conversion it is most apparent that religion is a potent force in bringing order out of confusion. If it is countered that people seem to get along quite happily without any religious conversion, conception, or belief, Niebuhr replies that as long as convictions 'transcend the bounds of rationality, as must all ultimate confirmations about what life is or ought to be, they are religious' (CRSW, p. 38). The faculty of human reason can only operate after certain ultra-rational presuppositions have been made.

Niebuhr is not very informative in this early phase of his theology as to what he means precisely by 'ultra-rational presuppositions', but an example of activity performed in accordance with ultra-rational presuppositions is 'moral preference'. He explains:

> Our ultimate moral preferences are ultra-rational. They need not in every case be consciously religious, and they are frequently accepted so uncritically and are so thoroughly a part of the world which we share with the group in which we live, that their rationality is taken for granted. But if they are traced back, they are always found ultimately to be derived from a total view of what life is and ought to be, which is religious. (CRSW, p. 70)

All moral preferences are related to a 'total view of life'. Therefore, if there is social injustice, and the moral preferences are satisfied with the alleviation of some immediate distress but remain oblivious of the root causes, then the 'total view of life' or the 'ultra-rational' framework must be inadequate. Niebuhr clarifies this thesis later when 'academic pressure' sharpens his discipline, and he eventually locates the contours of this framework, this 'total view of life', in the Jewish and Christian scriptures. This is the origin of what he later refers to as the 'mythical method'. But at this stage the most positive description of the character of religious faith is:

> [I]t must remain ultra-rational to the end, because it makes the world that is external to man relevant to his enterprise, an absurdity according to every canon of pure rationality, but an absurdity which has in it the root of ultimate wisdom, and which is perpetrated by many unconsciously, even while they disavow it. (CRSW, p. 44)

Since religious affirmation involves more than the assent of reason

29

the effects are greater than affirmations of rational principles can cause. Niebuhr describes two other features of the Christian religion which might be of interest to students of social work. First, there is the therapeutic value of the assurance of grace and forgiveness. This is a religious way of saying that there are healing and redemptive forces at work in life. Second, there is the sense of security which religion provides which in turn cultivates an essential optimism about life. This very often inspires a spirit of heroic courage.

The resources of religion operate best in intimate communities. 'Religion has achieved its highest triumphs in family life' (CRSW, p. 48).

> Where religion encourages attitudes of mutual forbearance and forgiveness, and where it emphasizes the sacramental character of the family union, thereby assuming its permanence, an atmosphere is created in which difficulties are resolved much more easily than in a purely secular atmosphere. (CRSW, p. 48)

However, if the religious impulse fails to locate any direct and immediate application the impulse loses virtue and potency. Therefore if religious benevolence is to become more than mere philanthropy it must be combined with an 'astute social intelligence' in order to guide the will through complex social relations. In other words it is important for adherents to become politically and socially aware if the religious impulse is to prove beneficial to the social order. The implication of this is that 'astute social intelligence' will be required in any description of the 'ultra-rational' framework, or the 'total view of life'.

The best example of the religious impulse combined with 'astute social intelligence' is to be found, argued Niebuhr, in the activities of the Communist Party. This bluntness has a serious intent apart from prodding an audience of student social workers whose attention may have drifted while listening to a preacher. By studying Communism it is possible to discover the weaknesses of the liberal Protestant religion. The work of the Communist Party among the underprivileged and the disadvantaged was singled out for eloquent appraisal, quite a contrast to the paltriness of philanthropy:

> If we want to see the power of religion functioning creatively, with all the furor and all the fervor which characterize vital religion, with all the peril of fanaticism which belongs to anything creative, we have to turn to a sect which is most

vociferous in disavowing religion—the communists. (CRSW, p. 59)

In contrast to 'proletarian religion', the middle-class religion, liberal Protestantism, is characterized by its sentimentality. Its vision of a loving God does not lead to a true conception of human sin. Its view of human nature is too one-dimensional. Niebuhr then contrasts the middle-class religion with 'classical religion'. By this expression he means the 'classical texts of Christian theology' usually typified in the works of St Augustine, but in this context the meaning is not clarified. Classical religion is contrasted with middle-class religion because the former has a paradoxical estimate of human nature. In the insight of 'true religion' God is not only a loving God, but also a holy God. Human beings are not only children of God, they are also sinners. In 'classical religion' there is always this double emphasis, human godliness and human sinfulness. These insights cannot be expressed in rational language. 'True religion' can only be expressed using 'poetic symbolism'.

Therefore in order for religious benevolence to exceed the bounds of mere philanthropy the true nature of religion must first be determined. This involves combining 'astute intelligence' with the poetic symbolism of 'classical religion'. Astute intelligence involves employing some elements of the Marxist critique of modern society, and poetic symbolism involves a reappraisal of classical religion because of its paradoxical estimate of human nature. To express this in its simplest terms: the modern Protestant religion must recreate a 'total view of life' by reassessing the paradoxical estimate of human nature found in classical theology and combining this with elements of the Marxist worldview which guides social activism in the appropriate direction. When Niebuhr develops this argument it involves a deeper investigation into what is meant by 'poetic symbolism' and a greater appreciation of the biblical source of this symbolism.

Niebuhr's route back to the Bible follows two paths. He accepts the science of historical criticism of the biblical texts completely rejecting reactionary fundamentalist exegesis. Second, since Marxism is considered to be a religion ultimately derived from the Christian worldview its critique of liberalism must be a religious critique. Marxism is therefore considered to contain elements of the Christian religion which liberal Protestantism either overlooked or interpreted incorrectly. This element is the eschatological dimension, the scriptural teachings and symbols about the end of this form of worldly existence.

In *Contribution*, though, Niebuhr is concerned with the ethical activity of the Communist 'religion' rather than its 'eschatology'. Astute social intelligence involves the recognition that all essential power in modern society is economic power, and the basis of economic power is the power of ownership. Economic power is always capable of bending political power to its will. Therefore: '[t]he private ownership of the productive processes and the increased centralization of the resultant power in the hands of a few, make inevitably for irresponsibility' (CRSW, p. 77).

But here, and throughout Niebuhr's work, 'productive processes' always refers to factories and machines. Niebuhr does not consider the ownership of the human labour which has been sold to the capitalist in such a way as to create 'surplus value'. Niebuhr never questions the possibility of the unethical nature of this basic social relation of capitalism.

Niebuhr concludes *Contribution* by comparing social workers with religious philanthropists. The purpose of this is to make the point that both forms of social activity are related to the prevailing individualistic ideology. The weakness of this ideology is related to its lack of an eschatological element, and this weakness has been revealed by an atheistic religion.

He argued that if social workers were content with making life more sufferable within the structure of an unjust social order then this activity belongs to the same category as religious philanthropy. The one great cause of injustice is the irresponsible use of power. The recession has meant that social conflict is inevitable, and the only way of reducing the conflict is through political organization of the exploited classes.

> [This] will make those who hold inordinate power more inclined to yield it under pressure, than to meet with threats of violence the social and political pressure put upon them. . . .
> The very genius of political force is that it has always possessed certain moral and spiritual elements. Once every degree of moral trust and good will is destroyed among various classes in society, it becomes inevitable that the conflict of power between them should result in violence. (CRSW, pp. 84, 85)

Social and religious idealists who fail to understand the brutalities of inter-group life and 'who do not understand the inexorable movement of economic power' (CRSW, p. 86) do so because of the natural limitations of their class.

The basic conclusion of the book is that social analysis is indispensable in forming the religious vision. Psychological insights are often familiar to Christianity because in its 'vital' forms it has always possessed insight into the motives of the human heart. But Christianity has lost its familiarity with social problems because of the ethical individualism of the predominant form of the religion. Its religious vision has narrowed itself to the individual life and it has made personal immortality and personal perfection the goal of religious striving. In doing this it has forsaken a basic biblical insight, that the prophets and the gospel possess the vision of a redeemed society.

Whereas liberal Protestantism is oblivious of the selfishness and brutality of inter-group behaviour, the proletariat religion has derived its insights into human nature by establishing the class war as the basis of social analysis. This religion has restored a vital element which modern religion has disregarded, the apocalyptic dimension of classical religion.

Niebuhr's conclusion has little point of contact with students of social work, but it fits neatly into his developing theology. The problem is that capitalist society seems to be on the brink of collapse. Because of the individualism of the predominant religion it lacks the religious resources to deal with the crisis. It is threatened by an atheistic religion which was capable of forecasting the crisis because of its valuable insight into human nature. These insights have been partially derived by portraying social development in terms of apocalyptic mythology, ostensibly reviving what liberal Protestantism had eradicated from classical religion. The future theological task therefore involves appropriating the insights into human nature available in classical religion and presenting them in such a way that they find points of coherence with the ethico-political problems of industrial society. This is what Niebuhr set out to achieve in the 1930s.

From *Contribution* it is clear that Niebuhr's theological critique of liberal culture is derived from a secular source. For this reason Barthians, who believe that theological thought does not have to harmonize with secular thought, accused Niebuhr of using experience to determine faith. Niebuhr's reply, the substance of which is demonstrated in *Contribution*, is that theological knowledge involves a 'conception of the circular relationship between faith and experience'.[5] Historical events that are experienced illuminate certain aspects of the Christian faith, and certain aspects of the Christian faith, when interpreted correctly, illuminate the obscurities in historical events. This is the basis of Niebuhr's theology.

With this in mind it is surprising that an important interpreter of Niebuhr can write: 'It was Karl Barth who provided for Niebuhr the theological weapon for puncturing the complacency of American liberal churchmen'.[6] On the other hand perhaps it is not surprising when that same writer dismisses *Contribution* as 'a slimmer book, hurriedly written and superficial in its arguments'.

NOTES

1   William E. Leuchtenburg, *The Perils of Prosperity* (Chicago, 1958), p. 241.
2   Charles W. Kegley and Robert W. Bretall (eds), *Reinhold Niebuhr: His Religious, Social, and Political Thought* (New York, 1956), pp. 5, 6.
3   The five articles published in 1930 were: 'Church in Russia', 'The land of extremes', 'Russia makes the machine its God', 'Russian efficiency', and 'Russia's tractor revolution'.
4   William James, *The Varieties of Religious Experience* (Longmans, Green, and Co., New York, 1914), p. 189.
5   Kegley and Bretall, *op. cit.*, p. 16. Niebuhr is referring to criticism from theologians who support the neo-orthodoxy of Karl Barth. Niebuhr never refused an opportunity for attacking Barth's theology.
6   Paul Merkley, *Reinhold Niebuhr: A Political Account* (Montreal and London, 1975), p. 74.

3

Collective Inertia

Reinhold Niebuhr's theological interpretation of Communist Party activities at the beginning of the Depression indicates the general nature of his thought. Historical events contribute to theological understanding and the poetic/symbolic ultra-rational framework of the Christian religion contains resources for interpreting paradoxical human behaviour. This means that a study of Niebuhr's theology involves knowledge of the historical events which helped to shape that theology. It also follows that an abstract approach to this theology is impossible. For example, one study of Niebuhr's work begins by acknowledging that a point of departure must be chosen when approaching any system of thought, and that such a choice indicates certain interpretational presuppositions. The writer then describes the choice to be adopted as 'man and society' studied 'separately and comparatively' and he proceeds with the subtitle 'Doctrine of man'. This presupposes that the ahistorical concepts of both 'man' and 'society' shaped Niebuhr's theology, and that such a theology would be applicable to any time and place.[1]

Essentially Niebuhr's theology reflects the tension which exists between two sociological paradigms for interpreting the reality of world society. One view is that the world is a collection of separate entities of varying size and power called States. These States interact on the basis of self-interest and security, they make and break alliances, and they exist in a balance of power. The study of world reality using the nation-state as the basic unit of analysis is the *pluralist* approach. The second view is that the basic historical and international forces are class forces, a system of horizontally

35

arranged hierarchies formed by their relation to the basic economic forces of the world. This is the basis of the *structuralist* approach.[2]

UNITED STATES LABOUR RELATIONS IN THE 1930s

In the Depression years there was a dramatic rise in the number of workers belonging to unions.[3] It was a combination of the determination of working people to resist victimization and the distress of the Depression, and a series of federal laws to encourage the unionization of the workforce. The National Industrial Recovery Act of 16 June 1933 contained as clause 7a a statement that workers had the right to bargain collectively with their employers through representatives of their own choosing. The law implied that employers were not allowed to stifle unions or interfere with the activity of workers in forming unions. The purpose of the Act was to stimulate economic recovery through the National Recovery Administration.

However, there were widespread violations of clause 7a and although a Labor Advisory Board was set up to hear complaints, this body was unable to keep track of all the violations. Senator Robert F. Wagner, a New York Democrat, argued that strong unions would lead to higher wage increases. With the increase of workers' spending power, demand would be stimulated and economic recovery would be achieved. Wagner threatened congressional action on any employer violating workers' rights. Roosevelt had no desire to alienate Wagner or the expanding labour movement, and on 5 August 1933 he created the National Labor Board, a seven-man board for investigating labour disputes.

Neither the NLB nor the National Labor Relations Board which replaced it proved very effective. When employers had elections forced upon them to decide whether or not to unionize, they used to get round it by rewarding 'loyal' workers (those who voted against forming a union) while dragging out negotiations with the trade union group. In the case of employers like Henry Ford, blatant anti-union tactics were used. In May 1937 Henry Ford's private police force mercilessly beat union organizers. Throughout 1933 and 1934 the powerful auto corporations waged war against unionism. They fired activists, imposed company controlled organizations, and refused to bargain with worker representatives. Workers dubbed the NRA the 'National Run Around' because its recovery programme seemed ineffectual.

On 27 May 1935 the US Supreme Court declared the National Industrial Recovery Act unconstitutional. However, by 5 July 1935 the National Labor Relations Act became law. Also known as the Wagner Act, it established the basic machinery for industrial relations. It shifted the focus of labour conflict from confrontation to the hearing rooms and courts. After 1937 and the favourable constitutional ruling by the Supreme Court, the number of deaths in labour disputes fell.

Up to 1935 the main body for organizing labour was the AFL. With its close affiliations with liberal clergy, and its heavy involvement with craft workers, it was structurally unsuited to organize mass production workforces. Robert H. Ziegler writes:

> AFL conventions were tedious affairs. Guest speakers, pious clergymen, and stodgy union chiefs droned on from a dais lined with venerable labor leaders and honored public officials. Floor debate rarely disturbed the somnolent convention hall. Delegates from the affiliated unions and from the city and state federations, bedecked with gaudy convention badges, paid little attention to the proceedings, which largely rubber-stamped the resolutions emanating from the tradition bound Executive Council.[4]

In contrast to this John L. Lewis, the miners' president, was an ebullient character who was instrumental in forming the breakaway Committee for Industrial Organization. Its purpose was to organize mass production workers. Throughout 1936 the CIO made spectacular gains, and in this presidential year it became a powerful political force. It supported the re-election of Franklin Delano Roosevelt, fearing that a Republican victory would bolster anti-union employers. It even gave financial support for Roosevelt's campaign. Following FDR's victory there were sweeping gains for the CIO in the steel industry and the auto factories.

The AFL had discriminated against black workers. This group of workers usually regarded the labour movement as their enemy and they praised employers such as Henry Ford for giving them a job. Employers often used black labour to break strikes. CIO officials realized that black workers laboured in key areas of production and they encouraged them to unionize. The CIO also welcomed radicals, the Socialists and the Communists. When critics suggested that the Communists might try to dominate the CIO Lewis replied, 'Who gets the bird, the hunter or the dog?'[5]

Whereas the AFL sought a hearing in pulpits, the CIO sought

political influence. Because mass production workers were highly mobile the type of private welfare system adopted by the AFL unions was inadequate and they had to look to the government for the creation and expansion of the social welfare system. These political ambitions coincided with Roosevelt's views on the subject. As early as 1931 Governor Roosevelt had told a special session of the New York state legislature that 'aid must be extended [to the unemployed] by Government, not as a matter of charity but as a matter of social duty'.[6]

INTERNATIONAL RELATIONS AND THE UNITED STATES

After the Great War the US emerged as the most economically powerful nation. But the Allies' difficulties in collecting reparations from Germany led in turn to difficulties in repaying war loans. Also the US tariff policy did nothing to stimulate the world economy. The Hawley—Smoot tariff of 1930 was 40 per cent and this led in turn to a world-wide increase in tariff rates, import quotas, exchange restrictions, and other impediments to the growth of free trade. This economic nationalism had such dire effects because the US controlled so much of the world's material wealth and industrial production, and possessed such a large share of capital resources.

Foreign policy became increasingly characterized by a retreat into traditional isolationism. Political commitments with the nations were not to interfere with America's freedom of action. America's moral and ethical role in world affairs was emphasized rather than its political role. The isolationist tendency was not confined to any one group or party, it cut across all the barriers. This attitude and its international influence is symbolized in the Kellogg—Briand anti-war treaty of 1928 signed by 64 nations. This treaty meant that war as a facet of foreign policy was illegal. A few concessions were made such as the French insisting on the right to use force to defend themselves, and Britain accepted that war was illegal except in certain parts of the world known as the Empire.

The isolationist tendency was further encouraged by the findings of the Senate-appointed committee to investigate the involvement of arms manufacturers in the Great War. It was chaired by Republican Senator Gerald P. Nye, and the secretary of the Munitions Investigating Committee was the lawyer Stephen Rauschenbusch, the son of the Social Gospeller Walter Rauschenbush. The committee concluded that American involvement in the Great War was the result of a conspiracy between Wall Street bankers and munitions manufacturers. Selig Adler comments:

> Historical revisionism engendered a climate of opinion that made congressional neutrality legislation all but inevitable. Past diplomatic errors were belabored while contemporary aggressors were allowed to prepare for the spoliation of the world. Seldom in the annals of the United States had a popular misreading of history been so fraught with danger for the future.[7]

Despite the fact that war was illegal, Mussolini attacked Ethiopia in 1935, and Hitler marched into the Rhineland in 1936. The US response was the Neutrality Act of 1937, passed in the House by 376 votes to 13, and in the Senate by 63 votes to 6. It imposed a mandatory arms and ammunitions embargo on all warring States, and upheld the embargo even as late as 1939.

CLASS AND NATION

Niebuhr's experience of the class war increased with his activities as a member of the FSC. One of the group's assignments in 1932 was to investigate a mining dispute in Pineville, Kentucky. The FSC committee had been invited to Pineville by the county attorney and the citizens' committee after 21 New York clergymen had memorialized the Senate to pass the Costigan–Cutting Bill which provided for a Senatorial investigation of the coal counties of Kentucky. The area had been receiving unfavourable publicity because an attorney defending striking miners had been beaten up, and the writer Waldo Frank had received similar treatment.

In an article for *The Christian Century* Niebuhr condemned the middle class for resisting the efforts of the miners to achieve social justice. The miners' demands had been considered 'unchristian'. But the people had also condemned the miners for demanding union rates of pay after their wages had fallen from $1.25 a ton to 25 cents a ton. At the same time the churches were encouraging charity towards the miners. Niebuhr concluded that whenever the love ideal of Christianity degenerates into pure philanthropy without regard for the difficult task of achieving social justice, it becomes a cloak hiding the face of social justice.

In 1935 Niebuhr founded the journal *Radical Religion* to become

39

the forum for FSC issues. Apart from Niebuhr, other regular contributers were H. Richard Niebuhr, Eduard Heimann, Paul Tillich, and Francis Henson. In its editorials he condemned Roosevelt's 'whirligig reforms' and argued that it was impossible to cure the ills of capitalism within the presuppositions of capitalism itself. However, by 1936 Niebuhr too began to baulk at the thought of a Republican victory in the presidential election. It entered his conscience that a vote for Norman Thomas was one lost for Roosevelt, and Niebuhr had to admit that under FDR the Democratic Party had travelled further to the left than anyone would have thought possible. Towards the end of the decade Niebuhr's admiration for Roosevelt and his reforms increased.

In addition to class and economic issues, Niebuhr was also attentive to international developments, particularly with regard to American foreign policy. During the 1930s he had paid close attention to political developments in Germany. He looked on the class struggle within that nation as an omen for civilization. He felt that the economic constraints placed upon Germany by the Allies and especially by America were playing into the hands of the capitalists. 'We are the first empire in the world to establish our sway without legions', he had said in 1930. 'Our legions are dollars.'

> We are living in an economic age, and the significant power is economic rather than military. In moments of crisis the banker may find it necessary to call upon the marines; but the civilized world is fairly well disciplined and permits its life to be ordered and its social and political relationships to be adjusted by the use of economic force without recourse to the more dramatic display of military power.[8]

In 1931 Niebuhr encouraged foreign policy makers to renounce claims for reparations and war debts, and to abandon the tariff protection policy which was inimical to the world economy. He warned that if these economic constraints were not lifted then war would be inevitable. The surest sign of a coming war would be the political collapse of Germany, either to the fascists or to the Communists.[9]

In 1941 Niebuhr summed up his attitude towards American foreign policy in an article for *Christianity and Crisis* entitled 'Repeal the Neutrality Act!'[10] The Act itself was described as 'one of the most immoral laws ever spread upon a federal statute book'. It was condemned for its 'misguided idealism' and its 'denial of moral responsibility'.

The peoples of America and Europe are now becoming members one of another. We belong to a common community and we have acquired immense communal responsibilities as a result of that fact. To deny these responsibilities is unchristian and unethical. This is exactly what the Neutrality Act did.

CLASS CONFLICT AND STATE CONFLICT

Moral Man and Immoral Society was published in 1932. It is the exposition of a theme found in the two earlier books, that moral values, when transmuted into collective activity, result in behaviour which seems immoral when seen from the individual standpoint. It bases its social critique on the absolute perspective provided by the Christian religion, and it is a corrective to the liberal Protestant belief that the simple ethic of Jesus applies to social realities, which in practice ignores the brutal realities of group behaviour. It faces up to the realistic situation that technological achievements have increased the extent and intensity of social cohesion, creating an interdependent international community. However, this international community is involved in both class conflict and conflict between states. Despite the fact that these realities govern the world system the American religious idealism is oblivious of their consequences.

> [T]he expanding economy of America obscured the cruelties of the class struggle in our economic life, and the comparative isolation of a continent made the brutalities of international conflict less obvious. (MM, p. 79)

The book explores the rational and ultra-rational possibilities and limits in dealing with both forms of social conflict, and then studies group behaviour from both perspectives, that is from the perspective of the group as nation/state, and from the perspective of the group as class. Finally revolutionary socialism and evolutionary socialism are studied in relation to the morality of violence and coercion, and their different methods of achieving social justice.

Niebuhr considered this book to be his 'first major work'. Like the two previous books the attack is focused upon liberal Protestantism for attempting to provide an individualistic ethic for a social reality which is governed by the interaction of groups. From the vantage point of Christianity with its poetic symbolism of the end of

41

time (i.e. eschatological myths), the liberal Protestant ethic is found to be inadequate.

> Wherever religion concerns itself with the problems of society it always gives birth to some kind of millennial hope from the perspective of which present social realities are convicted of inadequacy, and courage is maintained to continue the effort to redeem society of injustice. The courage is needed; for the task of building a just society always seems to be a hopeless one when only present realities and immediate possibilities are envisaged. (MM, p. 61)

This type of activity was termed 'behaviour by illusion' by the sociologist Vilfredo Pareto. This idealism for nerving social action is contrasted with the sentimental idealism of liberal Protestantism. Niebuhr characterizes this as follows:

> In spite of the disillusionment of the World War, the average liberal Protestant Christian is still convinced that the kingdom of God is gradually approaching, that the League of Nations is its partial fulfilment and the Kellogg Pact its covenant, that the wealthy will be persuaded by the church to dedicate their power and privilege to the common good and that they are doing so in increasing numbers, that the conversion of individuals is the only safe method of solving the social problem, and that such ethical weaknesses as religion still betrays are due to its theological obscurantism which will be sloughed off by the progress of the enlightenment. (MM, pp. 79–80)

Niebuhr begins *Moral Man* with what he considers to be a realistic description of the world. The human activity of subduing and controlling natural forces through technical knowledge has created a civilization in which the extent and intensity of social cohesion is greater than that of any previous era. However this same power which has dominated nature is held disproportionately within the human race and it manifests itself in the increasing polarization of the classes of human society. The uneven distribution of power in society has meant that social justice becomes an increasingly difficult achievement. In other words, the form which society has adopted to increase its domination of the natural world has at the same time increased social inequalities, and the greater the intensity of social cohesion, the more starkly this contradiction is revealed. Faced with these realities of power the traditional liberal virtues of

42

education, benevolence, and goodwill are insufficiently powerful instruments for creating a just society. All relationships between large groups, once the power factor is accepted, intrinsically involve a measure of coercion. Human political activity is the arena where the ethical and coercive factors of human existence meet, but the predominant factor is the coercive element and the motive force of coercion is rooted in economic interests.

The brutal facts of collective life would easily rob the average individual of confidence in the human enterprise were it not for the existence of an ideology to justify the powerful and 'to hide the nakedness of their greed' (MM, p. 8). An ideology functions to prevent despair because collective human activity is very often an outrage to the individual conscience.

But an ideology can never completely justify power because power expresses itself paradoxically. Power sacrifices justice to peace within the State, but this power conflicts with other powers between international communities and destroys the peace. Thus power prevents anarchy in intra-group relations but encourages anarchy in inter-group relations. The powerful classes organize a nation and the powerful nations organize a crude society of nations.

> The problem which society faces is clearly one of reducing force by increasing the factors which make for a moral and rational adjustment of life to life; of bringing such force as is still necessary under responsibility of the whole of society; of destroying the kind of power which cannot be made socially responsible (the power which resides in economic ownership for instance); and of bringing forces of moral self-restraint to bear upon types of power which can never be brought completely under social control. (MM, p. 20)

The vision of a perfect social order, that is, the ultimate religious vantage point, is one which is not capable of realization in actual history and must be content with increasing approximations.

Once the complex problem of social justice in modern society has been presented, Niebuhr compares two methods of approaching a solution. He considers the resources and limitations of both the rational and the ultra-rational (religious) approaches to the problem. The belief that rationalism would eventually create social justice has been a perennial hope. It is the creed of the Enlightenment, and the creed of modern leaders. But it must be realized that social impulses are more deeply rooted than the rational capacity. Reason is capable of increasing the moral

43

capacity, but the growing power of the rational faculty is not a guarantee of growing morality.

Reason can check selfish impulses, making for social and internal order and justice by placing restraints upon the desires of the self in the interests of social harmony. But pure moral action in complex and collective relationships is an impossible goal.

> Rationalism in morals may persuade men in one moment that their selfishness is a peril to society and in the next moment it may condone their egoism as a necessary and inevitable element in the total social harmony. (MM, p. 41)

Niebuhr cites the example of Utilitarianism as providing the middle class with the moral justification for following its own interests. Reason is capable not only of justifying egoism, but of giving it a new force. The will-to-live is transmuted into the will-to-power, self-preservation into self-aggrandizement. The impulse of self-interest is capable of harnessing reason, and the net result is hypocrisy. The larger the group, the more certain it is that self-interest becomes a governing factor. Technical efficiency has made it possible to increase the size of the group and the dominant groups within the nations have extended their power beyond the nation. In sum: 'A technological civilization has created an international community, so interdependent as to require, even if not powerful or astute enough to achieve, ultimate social harmony' (MM, p. 49). But the interdependent nations are composed of classes which possess disproportionate power.

> This social inequality leads not only to internal strife but to conflict between various national communities, by prompting the more privileged and powerful classes to seek advantages at the expense of other nations so that they may consolidate the privileges which they have won at the expense of their own nationals. Thus modern life is involved in both class and international conflict. (MM, p. 49)

Rational resources for providing an adequate ethic to cater for the collective realities of human life are considered to be inferior to ultra-rational resources. They are incapable of providing a 'transcendent fulcrum' or an 'impartial perspective' because 'they always remain bound to the forces they are intended to discipline' (MM, p. 44). Once the group size increases, the inadequacy of rationalism in providing a perspective, and an impetus, for social knowledge and action is brought out in clearer relief. When the modern world in its totality is considered the nature of intergroup relationships is complicated by the fact that group boundaries are both vertical and horizontal: vertical in the sense of a collection of interacting states, and horizontal in the sense of class divisions transcending state entities. Hopes for international peace seem vague because there is no power to control these interacting forces, no social restraint on collective egoism. There is no rational scheme capable of incorporating the whole in a total harmony because each scheme can be shown to be the projection of a particular self-interest. The very concept itself is self-aggrandizement.

When Niebuhr turns to the possibilities and limits of religion in assisting with the organization of social life he presents arguments which appeared in the previous book *Contribution*. He does not expand on what he means by 'ultra-rational' framework; this is a topic for consideration later. In *Moral Man* he is content to characterize religion as 'a sense of the absolute' (p. 52), echoing Schleiermacher, and explaining that the ultra-rational framework issues from the 'poetic imagination'. Religion 'uses the symbols derived from the human personality to describe the absolute and it finds them morally potent' (MM, p. 53). It will be observed that this definition of religion is essentially identical with Feuerbach's.[11] Defining religion in terms of the personal means that the ethics related to the religious imagination are more appropriate for individual relationships than they are for the more abstract social relations created by a mechanical civilization. The main difference between a rational ethic and a religious ethic is that the former seeks to bring the needs of others into equal consideration with those of the self, and the latter meets the need of the neighbour without carefully weighing and comparing the needs of the self. This means that the religious ethic is purer than the justice prompted by reason.

Although the religious imagination personalizes the absolute there is always, in every vital religion, the conception of an ideal society of love and justice. 'The religious imagination', writes Niebuhr, 'is as impatient with the compromises, relativities, and imperfections of historic society as with the imperfection of the individual life' (MM, pp. 60-1). It is this aspect of the classical religious imagination that has been secularized by Marxists. The impetus for this movement of secularization, according to Niebuhr, was initiated by the sentimentality of the liberal Protestant vision and culture. However, the religious/moral forces will never achieve the redemption of society because of 'constitutional limitations'. Niebuhr here is simply reaffirming that religion works best and is most ethically sensitive in the more intimate social relations.

The limitations of religion as a resource for assisting in the building of stable societies are related to the fact that religion, in addition to fostering the sense of humility before the absolute on the positive side, can also become self-assertion before the absolute on the negative side. In this latter sense religion can become a weapon in the struggle for social supremacy, justifying self-interest in terms of the absolute. For example,

> [t]he power, by which the middle commercial classes defeated the landed aristocracy in the political and economic battles of the past three centuries, was partially derived from the puritan sense of the religious worth of personality and of the spiritual character of secular pursuits. (MM, p. 65)

Weber's thesis therefore shows how easy it is for an individual or a group to regard itself as an instrument of the divine purpose, and become a sublimation of the will.

But it is equally wrong, argues Niebuhr, to swing in the opposite direction and allow the sense of the absolute to express itself in the subjection of the individual to the divine will. In this respect Niebuhr distances himself from what he takes to be the main implications of the neo-orthodox theology of Karl Barth where

> [t]he emphasis upon the difference between the holiness of God and the sinfulness of man is so absolute that man is convicted, not of any particular breaches against the life of the humanity [sic] community, but of being human and not divine. Thus, to all intents and purposes, creation and the fall are practically identified and, everything in human history being identified with evil, the 'nicely calculated less and more' of social morality lose all significance. (MM, p. 68)

Both the sublimation and the subjection of the will result in an identical separation of religion and morality. Therefore the sharp dualistic contrast between good and evil in religion reveals permanent limitations of the religious imagination by obscuring aspects of the moral life.

Once Niebuhr has assessed the resources and limitations of rational and religious approaches to the creation of social justice, he turns his attention to a description of human groups on a global perspective. He looks at the problem from both the pluralist and the structuralist perspectives, that is, the world of nation states, and the world of social classes. In each case he considers the morality of the group behaviour patterns.

The nation state is the group of strongest social cohesion with the most undisputed central authority and the most clearly defined membership. The basic characteristic of behaviour in state interactions is selfishness. Nations are selfish first because there is not sufficient contact between the groups to stimulate the flow of sympathy. Second, and more important, nations are groups whose cohesion depends more on coercion and emotion than on mind, and,

> since there can be no ethical action without self criticism, and no self criticism without the rational capacity of self-transcendence, it is natural that national attitudes can hardly approximate the ethical. (MM, p. 88)

National self-transcendence depends upon the rational capacity for self-criticism, but self-criticism is often regarded as a type of disloyalty and inner disunity and weakness.

The selfishness of nations can be mitigated by depriving the governing groups of their special privileges. When this occurs their interests will be more nearly in harmony with the interests of the total national community. The present situation is characterized by the fact that the 'economic overlords' have special interests in the profit of international trade, in exploiting weaker countries, and in the acquisition of raw materials and markets, and these interests are only remotely relevant to the needs of the people as a whole. Also the capitalist system produces goods and accumulates capital, neither of which can be absorbed in the nation by consumption and investment. This necessary expansion requires protection, and the whole community is called upon to provide this protection which in the end serves the interests of only a few people.

> If a socialist commonwealth should succeed in divorcing privilege from power, it would thereby materially reduce the selfishness of nations, though it is probably romantic to hope . . . that all causes of international friction would be abolished. (MM, p. 90)

In saying this it is clear that the pluralist paradigm is the most decisive in Niebuhr's thought and he does not regard the present form of the nation state as a function of the capitalist world economy. Niebuhr imagines that nations would retain something of their present form even within a world socialist commonwealth.

47

A third feature of the proverbial selfishness of nations is the force of patriotism. The irony here is that patriotism transmutes a basic individual unselfishness into national egoism. But there is also an element of projected self-interest in patriotic altruism and therefore national egoism can be said to be a combination of unselfishness and vicarious selfishness.

In addition to their selfishness, nations are also hypocritical because they seek to hide their selfishness. The ruling elites act to maintain legitimation by seeking moral approval, pretending to represent universal values and ideals. It is the sublimation of the religious impulse which accepts this legitimation, and state rituals seek to enhance it.

The selfishness and hypocrisy of nations is therefore a problem as far as international justice is concerned. There is no community which transcends the conflicts of interest which arise between individual nations and which has an impartial perspective upon the conflicts. The class structure of modern society would prevent the impartial functioning of such a body if one existed. Again it is clear that the pluralist paradigm governs Niebuhr's thinking because he is always thinking in terms of competing interests divided into national units rather than the shared interests across national boundaries. These units are not segregated with the interests of the proletariat in mind. Thus, for Niebuhr, the capitalist system is incapable by its very nature of creating a stable international order, and 'anarchy' will continue.

> The sharpening of class antagonisms within each modern industrial nation is increasingly destroying national unity and imperilling national comity as well. It may be that the constant growth of economic inequality and social injustice in our industrial civilization will force the nations into a final conflict, which is bound to end in their destruction. (MM, p. 112)

Niebuhr's study of the class war in Germany, and his analysis of the causes of national self-interest and hypocrisy, led him to predict the inevitability of a grave conflict in the future as early as 1932. In the same year the Under-Secretary of State, William R. Castle, in an address before the American Conference on International Justice held in Washington rejected a plea for an amendment in the Kellogg–Briand Pact which had wanted to assert that any nation breaking the pledge should be declared war on by the other members. Mr Castle said it was a contradiction in terms to use war to prevent war.

Following this analysis of the national group, Niebuhr next concentrates on class groups, the 'privileged classes' and the 'proletarian class'.

The 'dominant and privileged groups' roughly comprise the traditional Marxist concept of the bourgeoisie plus a number of groups which comprise the middle classes. The moral attitudes of this group are characterized by self-deception and hypocrisy. They tend to identify their own interests with general and universal interests, and claim universal values to defend their privileges; they assume the rewards they receive are just payments for their function in society; they claim moral superiority, equating their rewards with evidence of diligence and a righteous life; they claim their artistic and cultural interests justify their privileges; and finally they present themselves as apostles of law and order. Nevertheless this does not prevent them from preserving their privileges by the use of coercion and even violence. Their hypocrisy and dishonesty becomes apparent when they are quick to censure the violence of those who oppose them.

Some of their pretensions are consciously dishonest, but most are ideological. It means that the religion and culture they appeal to in defence of their position, power, and privilege, are partially created by that class and reflect their perspectives. Hence moral suasion is an insufficient weapon to use when dealing with them because the categories and patterns of thought are already weighted in their favour.

Niebuhr finds the ethical attitudes of the proletarian class to be a combination of moral cynicism and unqualified equalitarian social idealism. Their moral cynicism arises out of their ability to pierce the mists of bourgeois pretensions. Their social idealism is unqualified because history does not furnish much hope of achieving the type of social justice which this class imagines as a possibility. Just as the privileged classes attribute universal values to themselves, so too Marxism attributes universal values to the proletarian class. It is a religious interpretation of proletarian destiny.

The Marxian imagines that he has a philosophy or even a science of history. What he has is really an apocalyptic vision. (MM, p. 155)

Even while Niebuhr is considering groups from the structuralist perspective his pluralist conceptions of the State are still uppermost in his mind. He rejects as cynicism the Marxist idea that the State reflects bourgeois interests (p. 148). He therefore implies that the State is a neutral structure totally dependent on the political power pulling the strings. He also rejects as 'impossible' the Marxist theory of surplus value. Both these rejections of key elements in the Marxist analysis have the effect of imparting ahistorical permanence to the structures of capitalism even when he is supposedly attacking capitalism and warning of its demise. Niebuhr thinks in terms of the political power in the State structure being capable of reducing excessive privilege rather than approaching an analysis of the State as a necessary structure established for the general interest of capital accumulation. And the unqualified rejection of the Marxist theory of surplus value removes both a central feature of Marxist analysis, and the feature which, if substantiated, is clearly the most immoral aspect of modern society because it is not based on the particular immoral activities of individual bourgeoisie, but is inherent in the very structure of the system.

The purpose of this section is to determine

> how society can eliminate social injustice by methods which offer some fair opportunity of abolishing what is evil in our present society, without destroying what is worth preserving in it, and without running the risk of substituting new abuses and injustices in the place of those abolished. (MM, p. 167)

However, if the structural exploitation of labour is not recognized and is therefore not regarded as an evil, and the relationship between the bourgeois State and capital accumulation is not recognized and the State is regarded as neutral, then these ideas will influence the result of any analysis which is undertaken.

REVOLUTIONARY AND EVOLUTIONARY SOCIALISM

Niebuhr analyses two methods of eliminating social injustice and considers the ethical implications of each method. The problem lies in the fact that the dominant and privileged group in modern society attained and maintains its pre-eminence with an individualistic ethic which it believes is capable of establishing social justice. Such a belief is futile and hypocritical and will only exacerbate social injustice. An ethic by which a group rose to power cannot be used to mitigate that power and any pretence that it can will involve that group in hypocrisy.

The question of revolution involves the question of violence. The middle classes are wrong, asserts Niebuhr, in their assumption that violence is intrinsically immoral. The proletarian engaged in revolution does not have less moral motives than those who defend special privileges by more covert means of coercion.

> A political policy cannot be intrinsically evil if it can be proved to be an efficacious instrument for the achievement of a morally approved end. (MM, p. 171)

The assumption that violence and revolution are immoral rests on two errors. The first error is that there is a difference in kind between violence and coercion. On the contrary, argues Niebuhr, '[o]nce we admit the factor of coercion as ethically justified . . . we cannot draw any absolute line of demarcation between violent and non-violent coercion' (MM, p. 172). The second error is that there is a necessary connection between the motive for an action and the instruments chosen to pursue that action.

The real situation is that moral values are in a state of competition and they reflect the class war, each class having its own moral values. The characteristics of middle-class morality when applied to the social problem are hypocrisy and sentimentality. They are hypocritical because they are swift to condemn violence and swift to use it in the international situation. They make much of freedom and are swift to repress freedom when their privileges are threatened. They are sentimental because they hope to insinuate their individualistic ethic into a problem which lies beyond the competence of such an ethic. The characteristics of proletarian values are brutality and cynicism when applied to the social problem. They know that only collective action will yield results and the hypocrisy of those who deny this makes cynics of them. Niebuhr concludes:

> If a season of violence can establish a just social system and can create the possibilities of its preservation, there is no purely ethical ground upon which violence and revolution can be ruled out. . . . Once we have made the fateful concession of ethics to politics, and accepted coercion as a necessary instrument of social cohesion, we can make no absolute distinctions between non-violent and violent types of coercion

51

or between coercion used by governments and that which is used by revolutionaries. . . . The real question is: what are the political possibilities of establishing justice through violence? (MM, p. 180)

Niebuhr attempts to answer this question without reference to any particular type of violence and without specifying any particular targets of violence. He singles out four points which would affect the outcome of a campaign of violence. First, many workers have reached a degree of affluence which was not predicted in the original Marxist analyses. Second, the composition of classes in modern society is far more complicated than that originally envisaged in Marxism. Third, the divisions among the ranks of the proletariat are complex and must be brought into consideration. Fourth, Marx was correct in his predictions about cyclical crises in capitalism, but history seemed to be indicating that these crises led to fascism rather than Communist revolution. Because of these facts, Niebuhr concludes, the industrial West is not ripe for revolution and will not be in the immediate future unless there should be another world war. Communism will stand more chance of success in the agrarian East. 'So much for the possibilities of establishing an equalitarian world by violence' (MM, p. 191).

The conclusion is that the use of violence on behalf of the working class would be wrong because the use of violence would not succeed in the objectives of establishing social justice.

Niebuhr then brings another consideration into focus. He wonders whether it is possible to maintain a society where production is for need and allocation is selfless. Again there is a negative answer because the vision of such a society disregards the perennial limitations of human nature. Human beings will always be creative enough to enlarge their needs beyond minimum requirements, and will always remain selfish enough to feel the pressure of individual needs more than the needs of others. Niebuhr therefore assumes that human nature will remain much the same as it is under the present capitalist system. Therefore violence is not to be recommended as a policy for establishing social justice because it will not succeed, and even it it did succeed it would not maintain its success.

If violence can be justified at all, its terror must have the tempo of a surgeon's skill and healing must follow quickly upon its wounds. (MM, p. 220)

Having dismissed the possibility of violence and revolution on pragmatic grounds, Niebuhr considers the alternative method of establishing social justice through evolutionary means. Establishing socialism by this method is dependent on the trade union movement. The Depression sharply delineated the issues involved. The combination of political and economic power becomes a necessity in the fight against the political and economic power of the business community. According to Niebuhr, the State attacks workers because it is under the influence of the dominant classes. They have reduced the power of the strike through legislation, they use federal injunctions in labour disputes, they enforce compulsory arbitration, and they use troops to smash effective strikes. Despite these realities workers still believe that a democratic state can be used to establish social justice. Niebuhr's study of European socialism encouraged his belief that greater justice could be achieved through parliamentary action, and the State used to mitigate inequalities. Nevertheless after viewing the situation in America he is forced to conclude that the industrial workers would not gain enough support from other groups to establish a political majority. He adds:

> If these conclusions are valid we would be forced to the further conviction that there is no single political force which can break through and completely reorganize the present unstable equilibrium of forces in modern society. If such a conclusion should be correct (always with the reservation that another war might completely change the picture), it would become necessary to abandon the hope of achieving a rational equalitarian social goal, and be content with the expectation of its gradual approximation. (MM, p. 219)

There are two hazards inherent in evolutionary socialism. The first is that once there is any diminution in the eschatological element there is a corresponding loss of fervour for the political enterprise. For this reason it is important that extreme left-wing elements in the political activity are not rejected. They are needed to keep the goals of the political activity clearly in mind. Second, their presence acts as a foil to the tendency of working-class leaders to be sucked into the world of privilege and forget the viewpoint of the toilers in society. Socialists easily fall into the trap of espousing the causes of the enemies of labour under the pretence of peace for the State, or the principles of law.

MORAL DUALISM

The purpose of *Moral Man* was to illustrate that liberal Protestantism possessed an inadequate social ethic because it was based on an unrealistic assessment of the human situation. The book also elaborated the theme that Christianity has difficulty in applying itself to political ethics. Nevertheless a political morality is required and it must combine the insights of the political realist who accepts the necessity of coercion, and the moral idealist who wants to extend social intelligence and increase moral goodwill. Such an ethic realizes that there must always be conflict, but it must try to prevent futile conflict. 'Moral reason must learn how to make coercion its ally' (MM, p. 238). If social conflict is inevitable, then there is greater moral justification in it if it aims at greater equality rather than the perpetuation of privilege. 'Equality is a higher social goal than peace' (MM, p. 235).

But where does the Christian religion stand in all this? Moral counsels in the political realm are diametrically opposite to those of religious morality. Religious morality tends to perpetuate injustice 'by discouraging self assertion against the inordinate claims of others' (MM, p. 262). But a political morality justifies 'not only self assertion but the use of non-rational power in reinforcing claims' (MM, p. 262).

> The religious ideal in its purest form has nothing to do with the problem of social justice. (MM, p. 263)

The ethic of Jesus does not consider the social consequences of the recommended moral actions because 'he viewed them from an inner and transcendent perspective' (MM, p. 264). In this way they are relevant to all social conditions. Religious ideals work best in intimate communities and as the groups become more diffuse the self-sacrificial norm in relationships gives way to mutuality. However mutuality can only be maintained if it is informed by a passion which is greater than mutuality. This is summarized by Niebuhr as: 'Love must strive for something more than justice if it would attain justice' (MM, p. 266).

To give a practical illustration Niebuhr draws attention to the American Negroes. They have consistently compounded the religious virtues of forgiveness and forbearance, 'yet they did not soften the hearts of their oppressors by their social policy' (MM, p. 268). Niebuhr advocates a certain type of action based on his analysis in *Moral Man*. He wrote:

The emancipation of the Negro race in America probably waits upon the adequate development of this kind of social [non-violent resistance] and political strategy. It is hopeless for the Negro to expect complete emancipation from the menial social and economic position into which the white man has forced him, merely by trusting in the moral sense of the white race. It is equally hopeless to attempt emancipation through violent rebellion. (MM, p. 252)

And he gave some practical illustrations:

Boycotts against banks which discriminate against Negroes in granting credit, against stores which refuse to employ Negroes while serving Negro trade, and against public service corporations which practice racial discrimination, would undoubtedly be crowned with some measure of success. Non-payment of taxes against states which spend on the education of Negro children only a fraction of the amount spent on white children, might be equally an efficacious weapon. One waits for such a campaign with all the more reason and hope because the peculiar spiritual gifts of the Negro endow him with the capacity to conduct it successfully. (MM, p. 254)

Moral Man ends with the conclusion that there is no possibility of harmonizing a religious ethic which counsels self-sacrifice with a political ethic which counsels the assertion of rights.

It would therefore seem better to accept a frank dualism in morals than to attempt a harmony between the two methods which threatens the effectiveness of both. (MM, pp. 270−1)

Notes

1   T. Minnema, *The Social Ethics of Reinhold Niebuhr* (Kampen, 1958).
2   These two approaches to the study of world society are outlined by Ralph Pettman in *State and Class: A Sociology of International Affairs* (London, 1979), pp. 56ff.

3 Labour union membership as a percentage of total labour force

Year	Union membership	Percentage of labour force
1930	3.6 million	6.8
1933	2.9 million	5.2
1935 (Wagner Act)	3.7 million	6.7
1937	7.2 million	12.9
1940	8.9 million	15.5

Figures quoted from Harvard Sitkoff (ed.), *Fifty Years Later: The New Deal Evaluated* (New York, 1985), p. 52.

4 Robert H. Zieger, *American Workers, American Unions 1920–1985* (Baltimore and London, 1986), p. 43.
5 *Ibid.*, p. 55.
6 Sitkoff, *op. cit.*, p. 69.
7 Selig Adler, *The Uncertain Giant 1921–1941* (London, 1965), p. 166.
8 'Awkward imperialists', *Atlantic Monthly* 145 (May 1930), pp. 670–5.
9 'Economic perils to world peace', *The World Tomorrow* 14 (May 1931), pp. 154–6.
10 20 October 1941.
11 Two examples of similar definitions:

Man—this is the mystery of religion—projects his being into objectivity, and then again makes himself an object to this projected image of himself thus converted into a subject.

God is the highest subjectivity of man abstracted from himself; hence man can do nothing of himself, all goodness comes from God.

Ludwig Feuerbach, *The Essence of Christianity* (tr. George Eliot) (New York, 1957), pp. 29–31.

4

Civilization and Myth

By 1934 Niebuhr's thoughts were more to do with the rise and fall of civilizations than the problem of what to do with the unemployed youth. The Depression and the world crisis of capitalism, coupled with the gloomy prognostications of Oswald Spengler and the social philosophy of Marx, had convinced Niebuhr that the West had reached the end of an era. Roosevelt's New Deal policies were dismissed as superficial. Viewed on Niebuhr's grand scale, present social realities clearly indicated the demise of a once powerful system. He failed to realize the significance of the New Deal at the time because although he acknowledged the fact of US economic hegemony, he failed to realize the actual strength of the United States in the world economy, and so underestimated the long-term significance of the New Deal.

In 1934 he published *Reflections on the End of an Era*. *Moral Man* had been an essay in social analysis which elaborated one of Niebuhr's themes but it had said little about the ethic of Jesus and even less about the ultra-rational framework which surrounds all systems of coherence. It is this latter theme which receives attention in *Reflections*. But his elaboration of this framework is only presented after first developing social analysis. It is therefore necessary to sketch briefly some further background details.

'ROOSEVELT, NOT REVOLUTION'

The main political developments in the 1930s were not as

spectacular as the upheavals in the social conditions. There was a marked swing to the Democratic Party and Franklin Delano Roosevelt won the presidential election of 1932. Roosevelt proposed the 'New Deal' for the people of America. He thought that Hoover's confidence in the business community had been misplaced. Instead he argued for the progressives' assumptions about the extension of government action in controlling the economy. He was determined to preserve both democracy and capitalism.

Roosevelt swept to power in 1932 with 57.4 per cent of the popular vote. Hoover polled 39.7 per cent, and the Socialist Party candidate, Norman Thomas, and the Communist candidate, William Z. Foster, shared 2.9 per cent of the vote. Roosevelt had the support of every region of the United States. The urban working class voted for him even though most of their leaders did not endorse him. He calculated that there was little chance of a revolution. Most of the people on whom the left depended were influenced by either religious or nationalistic faiths and were basically hostile to revolutionary philosophies. Also, many were so demoralized by the Depression that they could not rouse any enthusiasm for political activity or thought. In the 1932 election 40 per cent of adults did not cast a vote.

The most obvious feature of the New Deal was the greater role for central government in the economic life of the country. Its programmes deliberately promoted the capitalist system. Roosevelt tried at first to co-operate with business leaders, but he became increasingly critical of them, and he moved his concern towards the welfare of the lower income groups.

The New Deal was not an economic revolution and it did not end the Depression. In 1939 unemployment was still high at 17.2 per cent. The Depression ended with the onset of war in Europe. The munitions industry boomed, and after Pearl Harbor, prosperity returned. By 1944 the unemployment figure was 1.2 per cent.

The New Deal programmes were not Keynesian despite the fact that Roosevelt and Keynes had met. It was only during the war, and through the work of economists such as J. K. Galbraith and Paul A. Samuelson, that Keynes's ideas began to take a hold. There were four main areas of federal activity: banking, labour, agriculture, and business.

In the banking sector the creation of the Federal Deposit Insurance Corporation was responsible for re-establishing confidence in the system. Bank failures had been occurring at an alarming rate. In 1920 there were 30,909 banks with $53.1 billion assets in total. By 1933 this had fallen to 14,771 banks with $51.4 billion assets. By 1940 there were 15,076 banks with $79.7 billion assets. The policies brought bank failures to a virtual end, and depositors were cushioned in the event of any bank having to close. The New Deal also separated commercial from investment banking, which ended the practice of using depositors' funds to speculate in risky investments.

The effect of the New Deal on labour relations was covered briefly in the previous chapter. In agriculture, the Agricultural Adjustment Act led to central control of farm production. It was funded by a tax on the food processors (later judged illegal by the Supreme Court). The New Deal also sponsored the Farm Credit Administration which granted long- and short-term loans. The Resettlement Administration tended to the needs of very poor farmers, and the Rural Electrification Administration brought power to areas which had been ignored by the private utilities.

The Depression gave rise to the conviction that the free market was hopelessly flawed. The National Recovery Administration sought to keep prices up by limiting the output of industrial products. There was also protection for airline and trucking companies from 'chaotic' or 'excessive' competition under the auspices of the Interstate Commerce Commission.

There was no underlying philosophy to the New Deal and programmes sometimes conflicted with each other. Its effect was to give government recognition to various interest groups and to assist the success of creative enterprises. There were three major lines of economic thought discernible but they did not always complement each other. The first line of thought advocated National Public Planning, and it was represented by economists such as Rexford G. Tugwell, Gardiner C. Means, and Mordecai Ezekiel. They wanted a thorough reorganization of the industrial system with government experts planning production and distribution. They did not favour government ownership although they felt that it would benefit certain utilities if they were publicly owned. The second line of thought advocated the ideas of a business commonwealth. They wanted more co-operation between businesses and fairer competition. The third group were decentralists, and they favoured the stimulation of small enterprises and regulation of Wall Street.

These three ideas can be isolated as motivating factors in the New Deal, but they were not always in harmony. Nevertheless between them they established the basis of the mixed economy.

59

In addition to these four major areas of concern there was also radical change in the welfare system. The Civilian Conservation Corps (CCC) was a relief agency which put men to work on reforestation and soil conservation. Initially it enrolled 250,000 unemployed young men, 25,000 First World War veterans, and 25,000 woodsmen. The Federal Relief Administration was a body set up to give grants to states for similar projects. The Federal Emergency Relief Administration (FERA) was able to grant funds to colleges and universities for employment of students on part-time work projects. It also distributed food surpluses supplied by the AAA to families on relief. The Civil Works Administration (CWA) set up 180,000 work projects employing 4 million, mainly in construction work. But it also provided jobs for teachers, engineers, architects, artists, and nurses.

In August 1935 the Economic Security Act established unemployment insurance plans, old-age assistance, and the extension of public services to promote public health, for children and mothers, rehabilitation of the handicapped, and aid to the blind. A new federal agency was set up to administer it, the Social Security Board. It would give 'at least some measure of protection' to 30 million people.

By February of 1934 the CCC, FERA, and the CWA provided general relief for 28 million people, 22 per cent of the population, in 8 million households.

William E. Leuchtenburg offers a concise summary of the achievements of the New Deal. 'What then did the New Deal do?' he asks.

> It gave far greater amplitude to the national state, expanded the authority of the presidency, recruited university trained administrators, won control of the money supply, established central banking, imposed regulation on Wall Street, rescued the debt-ridden farmer and homeowner, built model communities, financed the Federal Housing Administration, made federal housing a permanent feature, fostered unionization of the factories, reduced child labor, ended the tyranny of company towns, wiped out many sweatshops, mandated minimal working standards, enabled tenants to buy their own farms, built camps for migrants, introduced the welfare state with old-age pensions, unemployment insurance, and aid for dependent children, provided jobs for millions of unemployed, created a special program for the jobless young

and for students, covered the American landscape with new edifices, subsidized painters and novelists, composers and ballet dancers, founded America's first state theater, created documentary films, gave birth to the impressive Tennessee Valley Authority, generated electrical power, sent the Civilian Conservation Corps boys into the forests, initiated the Soil Conservation Service, transformed the economy of agriculture, lighted up rural America, gave women greater recognition, made a start toward breaking the pattern of racial discrimination and segregation, put together a liberal party coalition, changed the agenda of American politics, and brought about a Constitutional Revolution.[1]

DISINTEGRATION OF A SOCIAL SYSTEM

Niebuhr did not share the optimism of the New Dealers:

> When it becomes apparent (as it must in the long run) that political control of private capitalism cannot produce sufficient equality of income to eliminate overproduction and unemployment the stage will be set for a sharper delineation of the social struggle in our American life. (REE, p. 80)

Instead, Niebuhr set the American problem in the context of the world capitalist system as a whole. He reminded his readers that civilizations rise and fall, and that Western civilization was now in an irreversible 'process of disintegration', it was governed by a 'senile social system', and that it was suffering from an 'organic sickness'. *Reflections* is an attempt to offer 'adequate spiritual guidance' for the task of building a new social system. To do this it is necessary 'to combine political radicalism with a more classical and historical interpretation of religion' (REE, p. ix). In practice this means that Niebuhr will combine some aspects of Marxist social analysis with some aspects of biblical mythology in an effort to give form to the 'ultra-rational' framework which serves as a principle of coherence for situating life and experience.

Niebuhr considered that the problems facing society were far greater than could be solved by the haphazard philosophy of the New Deal.

> A social or political system, a ruling class or an economic organization may be persuaded to mend some of its incidental

defects; but it can hardly be persuaded to recognize that its day is done. (REE, p. 30)

The capitalist system has become an anachronism, he argued. The centre of its injustice is the private ownership of the means of production, and the fact that it produces goods on a massive scale but does not provide the wages or the employment to create the capacity for consumption which it requires to survive. The capitalist system is in the process of universalizing itself, that is its momentum, but it can live healthily only as long as it fails to universalize itself. The more expansive the system, the more obvious appear the contradictions. Modern technical achievements have made for transnational mutuality and international reciprocity, but the competitive basis of the economic system makes the realization of a universal society impossible.

The fact that Niebuhr supported a candidate who polled less than 3 per cent of the popular vote is explained by the observation that

the burden bearers of the world are always inclined more to patience than to heroic rebellion. They are slow to express their resentments and even slower to make them the basis of political policy. (REE, p. 52)

Therefore, 'judgements upon social evil are executed only after the evil has cumulated to intolerable proportions' (REE, p. 52).

The Depression is explained as follows:

For this reason the putrid remains of what was once living and is now dead frequently create a pestilence in society before they are decently buried. (REE, p. 52)

The New Deal strategies are only postponing the inevitable collapse:

Moribund social systems disintegrate slowly not only because the instruments of their destruction are fashioned so gradually but because they are of tougher fibre than the prophets of a new day realize. They may defy death even long after the diseases of senility have wasted their strength and their foes have given them the mortal wound. (REE, p. 52)

The most extreme case of the disease is fascism, and for Niebuhr the New Deal is a drift towards fascism. J. M. Keynes is characterized as a doctor of a moribund social system, but it is futile to expect societies to avert the deadly vengeance of history. A further symptom of the disease is the threat to democracy:

A dying capitalism is under the necessity of abolishing or circumscribing democracy, not only to rob its foes of a weapon, but to save itself from its own anarchy. The competitive freedom of *laissez-faire* capitalism becomes a dangerous hazard in the day of crisis, and it is therefore replaced by state capitalism in which the state both restricts the freedom and supports the weakness of the old property system. Even when the political development is not avowedly fascist the tendency to substitute state capitalism for the old *laissez-faire* economy is obvious, as for instance in England and America. (REE, p. 56)

Niebuhr feels that the imminent collapse of Western civilization, which is but another example of the inexorable processes of history, will be more rapid than previous collapses because technical progress has 'sharpened the instruments' of vengeance. Because modern technology has also increased the intensity of social cohesion the society will collapse much more rapidly than an organic society. There remains the possibility, however, of the old system yielding to new forces without too much of a struggle, in which case history is lenient and it will allow the old civilization to preserve 'a remnant of its glory' (REE, p. 68).

On the other hand while the virtues of one civilization may be transferred to a new social order it is inevitable that vices will be also transferred. This is how Niebuhr characterizes Communism:

One of the pathetic aspects of human history is that the instruments of judgment which it uses to destroy particular vices must belong to the same category of the vice to be able to destroy it. Thus some evil, which is to be destroyed, is always transferred to the instrument of its destruction and thereby perpetuated. (REE, p. 94)

Communism is also characterized as:

the victim and not the nemesis of capitalistic civilization, destined not to correct the weaknesses of a bourgeois culture but to develop them to the last impossible and absurd consistency. (REE, p. 103)

In sum, Niebuhr's sociology with medical imagery is explaining that the current economic crisis requires more drastic attention than is being given by the liberal economists and politicians. Roosevelt's policies are essentially prolonging an unjust social system, but a study of history reveals that they will not succeed because the injustices are too extreme and the contradictions of the economic system will eventually undermine these efforts.

MYTHOLOGICAL FRAMEWORK FOR SOCIAL ANALYSIS

Having characterized the contemporary social crisis in medical imagery Niebuhr embarks on the main purpose of the book, which is to characterize the same reality in religious imagery. If the present crisis can be situated in a religious framework then it should afford some guidance in the perplexing realities of life. Niebuhr is picking up a theme he first expressed in *Does Civilization* and which has remained since then without elaboration or clarification.

There is a preliminary consideration of the weakness of liberalism which links with *Moral Man* and other previous works. Despite the high optimism of its individualism its philosophy has little sense of the organic communal relationships, and as such it is without an understanding of the inertia of nature most evident in collective human behaviour. It is only from a religious perspective that a vantage point can be secured for analysing modern crises. What is required is a sense or feeling for the total situation in which the human stands. The actual rational comprehension of the total situation can only be gained by a combination of many minds and many generations of life. To understand the present before such expert analysis is possible is the function of mythology. 'Meaning can be attributed to history only by a mythology' (REE, p. 123).

> A philosophy of history adequate to bring all of the various perspectives, from those of economists and political strategists to the insights of artists and moralists, into a total unity must be endowed with the highest imagination. It must combine the exact data of the scientist with the vision of the artist and must add religious depth to philosophical generalizations. An adequate philosophy of history must, in short, be a mythology rather than a philosophy. It is precisely because modern culture is too empirically rationalistic that it cannot do justice to the very history of which it is a contemporary spectator. It lacks a vision of the whole which would give meaning to the specific events it seeks to comprehend. (REE, p. 122)

An 'adequate mythology' is able to give meaning to facts of history which would otherwise remain incomprehensible. All worldviews are, according to Niebuhr, mythological, even those which claim to be based on rational precepts. Bourgeois optimism is essentially a 'mythology of progress' which believes that in the end mind will triumph over impulse, reason will triumph over the sub-rational forces of human nature. What this mythology fails to realize is that historical development is not the gradual triumph of the human spirit over the impulses of nature, but a conflict between collective organisms, between old and new civilizations. There are similarities to Spengler's naturalism, but whereas Spengler imagines civilizations growing and fading like flowers in the soil that produced them, Niebuhr imagines them contending against each other like animals. The conflict between the old and new is a conflict in which 'forces of nature are arraigned against each other' (REE, p. 124). His language at times resembles Canaanite mythology. 'History' must be conceived in terms of a 'combat between two social organisms, the new organism emerging from the womb of a dying one' (REE, p. 124).

Modern rationalism is wrong to reject apocalypticism because this mythology acknowledges one vital fact which is overlooked, which is that the forces of history do not correspond to ideals. What Niebuhr means by this is that conscious designs and plans to harness and organize historical forces always yield results which do not match the original conscious purpose. In this respect Marxist mythology stands midway between the liberal faith and the faith of Christian sectarians. With liberalism it emphasizes faith in human responsibility for the historic process. With the Christian sects it realizes that history is not developed merely by those who imagine they are developing the process. Marxism is still a mythology because it acknowledges that history has meaning (and history can only have meaning when there is some comprehension of totality) even when the forces of history are not conscious of meaning.

To illustrate the point that Marxism is more than a scientific economic determinism, Niebuhr compares certain aspects of Marxism to the Christian faith. The Pauline concept that God 'uses the wrath of man to praise him' is secularized in the theory that the enemies of the proletariat will eventually defeat themselves. The teaching of Jesus that the 'last shall be first and the first shall be last' is transformed into the teaching that when the proletariat assumes the end of the existing order it is at the same time an announcement of its own existence. The Christian teaching 'fear not little flock, it is your Father's good pleasure to give you the kingdom' is equivalent to the certainty of the revolutionary victory nerving the necessary social activity required to secure that victory. Finally, Marxism experiences the same difficulties faced by Christianity in balancing voluntarism and determinism. Marxism insists that though the historical process inevitably leads to the victory of the proletariat, the dialectic must be consciously directed by a vanguard of the proletariat, the Communist Party.

The most important feature of Marxism in relation to religion, according to Niebuhr, is the fact that Marxism belongs to the general category of Jewish apocalypticism rather than Hellenistic interpretations of life and history. Here Niebuhr develops conclusions found in the earlier work, *Contribution*. This does involve some contradiction with regard to the ethic of Jesus. Niebuhr argues that Christian orthodoxy has tended to follow the Greek pattern of thought rather than the Jewish, and the characteristic of Jewish thought, of Jesus himself, and the early Christian Church with its hope for the Parousia (the second coming of Christ), is that they regard the issues of life from the perspective of those 'who are immersed in a social situation and therefore desire not individual emancipation from history's injustices, but the achievement of justice in history' (REE, p. 133). Up to this point in his work Niebuhr has of course been stressing the idea that the religious ethic of Jesus is meant for intimate organic communities and is not directly applicable to social justice.

The importance of Marxism for Niebuhr lies in the fact that it has reintroduced an eschatological dimension into modern thought. It has revived, in a secularized version, Jewish apocalypticism, and in that sense it is both a critique of and a judgement on modern forms of Christianity which have too easily accommodated themselves to modern culture. Christian orthodoxy is a compromise between the faith and Greek dualism, and Christian liberalism is a compromise with naturalistic monism (i.e. scientific evolutionary theories). Neither of them is preferable to a possible compromise between Marxism and 'pure Christian mythology' (REE, p. 135). Niebuhr explains:

> [I]f Christianity is to survive this era of social disintegration and social rebuilding, and is not to be absorbed in or annihilated by the secularized religion of Marxism it must come to terms with the insights of Marxist mythology. There is truth in this mythology because it is more able to affirm moral meaning in contemporary chaos than orthodox Christianity, since the latter tends to regard all history as unredeemed and

unredeemable chaos. It is superior to liberal Christianity because Christian liberalism is spiritually dependent upon bourgeois liberalism and is completely lost when its neat evolutionary process towards an ethical historical goal is suddenly engulfed in social catastrophe. (REE. p. 135)

ADEQUATE MYTHOLOGY

When Niebuhr teaches that a total comprehension of the world is a mythological worldview it is equivalent to what Thomas Kuhn would regard as a 'paradigm'. This similarity was mentioned earlier. Niebuhr considers that all frameworks which serve to draw isolated facts of experience into a coherent whole are, in the end, ultra-rational, or mythological. Each framework serves as a paradigm because all the facts of experience can be interpreted on the basis of its presuppositions. Kuhn's thesis, that scientific experiments generally illustrate a scientific law until the results of other experiments seem to contradict that law, bears some similarity with Niebuhr's conception of the function of mythology. When the anomalies to the scientific paradigm increase in frequency a new paradigm supplants the old because it no longer offers a framework of interpretation.

Niebuhr argues that modern life and experience is dominated by two mythological worldviews or paradigms which are contending with each other for the allegiance of adherents. But in both cases they are inadequate because they fail in some important respects to impart meaning to all the facts of experience which assail the senses. It is Niebuhr's constant thesis throughout his work that the Christian religion supplies the basic mythology which is capable of imparting meaning to experience and which is continually being validated by experience. *Reflections* represents his first attempt to clarify this theme which was expressed in his first book.

The two mythological worldviews which dominate the modern world are described as 'bourgeois naturalism' and 'proletarian communism'. The former imagines that history moves gradually by evolutionary determinism towards an ethical goal. It is an optimistic worldview corresponding with the bourgeois ideals of free co-operation in a libertarian social order. The proletarian worldview is also optimistic but there is a catastrophic note in it. The present social order must disintegrate before the ideal order can be established. Both worldviews are religious because they understand a purpose in history which in reality is the projection of human ideals upon cosmic reality. They are, like classical religion, efforts to deal with the problem of evil and to make suffering bearable by imparting meaning to a process having a discernible end.

> To understand the universe is to conquer it; but to understand must mean in some sense to make it relevant to the human enterprise. Every world-view therefore, which finds the mechanisms of the cosmos either neutrally amenable or profoundly sympathetic to human ideals, is mythological and religious. (REE, p. 196)

Although they are both religious interpretations of life they are inadequate because they do not belong to what Niebuhr categorizes here as 'full-orbed religion' but more usually as 'high religion'. They do not belong to this category because they are monistic rather than dualistic. A dualistic religion is one which believes that meaning and purpose transcend any immediate event or historical reality.

There are various tests which can be applied to a worldview to judge its adequacy as a framework of coherence. Niebuhr rejects philosophical adequacy however on the grounds that every philosophy is in itself merely a rationalized worldview which cannot do justice to all the facts of paradoxical reality. If a worldview seems rational to a given age or era it simply means that it does justice to those facts which an age regards as important. The real difference between the naturalistic monisms of bourgeois and proletarian worldviews and the supernatural dualism of classical Christianity is to be found in ethical feeling. Wherever the moral imagination conceives ideals for life which history in any conceivable form is able to realize, then a dualistic worldview arises. Supernaturalism emerges therefore with the discovery of the inertia and the persistence of the egoistic impulse in nature including human nature. A source above the human is sought to explain the moral demands and an order of reality is recognized which surpasses human perfection. The Christian religion with its conception of a transcendent–immanent God does justice both to the moral necessities of human life and also to the facts of human experience,

> for experience constantly reveals harmonies, meanings and purposes which, by their very imperfection, suggest a perfection beyond them but which in spite of their imperfection

contain elements of the perfection which transcends them. (REE, p. 201)

This is precisely what the myth of Creation reveals. God is both transcendent and immanent, immanent in the sense that the creation is a revelation of his majesty and glory.

In monistic worldviews the rational human is conceived as triumphing over the chaos of nature and history. In the dualistic worldview of classical religion the human is conceived as the source of chaos and there is no escape from the self-destruction of conflicting egoisms within the realm of history.

TESTING MYTHOLOGIES

The test of a paradigm is its ability to incorporate potential anomalies. If too many anomalies appear, the principle of coherence which the paradigm provides is threatened. For Niebuhr, the most appropriate test of a worldview is its attitude towards the political realm. Here, the intractable problem of collective egoism as threat of anarchy or tyranny has to be met.

The three worldviews yield different estimates of the political ordering of society. Christian orthodoxy regards politics as the nemesis of the moral ideal and its weakness is either to encourage acquiescence in the order of the day, or to infuse an element of permanent legitimacy to an impermanent political order. Radicalism (i.e. Communism and other types of socialism) tends to look on political power as an instrument of the moral ideal without being sufficiently aware of how easily power corrupts the ideal. Liberalism, which fails to make a distinction between morals and politics, imagines that morality is easily applied to the political world.

Radicalism is considered to be initially more realistic than liberalism but in the final analysis it still operates as if it imagines that collective egoism can be abolished through political and economic activity. Christianity from the beginning possessed no illusions about political behaviour. The political realm has always provided the most vivid symbols for human sinfulness (e.g. the book of Revelation).

This criterion for assessing the adequacy of worldviews poses a problem for Niebuhr which is not acknowledged in the book. Niebuhr, as a pragmatist, always judged a theory by the question, 'Does it work?'. As the 1930s progressed his criticisms of

Communism and Marxism became much harsher in tone because of the form it had taken under Stalin in Russia. He began to look on Communist theory as inevitably producing a Stalin. Yet here, in *Reflections*, Niebuhr admits that 'no sound principle of political change emerges anywhere in Christian thought' (REE, p. 221). The question is, if this is the case, how can Niebuhr have so much confidence in asserting that Christian mythology provides the ultimate framework for understanding life and experience? Why should he continue to promote Christianity especially if it has helped to shape modern liberal society which has aggravated social injustice to intolerable proportions? It is this problem which eventually leads Niebuhr to search behind the forms of historic Christianity to what he regards as its pure expression in the scriptures.

In *Reflections* Niebuhr returns to the biblical source for the ethic of Jesus, and the mythological framework is mentioned but not emphasized. The ethic of Jesus is offered as a truth of experience and as an explanation as to why historic Christianity has been generally ineffectual with regard to political justice. The ethic of Jesus stresses the ideal of love, it does not offer concrete rewards, and it condemns the assertion of the ego. In short, it is the opposite of sensible political advice. Political activity without hope of reward is very often the preoccupation of fanatics, and the reluctance to assert rights very often ends in them being trampled underfoot. But paradoxically, the ethic is relevant to the experience of life, argues Niebuhr, because when life is conceived as an organic whole then any part which thrusts against the whole destroys the organic harmony. However, the rational realization of this fact does not check its occurrence and life must be organized and prepare itself for these collective impulses which threaten the whole. Thus the ethic of Jesus can never be adopted as a simple method of attaining self-realization in history. Liberal Protestantism transformed the ethic of Jesus into a social teaching under the influence of eighteenth-century rationalism and nineteenth-century liberalism. Classical Christianity faced the same problem by borrowing elements of the Stoic ethic and elaborating a Christian version of the natural law which answered to some of the demands of social justice.

The ethic of Jesus, even though in its pure form it is indifferent to politics, cannot be understood as individualistic perfection, because the concept of the Kingdom of God is a social concept. It is beyond human capacity to establish the ideal society, that could only be accomplished through the grace of God. This is the function of the apocalyptic mythology in which the ethic of Jesus is set. This mythology maintains the hope of social fulfilment, and indicates that its achievement is unattainable through human resources. Nevertheless co-operation with the divine purpose involves working towards social justice.

POLITICS, ETHICS, AND GRACE

Having analysed the social problem, and having described how the religious worldview is related to political philosophy, Niebuhr offers his own approach to the social and moral problems of contemporary America. It must be a political policy which contains resources to check egoistic impulses, it must be capable of exploiting the altruistic impulse to extend community, and it must recognize a religious base which challenges every concrete attainment. The prevailing worldview does not see life in its full dimension of nature and spirit. It does not acknowledge the stubborn inertia below the level of reason, and does not recognize the heights of self-sacrificial love above the liberal prudential morality.

An adequate worldview must cater for all three points. It must therefore be composed of a radical political theory, a theory of morals which allows for the prudence of liberalism and the disinterestedness of radical religion, and an idea of grace with its paradoxical attitudes towards human nature found only in classical religion.

A radical political theory in Niebuhr's thought is one where there is social ownership of the means of production. This would involve a strong political force to hold economic power in check, but it could also add to disproportions of power. This means that democracy must remain a perennial necessity.

Political radicalism often overlooks elements of mutual accord which develop in any social situation. It often lacks a virtue of liberalism, the virtue of tolerance. But liberal ethics separates reason and emotion, whereas in the ethic of Jesus reason is not set against impulse. Reason accepts altruism which is rooted in the natural impulse and enlarges it. The ethic of Jesus is a union of altruistic impulse and rational imperative. To illustrate this Niebuhr adds:

> The observation of Jesus, 'If you love those who love you what thanks have ye?' grows out of a spiritual insight in which

71

natural altruistic emotions have been heightened by rational force. (REE, p. 264)

The third element, the experience of grace, means recognizing and accepting the ultra-rational framework of the Christian religion. By grace, Niebuhr means the acknowledgement that nature and history possess meaning. It is the acknowledgement that God is revealed in nature and history (REE, p. 285). Thus, although the Depression is a revelation of judgement, history does supply examples of the revelation of divine mercy. This is why Niebuhr argued earlier that old social forces should yield to new social forces. The yielding is equivalent to the expression of contrition, and mercy follows contrition. A vital religion is one which catches glimpses of the ultimate in the imperfections of life and history.

The religion of Jesus is an example of vital religion. When Niebuhr turns to the biblical source to illustrate his argument he maintains the liberal Christian distinction between the religion of Jesus and the religion of Paul. As he developed his theology of myth he was unable to maintain this distinction with the same insistence. Niebuhr finds in Paul the origin of the Greek influence which led to Christian orthodoxy's pessimism regarding the political order. In the religion of Jesus there is both ethical tension and relaxation of that tension. There is the demand for perfection (Mt 5:48), but there is also the contrite recognition that perfection cannot be attained (Mk 10:18). The former establishes ethical dualism by acknowledging the transcendent source, and the latter establishes ethical realism by acknowledging the perennial imperfections of history.

Niebuhr finds that in the religion of Paul, however, the contrast between the dualism and the realism in the difference between the perfection of the Lord and the ethical possibilities of this life, creates a chasm between nature and God which requires more specific acts of grace. In more consistent dualism this leads to a conception of grace which is confined to those specific acts (e.g. incarnation), and confined to the mediations of a particular religious institution. This weakens the sense of history as a revelation of grace, and the ethical tension is divorced from the social dimension and conceived in purely individualistic terms. The consequence of this is:

that the moral vigor which is most relevant to the urgent moral problems of an era which must deal with the life and death of social systems is expressed outside the churches. (REE, p. 292)

Niebuhr does not develop many details about the mythical framework, but the true nature of myth must be realized if the Christian religion is to be a resource for the building of a new society.

> The experience of grace can only be expressed in mythological terms if it is not to become a peril to the ethical life. For only in concepts of religious myth can an imperfect world mirror the purpose of a divine Creator and can the mercy of God make the fact of sin and imperfection bearable without destroying moral responsibility for the evil of imperfection or obscuring its realities in actual history. (REE, p. 292)

Any attempt to rationalize the mythical framework endangers the truth of the religion. Christian orthodoxy, because of its Platonic dualism, has problems with the concept of the absolute expressed in the imperfections and relativities of history. Niebuhr considers the neo-orthodoxy of the Barthians in their reaction to liberalism is too extreme in its dualism, and it robs history of its meaning. Liberalism, by contrast, is too monistic, the consequence of which is to invest nature and history with the aura of the absolute and the perfect. These errors lead to unrealistic hopes for human progress; history is endowed with too much meaning. Niebuhr regards the naturalistic monism of Marxism as informed by the same error despite the initial concept of catastrophe. Naturalistic monisms do not understand the mythical implications of the Fall. It is an expression for the transformation of the natural impulse of egoism into the wilful conflict of life with life.

In the final chapter of *Reflections* Niebuhr has gone some way towards clarifying a recurring theme in his work. He has developed something of the content and purpose of the ultra-rational framework. Another expression for the recognition of this framework is 'the experience of grace'.

> Essentially the experience of grace in religion is the apprehension of the absolute from the perspective of the relative. The unachieved is in some sense felt to be achieved or realized. The sinner is 'justified' even though his sin is not overcome. The world, as revealed in its processes of nature, is known to be imperfect and yet it is recognized as a creation of God. Man is regarded as both a sinner and a child of God. In these paradoxes true religion makes present reality bearable even while it insists that God is denied, frustrated and defied in the immediate situation. (REE, p. 282)

All worldviews explicitly or implicitly possess a mythical framework, and Niebuhr's assumption is that the Christian religion, when understood correctly, is capable of refuting alternative worldviews or corruptions of its own mythology. Much of Niebuhr's later work will be a demonstration of the power of this mythology as a basis for interpretation and refutation.

NOTE

1 William E. Leuchtenburg, 'The achievement of the New Deal' in Harvard Sitkoff (ed.), *Fifty Years Later: The New Deal Evaluated* (New York, 1985), p. 228.

5

Ethics and Myth

In the spring of 1934 Niebuhr delivered the Rauschenbusch Memorial Lectures at Colgate-Rochester Divinity School, New York. These lectures were published in 1935 as *An Interpretation of Christian Ethics*. The book contains the familiar themes: the inadequacy of liberal Protestantism; the importance of understanding the character of collective human activity; the form of the ultra-rational mythical framework of 'prophetic religion'; the relationship between the ethic of Jesus and the mythical framework; and the religious contribution of the Marxist social critique.

The book is an elaboration of the material found in the final chapter of *Reflections*. The mythical framework of 'prophetic religion' is established in a discussion of the liberal critique of orthodox Christianity. This is followed by a biblical exegesis of selected sayings of Jesus with the intention of demonstrating how the ethic of Jesus coheres with the truths revealed in the mythical framework. The relevance of this ethic in the political sphere is discussed and contrasted with the weaknesses of both orthodox Christianity and liberal Christianity when applied to the same sphere. Finally, to satisfy the individualists, there is a discussion of the significance of this theology for the individual believer.

'ESSENTIAL CHRISTIANITY'

Niebuhr begins by dividing Christianity into two broad divisions, the orthodox churches and the liberal churches. Many critics have complained about Niebuhr's loose terminology, and his use of the word 'orthodox' certainly justifies these criticisms. In general it means the main form of Christianity from Augustine, through the mediaeval period, up to and including the leading figures of the Reformation. But it can also mean that form of Christianity which has remained unmoved by the rationalism of the eighteenth century and the discoveries of modern science. It stresses adherence to creedal affirmations. It is conservative, but not fundamentalist. The pre-Vatican II Catholic Church, for example, would be classified in Niebuhr's 'orthodox' category. The two groups of churches, the orthodox and the liberal, are found to be incapable of serving a useful function in the contemporary world:

> The orthodox churches have long since compounded the truth of the Christian religion with dogmatisms of another day, and have thereby petrified what would otherwise have long since fallen prey to the beneficent dissolutions of the processes of nature and history. The liberal churches, on the other hand, have hid their light under the bushel of modernity with all its short-lived prejudices and presumptuous certainties. (ICE, p. 14)

The orthodox churches have their truths embedded in an outmoded science, and their morality is confined to dogmatic codes which do not relate to shifting social mores. They have lost religious and moral meaning. The liberal churches, in their desire to prove that they do not share the anachronistic ethics or believe the incredible myths of orthodoxy, have obscured what is distinctive in Christian religion and morality. In their efforts to prove that religion and science are compatible they have merely clothed naturalistic philosophy and utilitarian ethics in fine phrases.

Niebuhr's concern is to express the Christian faith in such a way that it will provide an ethic which is capable of locating and dealing with specific problems of social justice, and at the same time is expressed in such a form that it is not outrageous to the modern scientific mind, nor a scandal to traditional faith. The Christian religion is a 'high religion' which means that it attempts to bring the whole of reality into some system of coherence. It is a religion 'straining after ultimate coherence' (ICE, p. 17). The parameters of this system of coherence are God the creator of existence and God the fulfiller of existence. The system is expressed in mythological language. It is the 'ultra-rational framework' of *Does Civilization*.

If the system of coherence is to make sense in a post-scientific world then it must acknowledge the fact that liberal Christianity emancipated traditional Christianity from dogmatic and literalistic interpretations of the mythical inheritance. By accepting the historico-critical method of biblical analysis it has made it possible to free what is eternal in the Christian religion. However, in its accommodations to liberal culture liberal Christianity has failed to take advantage of its methods of analysis. Just as orthodox religion degenerates into bad science if its mythological form is interpreted literally, so liberal religion degenerates into superficial religion in its attempts to rationalize its mythological setting. Scientific descriptions of historical sequences are easily 'corrupted into an untrue conception of total reality' (ICE, p. 22). Therefore the mythical content of traditional Christianity must be taken seriously:

> It is the genius of true myth to suggest the dimension of depth in reality and to point to a realm of essence which transcends the surface of history, on which the cause and effect sequences, discovered and analysed by science, occur. (ICE, p. 22)

Religious myth points to the ultimate ground and the ultimate fulfilment of existence, but because it has to express trans-historical truth in symbols and events in history it invariably falsifies history, as seen by science, to state its truth. Niebuhr adopts the Pauline expression 'As deceivers, yet true' (2 Cor 6:8) to express this.

Theology and philosophy are regarded as two stages in the direction from myth to rational consistency. For Niebuhr, theology is an attempt to construct a rational and systematic view of life out of the mythology of a religious tradition, and philosophy attempts to dispense with myth altogether in an effort to form rational consistency.

> This rationalization of myth is inevitable and necessary, lest religion be destroyed by undisciplined and fantastic imagery or primitive and inconsistent myth. (ICE, p. 24)

However,

> Every authentic religious myth contains paradoxes of the relation between the finite and the eternal which cannot be completely rationalized without destroying the genius of true religion. (ICE, p. 24)

This means that Niebuhr does not see himself as a theologian in the strict sense of the word. He is not interested in a systematic

77

presentation of a doctrine of God, a Christology, a theological anthropology, an ecclesiology or a pneumatology. His task is to distinguish between primitive mythology and authentic mythology, and to demonstrate how authentic mythology contains paradoxical wisdom which is continually being validated by life and experience. Authentic mythology consists of the great myths of creation and redemption in the Hebrew tradition, and the clue to their interpretation is the historical figure of Jesus Christ. On the other hand the teaching of Jesus can only be interpreted when it is set within this authentic mythology. Liberal Protestantism transformed the Christ of Christian orthodoxy, the 'true mythical symbol of both the possibilities and limits of the human' into 'the good man of Galilee, symbol of human goodness and human possibilities without suggestion of the limits of the human and the temporal' (ICE, p. 25). It removed the figure of the historical Jesus from the mythological setting. The consequence of this was to imagine sin to be an imperfection of ignorance which would eventually yield its power to human development. It lost the concept of the demonic in collective activity, the knowledge that collective human nature transforms partial virtues into consistent vices, such as loyalty into imperialism, for example.

The source of 'authentic' myth is the Hebrew prophetic movement, and the great myths of the beginning and end of existence are termed 'classical' myths. Niebuhr uses a number of different expressions for this throughout his work. Whenever he uses the terms 'Hebrew religion', 'prophetic religion', 'prophetic faith', 'biblical religion', 'biblical faith', he is referring to the religion expressed in the form of classical myths. It is a 'high religion'.

> Mythical thought . . . deals with vertical aspects of reality which transcend the horizontal relationships which science analyses, charts and records. The classical myth refers to the transcendent source and end of existence without abstracting it from existence. In this sense the myth alone is capable of picturing the world as a realm of coherence and meaning without defying the facts of incoherence. Its world is coherent because all facts in it are related to some central source of meaning; but it is not rationally coherent because the myth is not under the abortive necessity of relating all things to each other in terms of immediate rational unity. The God of mythical religion is, significantly, the Creator and not the First Cause. (ICE, p. 36)

The myth of Creation expresses the fact that God is both organically related to the world and distinct from the world. Thus the world can be thought of as a realm of meaning and coherence without having to insist that the world is totally good or that the totality of existence must be associated with the sacred. Within this framework the Hebrew prophetic movement was able to account for evil without making it identical to the genesis of life in the sense that it was ordained by God or that it was inevitable. Thus Hebrew spirituality possessed resources which prevented the development of either an unrealistic optimism where the world is endowed with an unmerited sanctity, or an unrealistic pessimism, where the world is conceived as a meaningless recurrence of cycles. The myth of the Fall means that evil is both an incomprehensible mystery and the consequence of human perversity. This mythical basis of the Hebrew religion imparts meaning to history without imparting undue reverence for the human as creator of history.

The myth of a Creator God also offers the possibility of conceiving God as judge and redeemer. The Creator God who transcends the world also, from this perspective, condemns the world as judge, but from the perspective of immanence, promises redemption both within the world and at the end of the world. Thus the myth of redemption is cast in such a form that naturalism (which imagines that nature and history are ultimately self-explanatory and redemptive) and mysticism (which can find no meaning in history and imagines redemption as other-worldly) are both conceived as errors.

Apart from naturalism and otherworldliness as threats to the insights of prophetic religion, Niebuhr also cites the sacramentalism of Catholic orthodoxy as a vitiation of prophetic mythology. By reinterpreting the eschatology of prophetic religion Augustine replaced redemption at the end of history with a reference towards a realm of transcendence above history, and the mediation between the world of nature and the world of history was provided by a sacramental institution.

The centre of Niebuhr's theology is not, therefore, Christology or anthropology or the concept of the hidden God as critics often infer. Its centre is, in a sense, sociological in that the experience of a social group becomes the norm for interpreting all experience. It adopts the classical mythology which the Jewish prophetic movement developed to describe its experience and self-consciousness as the chosen people of the one true God. Niebuhr's Christology, his anthropology, and his concept of the hidden God, are all derivatives of the primary source which is the Jewish prophetic movement. 'Vital Christianity' or 'essential Christianity' is a demonstration of how this mythical, ultra-rational framework provides a basis for understanding life and history in both its individual and social dimension. Historical experience continually validates the truth of this mythological framework, and the framework continually provides resources for refuting alternative suggestions of meaning which history produces to contend against it.

> Only a vital Christian faith, renewing its youth in its prophetic origin, is capable of dealing adequately with the moral and social problems of our age; only such a faith can affirm the significance of temporal and mundane existence without capitulating unduly to the relativities of the temporal process. Such a faith alone can point to a source of meaning which transcends all the little universes of value and meaning which 'have their day and cease to be' and yet not seek refuge in an eternal world where all history ceases to be significant. Only such a faith can outlast the death of old cultures and the birth of new civilizations, and yet deal in terms of moral responsibility with the world in which cultures and civilizations engage in struggles of death and life. (ICE, p. 44)

THE ETHIC OF JESUS

Needless to say the ethic of Jesus fits perfectly into the worldview of prophetic religion. It cannot be used to support the idea that ascetic withdrawal from the world is of more value than involvement in the world, and it cannot be used as a basis for expecting social life to ultimately conform to its norms.

Niebuhr demonstrates that the ethic of Jesus belongs to prophetic religion in three ways. First, he shows that the contrast between good and evil in both prophetic religion and the ethic of Jesus is not between perfection and imperfection, or between the temporal and the eternal. By referring to Mt 7:11, 'If you then, who are evil, know how to give good gifts to your children, how much more will your Father who is in heaven give good things to those who ask him?', he concludes that the contrast is between good and evil will. Jesus sees something of the character of God in the tenderness of parents towards their children, but also a symbol of God's love among 'evil' and not imperfect people. Since the evil will is not the consequence of finiteness, human life is not without symbols and echoes of the divine.

Second, he contrasts the universalism in the ethic of Jesus with the universalism of the Stoic ethic. In Stoicism, life beyond the narrow loyalties of life is to be affirmed because all life reveals a unifying principle, the divine principle. In the ethic of Jesus the motive for love is not that others are divine but that God loves all equally, and they are to be forgiven, which is the highest form of love, because they are all—including the self—equally far from God. This difference between the Stoic ethic and the gospel ethic is the difference between a pantheistic religion and prophetic religion. In prophetic religion ultimate moral demands can never be affirmed in terms of the actual facts of human existence. Human order and virtue and possibilities cannot become solid bases of the moral imperative. Moral demands can only be affirmed in terms of a divine reality which transcends human existence.

Third, the eschatological setting of the ethic of Jesus is again true to the insights of prophetic religion. The rewards that are promised in the Sermon on the Mount are for fulfilment at the end of time and not in some realm above temporality. The eschatological basis of Jesus' ethic indicates that

the ethical demands made by Jesus are incapable of fulfilment in the present existence of man. They proceed from a trans- cendent and divine unity of essential reality and their final fulfilment is possible only when God transmutes the present chaos of this world into its final unity. (ICE, p. 67)

It is stating mythically what cannot be stated rationally, that eternal reality can only be fulfilled in the temporal.

It must be mentioned here that Niebuhr's thought is confused regarding the eschatological setting. He is attempting to avoid the conclusions Albert Schweitzer arrived at regarding the apocalyptic thought of Jesus and an 'interim' ethic, an ethic which counsels patience because the present world order is soon to vanish. At the same time Niebuhr seeks to maintain an ethical activity based on reality and not illusion, for if it were based on an illusion, it would not be substantially different from a Marxist ethic which is based on the emergence of the classless society where evil has been gradually eliminated from the social order. Against the idea of an 'interim' ethic Niebuhr states: 'Apocalypticism in terms of a specific inter- pretation of history may thus be regarded as the consequence and not the cause of Jesus' religion and ethic' (ICE, p. 68). This

81

contradicts Niebuhr's assertion that the ethic of Jesus is set within prophetic mythology which already contains an apocalyptic element. On the second point, Niebuhr's argument about the eschatological context in prophetic religion not only contradicts his assertion that apocalypticism is a consequence and not a base of Jesus' ethic, it also leads to difficulties later on in Niebuhr's work when he rejects any possibility of a literal understanding of the Parousia. For here, against the illusions of Marxist eschatology, Niebuhr writes:

> All these promises of an ultimate reward are in no way in conflict with the rigour of the gospel ethic. They merely prove that even the most uncompromising ethical system must base its moral imperative on an order of reality and not merely on a possibility. Somewhere, somehow, the unity of the world must be or become an established fact and not merely a possibility, and actions which flow from its demands must be in harmony and not in conflict with reality. (ICE, p. 65)

In other words, there has to be a perfect order of reality in the future; otherwise the ethic of Jesus is based on an illusion and is inferior to the Marxist ethic which describes the necessary activity to achieve social justice in a classless society.

Niebuhr finds the central theme in the ethic of Jesus to be the condemnation of every form of self-assertion. The basis of self-love is the natural will to survive. It is an animal impulse which in human life becomes the temptation to assert the self against the neighbour. Therefore, there is to be no concern for physical existence; people are encouraged not to worry about how they are going to receive food and clothing. Birds do not worry about these things and God feeds them (Mt 6:25–32).

A natural form of self-assertion or expansion of the self is to acquire possessions. The ethic of Jesus counsels against acquiring possessions (Mt 6:19–24). A rich young man is advised to sell all his possessions and give the money to the poor and live an itinerant life in the company of Jesus (Mt 19:21), or a widow is held up as a good example because she gave away all her money for the upkeep of the temple (Mk 12:44).

Jesus attacked those who sought social approval, a subtle form of self-assertion and pride which particularly afflicts 'good' people (Mt 23:5–7). Jesus' attack on vindictiveness and his injunction to forgive are seen as examples of his intransigence with forms of self-assertion which have social and moral approval in any natural morality. The self is not to assert its interests against those who encroach upon it (e.g. 'love your enemies').

In natural human intercourse these demands are an impossibility. The ethic of Jesus is in conflict with the impulses and necessities of ordinary people in typical social situations. To elaborate these injunctions into social or political systems blunts the penetration of the moral insights. For example, when people (like liberal Christians for example) condemn violence in conflict it ceases to provide a perspective on the sinful element in any form of conflict. Pacifism is usually hypocritical because it is advocated by those who can afford to dispense with more violent forms of coercion.

Niebuhr finds Mt 10:39 neatly summarizes the ethic of Jesus: 'He that finds his life shall lose it: he that loses his life for my sake shall find it'. He comments:

This paradox merely calls attention to the fact that egoism is self defeating, while self sacrifice actually leads to a higher form of self realization. Thus self-love is never justified, but self realization is allowed as the unintended but inevitable consequence of unselfish action. (ICE, p. 62)

All this invites the conclusion that the ethic of Jesus cannot lead directly to a social ethic. It is an expression of the fact that the law of life is love, that to conform to the law of life is an 'impossible possibility', that the law of life stands in judgement over every actuality, that the example of conformity to the law of life ends on the cross, and that all human life, in its vertical dimension, is opposed to God since all life can only approximate the law of love.

Anything less than perfect love in human life is destructive of life. All human life stands under an impending doom because it does not live by the law of love. . . . The destruction of our contemporary civilization through its injustice and through the clash of conflicting national wills is merely one aspect and one expression of the destruction of sin in the world (ICE, p. 71).

Niebuhr's theological method of 'renewing the prophetic origin' involves, therefore, a reappraisal of the biblical sources, the primary myths of Creation, Fall, Atonement, and Parousia. The ethic of Jesus is presented in such a way as to demonstrate its coherence with this mythical pattern. Anticipating the later critique, it can be provisionally noted here that Niebuhr's theology will be vulnerable in the area of biblical analysis, both in its interpretation of biblical mythology and in its presentation of the ethic of Jesus. It assumes, for example, that all three synoptic gospels, Matthew, Mark, and Luke, can be drawn on randomly to support Niebuhr's interpretation. It assumes that the division is between the Jesus of history and the theology of Paul. The fact that each gospel is, like the Pauline corpus, a theological interpretation of the significance of Jesus, and the fact that all the gospels are further removed in time from the historical Jesus than are Paul's letters, are not considered to be worth mentioning. Also the myth of Creation, for example, is a much more complex subject than Niebuhr's simple designation 'prophetic' would suggest. The myth of Creation is depicted in two literary strands labelled 'J' and 'P' which originate in different periods and different social climates. In addition, the prophetic idea of Creation absorbs more Canaanite primal mythology than the two Creation stories of Genesis. Finally, the Wisdom schools display a more rational interest in the techniques of Creation. The importance of the Wisdom interpretation of mythology will become apparent in the study of Niebuhr's interpretation of eschatological symbols later.

LIFE OPPOSED TO THE 'LAW OF LOVE'

Niebuhr called his approach to theology the 'mythical method' (ICE, p. 92). He attempted to illustrate what he meant by the 'mythical method' by comparing a portrait and a photograph.[1] The difference between an artist's portrait painting of a subject and the photograph of a subject is typical of the difference between myth and science. A photograph presents immediate actualities faithfully, but the mood of the moment may obscure or falsify the spirit of personality. A good example of what Niebuhr means here would be the way in which 'mug' shots in a photographic booth always seem to turn the subject into a wanted criminal. By contrast a portrait artist will often select, accentuate, and even falsify, physiognomic details in an effort to capture the spirit of the personality. A good example of this was Graham Sutherland's 1954 commissioned portrait of Winston Churchill which was subsequently destroyed on the instructions of Lady Churchill. Niebuhr explains:

> The vagueness of the boundary line between the art of portraiture and that of caricature suggests how difficult it is to distin-

guish between deception in the interest of a higher truth and deception which falsifies the ultimate truth. (ICE, p. 94)

The 'mythical method' is an attempt to characterize the essence of the human experience of life and history by applying the classical Hebrew myths of prophetic religion (Creation, Judgement, Redemption, Fulfilment) to the human situation. It is from this basis that Niebuhr derives all his theological and anthropological conceptions. Thus the centre of Niebuhr's thought is not Christology (Lehmann).[2] Niebuhr's Christology is determined by his interpretation of prophetic mythology. Nor is it possible to begin a study of Niebuhr with 'Niebuhr's Doctrine of Man' as its point of departure (Minnema).[3]

Paul Tillich recognized and criticized this basis of Niebuhr's theology in 1956. He wrote:

Niebuhr does not ask, 'How can I know?'; he starts knowing. And he does not ask afterward, 'How could I know?', but leaves the convincing power of his thought without epistemological support.[4]

Tillich wants to know by what criteria Niebuhr chose a number of classical Hebrew myths to serve as a basis for knowledge about the human condition, and having chosen the myths, how is the choice justified? Niebuhr's simple answer is that these myths are chosen and continue to serve as an epistemological basis because life and experience continually demonstrate their validity as principles of coherence. Three of Niebuhr's most important subsequent works employ the 'mythical method' of knowing. The two volumes of *Nature and Destiny* are expositions of the mythical method of analysis, and both *Faith and History* and *The Self and the Dramas of History* represent further development and refinement of the method.

The mythical method with regard to the myth of Creation illustrates that pantheistic monisms and dualistic mysticisms lead to erroneous views about human nature and human history. In the case of the myth of the Fall, this prevents false ideas developing about the limits and possibilities of social cohesion, and also prevents false ideas about the nature of free will and determinism in moral activity. The Fall is a myth which depicts the human condition and all-pervading nature of sin. It speaks about the relationship between order and chaos, and it detects the principle of evil within the human heart 'at the juncture of nature and spirit' (ICE, pp. 86 ff.). The sense of sin, argues Niebuhr, is a consequence of measuring 'life in its total dimension' (ICE, p. 75). The human being can apprehend but not comprehend the total dimension of life. This means that the human is always capable of conceiving order, unity, and harmony, beyond the contingent facts of existence, but because of finiteness it lies beyond human capacity to establish these visions. Human beings are therefore both related to and separated from essential reality. The sense of God and the sense of sin is the same act of self-consciousness. In moral terms, there is a tension between the principle of love and the principle of egoism, between the obligation to affirm ultimate unity and the urge to establish the ego against competing forms of life.

This tension between order and chaos, aspiration and reality, is adequately expressed in the myth of the Fall.

> In this as in every significant myth of prophetic religion the permanently valid insight must be isolated from the primitive. (ICE, p. 82)

The myth teaches that evil is a human responsibility. It is an act of rebellion which threatens the unity of human existence. The symbol of the serpent does justice to the idea that the human rebellion is not the first cause of evil because the world was not created a perfect harmony. The figure of Satan (who in later mythology is associated with the serpent) is both a rebel and yet under the dominance of God. This symbolizes the paradox that disorder depends on order. Only highly cohesive nations can be a threat to world peace. Evil is not the absence of good, it is the corruption of good. The moral urge to establish order in the society and the world is mixed with the ambition to make oneself the centre of that order.

> Possibilities of evil grow with the possibilities of good, and . . . human history is . . . not so much a chronicle of the progressive victory of the good over the evil, of cosmos over chaos, as the story of an ever-increasing cosmos, creating ever-increasing possibilities of chaos. (ICE, p. 108)

The ethic of Jesus exposes in all its clarity that the law of life is love, and that in its vertical dimension there is a command to love God, and in the horizontal dimension a command to love others as God loves; the love of the neighbour should extend to the point of self-sacrifice. In reality the law in its vertical and horizontal dimension is incapable of fulfilment and life is opposed to both directions. Therefore whatever social order is established it fails to meet the requirements of the law of love in both directions. This aspect of Niebuhr's thought can only be clarified in the light of further developments in his interpretation of this particular myth.

Given the nature of the opposition to the law of life Niebuhr concludes that the perfectionist ethic of Jesus does not easily relate to the immediate social situation. Nevertheless, it is important to understand the relevance of the ethic of Jesus and for that 'it will be necessary for our [Niebuhr's] generation to return to the faith of prophetic Christianity to solve its problems' (ICE, p. 109). At the same time, 'it will be necessary for prophetic Christianity to develop a more adequate social ethic within terms of its understanding of the total human situation' (ICE, p. 109).

THE RELEVANCE OF THE IMPOSSIBLE

Any Chancellor of the Exchequer who suddenly announced that all citizens should no longer be anxious about how they were to acquire money or clothes because birds were not worried about these aspects of life would experience great difficulty maintaining a credible authority in the post. In all probability colleagues would tactfully recommend a course of hospital therapy for the minister. Stanley Hauerwas has advocated a nice way of getting round these practical difficulties in the ethic of Jesus:

> Christian social ethics . . . is not best written from the perspective of the Secretary of State or the President, but from those who are subject to such people. The task of the Christian people is not to seek to control history, but to be faithful to the mode of life of the peaceable kingdom.[5]

Every instinct of Niebuhr would have recoiled at such an abdication of responsibility on the part of Hauerwas. If the Christian religion bears the truth of life through the generations then it cannot be confined to little pockets of peaceful resistance here and there where people set a good example of social behaviour in the hope of attracting some attention to the motivation for their actions. It must be remembered that the first followers of the ethic of Jesus carried swords and were not slow to use them in self-defence.

In the previous chapter it was noted that Niebuhr was unable to find a sound principle of social change in any historic form of Christianity. It follows that if his principle of interpretation is to be of any value it must be able to explain why historic forms of

Christianity have failed in this regard, and at the same time it must be able to provide principles for social change which are something more than withdrawing from responsibility and hoping that being extraordinarily friendly towards each other will have the required effect in the social realm. Niebuhr's search for a principle has produced a modern form of the Reformation slogan *sola scriptura*, the teaching that scripture is the sole source of authority for the Christian and the Church.

The historic forms of prophetic religion must fail to realize some important aspect of their mythical heritage if they are to fail the social realm. Niebuhr's mythical method of analysis looks inward as well as outward and is deployed in the criticism of historic forms of Christianity. The ethic of Jesus, which is a consistent application of prophetic religion, disintegrates into two contrasting types of religion, Niebuhr argues. One tries to deny the relevance of the ideal of love, and the other tries to prove the relevance of the religious ideal to the problems of everyday existence by reducing it to conformity with a prudential ethic. These two corruptions are represented by Christian orthodoxy and modern secularism, and liberal Protestantism is included in the latter category.

Against Christian orthodoxy, the prophetic tradition insists that the ideal of love is relevant to the moral experience on every conceivable level. It is not a superimposed ideal upon life with no relation to the total human experience:

> The whole conception of life revealed in the Cross of Christian faith is not a pure negation of, or irrelevance toward, the moral ideals of 'natural man'. While the final heights of the love ideal condemn as well as fulfil the moral canons of common sense, the ideal is involved in every moral aspiration and achievement. It is the genius and the task of prophetic religion to insist on the organic relation between historic human existence and that which is both the ground and the fulfilment of this existence, the transcendent. (ICE, p. 115)

Against modern secularism and liberal Christianity:

> The impossibility of the ideal must be insisted upon against all those forms of naturalism, liberalism, and radicalism which generate utopian illusions and regard the love commandment as ultimately realizable because history knows no limits of its progressive approximations. (ICE, p. 128)

Niebuhr's argument for the relevance of the love ideal proceeds by a simple logic. Moral life implies a meaningful existence. A meaningful existence implies a system of coherence. Moral obligation is an obligation to promote harmony and overcome chaos in the direction of the system of coherence. Every historic order contains elements of anarchy. Moral obligation can only arise when it is based on a deeper unity and promise of a more perfect harmony than any realizable historic situation, or any immediate situation. Any lesser faith leads to premature identification with some contingent order which can either mean fanaticism if the order is not in control or complacency if the order is in control, or despair if there is no chance of control.

> The prophetic faith, that the meaningfulness of life and existence implies a source and end beyond itself, produces a morality which implies that every moral value and standard is grounded in and points towards an ultimate perfection of unity and harmony, not realizable in any historic situation. An analysis of the social history of mankind validates this interpretation. (ICE, p. 116)

The dominant attitudes of prophetic faith are gratitude and contrition, gratitude for Creation and contrition before Judgement. There is also hope in the ultimate harmony of existence but realism in the sense that this harmony can only be approximated by human endeavour.

In the political realm Niebuhr finds that equality is the rational political version of the law of love because it remains 'a principle of criticism under which every scheme of justice stands and a symbol of the principle of love involved in all moral judgments' (ICE, p. 119). The relevance of an impossible ethical ideal also makes it possible to value the positive contribution of Marxism by providing a perspective high enough to accept its insights without being oblivious of its pretensions. Niebuhr repeats the claim which had appeared in earlier works that Marxism has actually contributed an insight of prophetic religion which modern culture has lost. In the class war a religion which holds the law of life to be love 'stultifies itself if it does not support equal justice as a political and economic approximation of the ideal of love' (ICE, p. 141).

The image of Christ in both Christian orthodoxy and liberal Protestantism also reflects their moral stances:

> Christ is the revelation of the very impossible possibility which the Sermon on the Mount elaborates in ethical terms. If

Christian orthodoxy sometimes tends to resolve this paradox by the picture of a Christ who has been stripped of all qualities which relate him to man and history, Christian liberalism resolves it by reducing Christ to a figure of heroic love who reveals the full possibilities of human nature to us. In either case the total human situation which the mythos of Christ and the Cross illumines is obscured. (ICE, p. 130)

Niebuhr's doctrine of Christ or his Christology is fully developed in *Nature and Destiny* and subsequent works. In *Interpretation* he simply maintains that the interpretation must be within the framework of prophetic religion in a kind of reciprocal relationship. The Cross illumines the ethic of Jesus, the ethic of Jesus ends on the Cross; the Cross reveals the essence of prophetic religion, and the myths of prophetic religion illumine the significance of the Cross. Thus the great myths of Creation, Fall, and Fulfilment, illumined by the Cross of Jesus, provide a principle of interpretation which is capable of relating to every historic form of social order, and also capable of revealing the shortcomings of the attempted embodiments of its own prophetic heritage.

If a Chancellor of the Exchequer were suddenly to announce the ambition to create a just social order where no-one need worry about having enough money to ensure the basic necessities and dignities of human life, the message might not be believed but the question of the Chancellor's sanity would not arise.

NEGATIVE VALIDATION OF PROPHETIC RELIGION

Niebuhr began his career in Detroit with a strong awareness that the liberal Protestant education he had received was an inadequate preparation for the social realities he had encountered. Once Niebuhr adopted the mythical method of analysis he was able to provide a critique of all historic forms of Christianity. In *Interpretation* he confines himself to a critique of the orthodox and liberal forms of Christianity. In his later works Niebuhr subjected a whole array of theologies and philosophies to this type of critique.

If Christianity is to provide any sort of constructive guidance in political and social ethics it has to avoid the inherent tendency of historic forms to destroy the dialectic of prophetic religion. The tension is usually destroyed either by sacrificing time in history to eternity, or by giving ultimate significance to the relativities of history. Christian orthodoxy shows a tendency to develop the former and Christian liberalism the latter, the one issuing in pessimism regarding effectiveness in the social realm, and the other issuing in sentimentality. Niebuhr concludes that the reason why prophetic Christianity has been corrupted is because it has become the expression of the ruling classes of the two periods, the mediaeval period and the modern period.

In the mediaeval period Christianity destroyed the dialectic of prophetic religion by establishing the principle of order rather than the principle of love as the motive force in social and political activity. The impetus for this was the necessity of the Church adjusting to the world once the hope of an imminent Parousia had waned. The Church adopted the Stoic natural law which supposedly established universal standards of behaviour, not identical with the law of life as love, but nevertheless having equal validity as laws of God. Niebuhr accepts this inevitable development and is highly critical of those who detect in this the elements of a pagan apostasy. Such criticisms are informed by a moral sentimentalism 'which does not recognize to what degree all decent human actions . . . are determined by rational principles of equity and justice, by law rather than by love' (ICE, p. 155). The problem with the adoption of the natural law was that the Church placed too much emphasis on the natural law as applicable to the world of sin, the relative natural law, rather than the absolute natural law which demanded equality and freedom. This lack of balance was made possible because of the under-emphasis of the eschatological dimension.

> Whenever the prophetic faith that all things have their source in God is not balanced by the other article of prophetic faith, that all things have their fulfilment in God, ethical tension is destroyed and the result is similar to a pantheistic religious acceptance of life as it is. (ICE, p. 161)

In other words the myth of Creation and the myth of the Parousia must be interpreted in the total situation to maintain ethical tension. The end result of the principle of order is fascism, argues Niebuhr.

> The theory that government is justified mainly by the negative task of checking chaos is held in common by both fascism and Christian orthodoxy. It may be that the political principles of the former are, at least partially, derived from the latter. (ICE, p. 167)

Prophetic religion must balance gratitude and contrition. In

Christian orthodoxy Christian spirituality (i.e. contrition for sin) without a balance of Christian piety (i.e. gratitude for creation) leads to pessimism regarding the social and political situation. On the other hand Christian piety without the balance of Christian spirituality leads to a conservative attitude towards the organizing power of the day, and is therefore too optimistic about the social and political situation. One of the virtues of the Enlightenment was its insistence that critical intelligence is a prerequisite of justice. Such a critical intelligence provides a method for attaining a rational balance between optimism and pessimism, between spirituality and piety, with regard to the social and political realm.

The critique of liberal Protestantism within the pages of *Interpretation* is basically a repetition of earlier critiques. Niebuhr finds that it is a religio-moral version of *laissez-faire* economics where justice must be established by appeals to the moral ideal and with as little machinery as possible. Since economic power is the most basic power, political power is not possible without a reconstitution of the economic system, which is based in the inequalities of the property system. Anything less results in mere philanthropy on the part of Christian activism. This is merely naivety compared to Marxism whose 'analyses of the technical aspects of the problem of justice have not been successfully challenged, and every event in contemporary history seems to multiply the proofs of its validity' (ICE, p. 194). Niebuhr also includes in this section an attack on the sentimentality of pacifism with the knowledge that sooner or later the Western democracies would have to reckon with the demonic power of fascism.

LEAVEN IN THE SOCIAL FABRIC

Stanley Hauerwas tries to argue that Niebuhr failed to articulate an adequate ecclesiology. He writes:

> Drawing on the theme of justification, Niebuhr provided little place for the possibility of growth in the Christian life, and what growth in character and virtue demanded was a corresponding community of character and virtue.[6]

And more recently:

> Niebuhr paid almost no attention to the social significance of

the church—for finally, in spite of all the trenchant criticism he directed at America, America was his church.[7]

It was in response to this type of criticism that D. B. Robertson, as long ago as 1959, gathered 340 pages of articles on the significance of the Church in Niebuhr's thought and published them as *Essays in Applied Christianity*. It is therefore astonishing that, despite this anthology, and despite the fact that Niebuhr's own church grew from 65 members to over 800 members during his pastorate, critics continue to pursue this weary argument.

In the final section of *Interpretation* Niebuhr spells out a high ecclesiology that is almost Catholic. He sees Christian activity as a kind of 'refinement' in the social fabric of society, a kind of leaven. This type of social activity was a theme which emerged at the Second Vatican Council. Niebuhr simply established the important proviso that the structures of social justice are not created by this type of activity. The function of the Church as the Body of Christ is to provide a community of grace. Grace means that the moral fruits of religion are not acquired by a conscious effort to achieve them but are dependent upon a community. Niebuhr explains:

> The Church is the Body of Christ and the noble living and the noble dead in her communion help to build up in her the living Christ, a dimension of life which transcends the inclinations of natural man. It is consequently natural and inevitable that the faithful should regard genuine acts of love as proceeding from propulsions which are not their own and should confess with St Paul, 'I, yet not I, but Christ that liveth in me'. (ICE, p. 226)

Niebuhr also agreed with the Catholic doctrine that faith, hope, and love are 'theological' virtues which are added to the moral possibilities of 'natural man' by an infusion of grace. What Niebuhr did attack was a concept of sacramental grace which the Second Vatican Council also attacked. Grace cannot be confined narrowly to institutions. There are forces in life

> which can only be described as the grace of God. What men are able to will depends not upon the strength of their willing, but upon the strength which enters their will and over which their will has little control. (ICE, p. 228)

The Church is the essential ground which provides the grace and the faith to develop an adequate social ethic which makes sense to

93

Presidents and to people. A Christian ethic which is satisfied with anything less must be one which emerges from 'islands of neutrality' (ICE, p. 246).

NOTES

1   It has to be admitted that Niebuhr had not studied the art of photography.
2   Paul Lehmann, 'The Christology of Reinhold Niebuhr' in Charles W. Kegley and Robert W. Bretall (eds), *Reinhold Niebuhr: His Religious, Social, and Political Thought* (New York, 1956), pp. 251–80.
3   T. Minnema, *The Social Ethics of Reinhold Niebuhr* (Kampen, 1958).
4   Paul Tillich, 'Reinhold Niebuhr's Doctrine of Knowledge' in Kegley and Bretall, *op. cit.*, p. 35.
5   Stanley Hauerwas, *The Peaceable Kingdom* (London, 1984), p. 106.
6   Ibid., p. xxiv.
7   Stanley Hauerwas, *Against the Nations: War and Survival in a Liberal Society* (Minneapolis, 1985), p. 47.

6

Primary Myths of Biblical Religion

By the end of the 1930s four historical facts influenced the future direction of Niebuhr's thought. The threatened judgement on the capitalist system was not to be executed by Communism; Stalin had transformed the dictatorship of the proletariat into a tyranny; the Socialist Party in America was hopelessly isolationist; and the New Deal was having a measure of success in dealing with the severest crisis which capitalism had experienced.

PARTING OF THE WAYS

Niebuhr responded to these facts by recommending full support to the Allied war effort even though it meant saving the capitalist system; resigning from the Socialist Party; and supporting a third term for Roosevelt, and eventually working for the Roosevelt administration.

His support for the war came gradually. In 1934 he was arguing that war in Europe seemed inevitable but US neutrality might help to keep Great Britain out of it. Nevertheless, neutrality would help to preserve the capitalist system for additional decades. But that was preferable to the complete chaos which would result from war. In the latter half of the decade the editorials in *Radical Religion* were suggesting that Britain's inevitable role was to resist fascist aggression. Since this would eventually prove the case Niebuhr was impatient with the apparent reluctance of the democratic nations of Europe to use even the simple expedient of economic sanctions. He noted that in Britain 'the most effective opposition to Chamberlain has come not from Labour but from clear eyed imperialists like Churchill'.[1] Up to 1937 Niebuhr's general line had been that America could do little to avert a catastrophe in Europe, and American involvement would only ensure a massive escalation of the war. Even as late as 1938 he was still arguing that America should not get involved in supporting Britain's imperialist interests.

Gradually his opinions changed. Fascism must not be allowed to triumph over democracy and America must do what is required to ward off an international catastrophe. An editorial in *Radical Religion* (Fall 1940) admitted unjustified criticism of Roosevelt's 'preparedness program'. Then the 1940 April convention of the Socialist Party in Washington voted 159 to 28 for a total repudiation of US assistance to the Allies. Niebuhr could not agree to this and in May 1940 he resigned from the party. He argued that Norman Thomas was accepting Nazism and agreeing on spheres of influence on the collapse of the British Empire.

He also published a stream of anti-pacifist articles, and launched a new journal to reach more people more often than his *Radical Religion*. He called it *Christianity and Crisis*, and in its pages he argued for the Allied cause. He also warned:

Nazi tyranny intends to annihilate the Jewish race, to subject the nations of Europe to the dominion of a 'master' race, to extirpate the Christian religion, to annul the liberties and legal standards that are the priceless heritage of ages of Christian and humanistic culture, to make truth the prostitute of political power, to seek world dominion through its satraps and allies, and generally to destroy the very fabric of our Western civilization.[2]

He advocated 'all measures short of war' in support of the Allies, and he would not guarantee that the US would not get involved.[3] Then on 7 December 1941 the Japanese air force bombed Pearl Harbor and Niebuhr wrote:

For years we argued whether or not we should go to war. The implicit assumption of all of these arguments was that we had the complete power to make this decision. Then history descended upon us and took the decision out of our hands. We might have known that it would be like this. History is not as completely under the control of human decisions as either the interventionists or pacifists assumed.[4]

On the domestic scene, even before his resignation from the Socialist Party, he warned readers of *Radical Religion* that a vote for the Republican Party in the 1940 presidential election would be a reactionary vote undermining all that had been achieved by the labour movement. If they gain power, he wrote,

> [t]hey will seek to destroy the Wagner act, the social security legislation of the Roosevelt administration, the freedom of labor to organize and the relief of the unemployed. . . . There is no one of sufficient stature to bear the mantle of Roosevelt and win the election. Only he can overcome the treason which all the reactionary bourbons of the south will engage in. . . . All this means that Roosevelt . . . is the only hope of maintaining the real gains which have been made in the past years of the depression.[5]

When Roosevelt was elected Niebuhr wrote that despite the ambiguities of Rooseveltian liberalism the president's re-election was a heartening revelation of the ability of democracy to arrive at a right decision in a crisis. He even wrote a favourable review on a book by a leading light of the New Deal economics, Mordecai Ezekiel, *Jobs For All*.[6] He found Ezekiel's argument preferable to the thought of social upheaval and the threat of fascist reprisals.

But despite extensive political activity and journalism on international and domestic issues, Niebuhr was also at work in these years on his most important work of theology, *The Nature and Destiny of Man*.

MYTHICAL PROLEGOMENON

In 1937 Niebuhr published a book of 'sermonic essays' entitled *Beyond Tragedy*. The first chapter, 'As deceivers, yet true', explains the nature of 'the necessary and perennially valid contribution of myth to the biblical world view' (BT, p. x). The essay picks up the theme first mentioned in *Reflections*, and developed in *Interpretation*, that classical Hebrew mythology contains the essential truth about human nature but because it has to use historical images it risks corruption if its purpose is not discerned. It risks corruption because its use of language is deceptive. The interesting feature of this essay is that it provides the basic plan for the two volumes of *The Nature and Destiny of Man*. It presents a description of the primary biblical mythology which Niebuhr will later use as a standard to measure alternative systems of knowledge, and corruptions and developments of the myths themselves within the Christian tradition.

Niebuhr repeats the comparative example of the portrait artist found in *Interpretation*, and his exposition of the myths of Creation and Fall repeat the substance of the material found earlier except that he adds, concerning the Fall, an explanation about the perfection before the Fall. This state is

> an ideal possibility which men can comprehend but not realize. The perfection before the Fall is, in a sense, the perfection before the act. Thus we are able to conceive of a perfectly disinterested justice; but when we act our own achievements will fall short of this standard. (BT, pp. 12–13)

In *Interpretation* Niebuhr described how the ethical teachings of Jesus fitted neatly into the truths of classical Hebrew mythology and how the Cross could be interpreted as symbolizing the meaning of the ethic and the truth of the mythology. In this essay Niebuhr deals more specifically with the myths about the person of Jesus, that is, Christology. He covers the Incarnation, the Atonement, Jesus as the Second Adam, and Jesus as the Son of God.

The Incarnation is a mythical way of expressing the paradoxical fact that an event in history can reveal the character of history, and that without such a revelation the character of history could not be known. In this context he also explains his understanding of the distinction between general and special revelation. General revelation points to the reality of God but not the attributes of God. The character of God is not revealed as one who communicates with people. This conception of God, without the knowledge of special revelation, ends in pantheism. Special revelation is the communication of God's Word to people. It is like the difference between the scientific study of a person's behaviour and a meeting and conversation with the person whose behaviour is being scrutinized. It is only in the meeting and conversation that 'personality' is disclosed.

The myth of Christ as the Second Adam is interpreted as symbolic of the restored perfection of what 'man' was and ought to be, and Christ as the Son of God is symbolic of the truth that human life is in touch with the infinite, or, in Niebuhr's words, 'Human life stands in infinity' (BT, p. 16). The doctrines about the two natures of Christ were attempts to rationalize the paradoxical in these symbols. Niebuhr sees them as expressing ethical truth. They indicate that only infinite love is an adequate moral standard. Christ as the

Second Adam is the moral norm, and Christ as Son of God indicates that all human life has God as the source of existence and this knowledge is the basis of ethics. The fact that God loves all impartially is the basis for ethical interaction. Niebuhr accepts the myth of the Virgin Birth is another symbol for describing Jesus as Son of God, but it expresses this truth through historical distortion. Niebuhr therefore rejects the historicity of the Virgin Birth. Finally in this context, the Son is a mythological concept of the God of history, and the Father is symbolic of the God who transcends history.

Niebuhr stresses that the Incarnation is not redemption, it merely signifies that an event in history can reveal the character of history. The event in history which does reveal the character of history is the crucifixion of Jesus. The Atonement is the myth which explains the paradoxical truth revealed in the Cross of Jesus. It is a symbol of the redeeming power of God in Christ. The '[a]toning death of Christ is the revelation of ultimate reality which may become the principle of interpretation for all human experience' (BT, pp. 19–20). The Atonement is validated in human experience when historical evil is transformed into good. Without the Cross, the goodness of life easily leads to a false optimism, and what is tragic in life easily leads to despair.

It must be mentioned here that the Pauline use of the Second Adam mythology is not in line with Niebuhr's interpretation of the symbol. For Paul it is a symbol of the creative power of God who is transforming human existence. It is the Risen Lord who is the Second Adam, the first-born of a new creation and the human form which surpasses original perfection and which is the destiny of the human species on the general resurrection. Niebuhr does not interpret the symbol in this way because he has no theology of the resurrection of Jesus. The hope which Niebuhr speaks about is basically another word for faith:

Human existence denies its own deepest and most essential nature. That is tragic. But when that fact is understood, when men seek to make the standards of a sinful existence the norms of life but accept its true norm, even though they fail to obey it, their very contrition opens the eyes of faith. This is the Godly sorrow that worketh repentance. Out of this despair hope is born. The hope is simply this: that the contradictions of human existence, which man cannot surmount, are swallowed up in the life of God Himself. The God of Christian faith is not only creator but redeemer. He does not allow

99

human existence to end tragically. He snatches victory from defeat. He is Himself defeated in history but He is also victorious in that defeat. (BT, p. 19)

The victory is not in the resurrection of Jesus. If it were, Niebuhr would have mentioned the resurrection. However, the resurrection of Jesus does not feature in his theology until *Faith and History* (1949). The victory is the acceptance of the true norm, and the true norm is the self-sacrificing love of God for people. Once it is realized that God sacrifices his Son on the Cross, the true norm of life is revealed and human life need no longer deny its essential nature. At this point Niebuhr's theology bears strong resemblance to features of Bultmann's theology, although later Niebuhr will actually repudiate any similarity.

Finally Niebuhr explains the importance of the myth of the Parousia, the Second Coming of Christ. When Niebuhr writes about the Parousia his understanding of the myth includes the attendant eschatological myths related to it, that is, the General Resurrection, the Final Judgement, and the appearance and destruction of the Antichrist. Here in *Beyond Tragedy* he stresses that the myth 'involves all the profoundest characteristics of the Christian religion'. It is this myth which distinguishes Christianity from all forms of naturalistic utopianism (which means bourgeois and Marxist worldviews) and Hellenistic otherworldliness (which means consistent dualisms and mysticisms). The myth also places the corporate enterprise of humankind under ultimate judgement as well as individuals. The total human enterprise is always opposed to God.

APPLIED MYTHS

In 1939 Niebuhr was invited to deliver the Gifford Lectures at Edinburgh University. The lectures were subsequently published as the two volumes of *The Nature and Destiny of Man* in 1941 and 1943 respectively. This book marks a culmination of his work in the 1930s in that it gives substance to the ultra-rational framework and interprets reality on the basis of the primary Christian mythology, and it forms a prelude to his work of the 1940s and 1950s with its interest in the theology of history.

The point of departure for the study is the familiar theme of the inadequacy of the liberal Protestant religion in meeting the needs of the age. It is hoped that through a correct analysis of the social, political, and religious forces which have shaped the modern world, a more competent form of the Protestant religion will emerge.

Niebuhr considers that Western culture is a combination of two dominant paradigms. It combines elements of both the classical and the biblical worldviews. These were held in a balanced synthesis in the mediaeval culture. The destruction of the mediaeval synthesis resulted in the two forces distilling the two components from the synthesis, the Renaissance distilling the classical element and the Reformation distilling the biblical element. The liberal Protestant religion is considered to represent an attempt at bringing these two forces together. *Nature and Destiny* analyses what it considers to be essential knowledge if this synthesis is to be achieved. It is a question of determining '[h]ow far and by what means it may be possible to bring Renaissance and Reformation insights about human nature into terms of fruitful interrelation' (N&D I, p. 318). Modern culture is conceived as a 'battleground' of the two opposing views of human nature, with the Renaissance view much the stronger. Niebuhr attempts to demonstrate the relevance of the biblical view by demonstrating how it is capable of interpreting experience and refuting false interpretations of experience. To achieve this, Niebuhr applies the primary myths of the Christian religion.

It has been pointed out that *Nature and Destiny* is constructed around an exposition of the four myths, Creation, Fall, Atonement, and Parousia. Volume I deals with Creation and Fall, and Volume II with Atonement and Parousia. The myth of Creation is considered as it relates to human beings who are created in the image of God but who are nevertheless creatures subject to finitude.

The Fall is considered in its relation to the inherent dangers of being both a creature and an image of God. That is, the Fall is thought of as a failure of balance in the combination of the human as both creature and image of God.

The myth of the Atonement provides the key of interpretation for the whole work, and for nature, life, and history. The myth reveals wisdom and power, the wisdom being knowledge into the nature of history and ethics, and the power being grace in judgement and mercy over the human as justification, and grace as sanctification within the human.

The Christological titles, Jesus as Son of God, and Jesus as Second Adam, are related to the wisdom of the Atonement in that the former title refers to the divine sovereignty of God over history, and the latter title refers to Jesus as the ethical norm, Christ as revelation of what we ought to be and what we can never be within history.

Finally, the myth of the Parousia (which includes the attendant myths) is analysed at the end of Volume II but the insights afforded by this myth are not related successfully to the work. Niebuhr's next book on the theology of history, *Faith and History*, makes good this deficiency.

MYTH, EXPERIENCE, AND REVELATION

In the preliminary discussion, Niebuhr characterizes the classical and the biblical views of human nature. In classical thought, Platonic, Aristotelian and Stoic forms all share, according to Niebuhr, the concept of the uniqueness of the rational faculties, the *nous*. The consequence of this easily leads to the divine principle being equated with the rational faculty and the principle of evil being located in the body. This strict dualism does not provide a frame of reference which is able to construe history as meaningful. History is conceived in cyclical terms. The biblical view of human nature knows nothing of a mind- or soul-and-body dualism. The myth of Creation prevents the classical error of finding the principles of good and evil in the mind and body respectively. The myth of the Fall, which defines the essence of sin, locates its source at the juncture of nature and spirit.

Modern thought, which Niebuhr depicts as a triumph of the classical elements over the biblical, is placed into two broad categories, rationalism and vitalism. The modern problem is: Should human nature be understood from the point of view of the uniqueness of its reason, or from the point of view of its affinity with nature? Rationalism subordinates the processes of nature and history in its conception of human nature, and its social-economic base is the rising middle class which has now become the dominant bourgeois class. Vitalism, which seeks to understand the human through its affinities with nature, is considered to be a protest against the 'pretensions of rational man as essential man' (N&D I, p. 52). There are two forms of vitalism, romanticism and materialism. The former is the protest of the lower middle class and culminates in fascist politics, and the latter is the protest of the working classes and culminates in Communist politics.

Unfortunately in spite of the important truths about human

nature and history which romanticism and materialism have discovered, these philosophies are becoming instruments of a deepening decadence on the one hand and an abortive regeneration on the other. They do not see the problem of human nature in sufficient depth and therefore remain in the confusion, and sometimes accentuate the errors, in which modern culture has been involved from the beginning. (N&D I, p. 53)

Niebuhr presents a brief summary of the main trends in modern thought and analyses their weaknesses. They either overestimate the good in Creation or underestimate the evil of the Fall.

In each of these areas of thought we have suggested that the difficulty arises from the lack of a principle of interpretation which can do justice to both the height of human self-transcendence and the organic unity between the spirit of man and his physical life. The modern mind interprets man as either essentially reason, without being able to do justice to his non-rational vitalities, or as essentially vitality, without appreciating the extent of his rational freedom. (N&D I, p. 132)

The question arises: Why should the mythical framework of the Christian religion be accepted? How can we know? as Tillich would ask. For the first time in his work to date Niebuhr attempts an answer to the question. The answer he gives is firmly rooted in the liberal Protestant tradition and it is an extension of the principle which Schleiermacher used to ground his theology. In short, we know because the primary myths clarify our deepest feelings. But whereas Schleiermacher located the feeling as that of 'unqualified dependence' or the feeling of 'absolute dependence', Niebuhr, after acknowledging his approval, also adds: '[a]n equally important characteristic of the experience of God is the sense of being seen, commanded, judged, and known, from beyond ourselves' (N&D I, p. 137).

Niebuhr begins knowing by assuming the existence of God. This God is an 'unknown God' who reveals his existence to all individual humans. There is a dim sense of recognition, a mixture of inchoate feelings. This type of personal revelation is called 'general revelation' and is common to all by virtue of a shared human nature. These feelings may be interpreted in many different ways and give rise to many forms of religion but only in the biblical tradition do these feelings find ultimate coherence. When this personal revelation is combined with the social historical revelation to the Jewish people, which is termed 'special' revelation, only then does the inchoate assume a lucid form.

The 'special' revelation is codified in mythical stories which defy any attempt to construct a rational system around them. Creeds are steps towards rationalizing the myths, but they are always prone to stating rational absurdities which are a scandal to modern thought. The justification for using these particular myths rather than other myths or other systems of coherence ultimately rests on their performance in validating experience and refuting alternative explanations of experience. Their validation does not rest on the existence of any historic community which perfectly conforms its existence to the truths they reveal because all historic communities which claim them as their own fail either to live up to their teaching or to interpret them correctly.

According to Niebuhr there are three types of personal experience which the social-historical biblical mythology clarifies. It is an expansion of the idea found in *Interpretation* that the basic religious feelings are gratitude and contrition. In *Nature and Destiny* Niebuhr isolates the feeling of reverence, the sense of moral obligation, and the longing for forgiveness. Each one of these feelings corresponds to a conception of God as Creator, Judge, and Redeemer.

The 'special' revelations which clarify these feelings do not, however, include the myth of Creation. Niebuhr considers this to be a 'primitive' myth which is 'retained' in the Bible because 'it preserves and protects the idea of the freedom of God and His transcendence' (N&D I, p. 143). It does not qualify as historical revelation. This begins with the counterpart of the sense of moral obligation, the covenant community of Israel. However, the myth of Creation should be included in the category of 'special' revelation. It is retained in the Bible not for the reason Niebuhr gives but because the myth was theologically connected to Israel's saving history.[7]

Nevertheless the sense of moral obligation is rooted in the covenant relationship where the ideal possibility is set before Israel, and where the prophets condemn Israel for failing to live to the ideal standard. What is learnt in this experience is that any nation, culture or civilization brings judgement upon itself because of its sin. The catastrophic events of history are revelations of God which resonate with the dimly perceived sense of being judged in the personal sphere.

The Old Testament does not provide a 'special' revelation to correspond with the longing for forgiveness, argues Niebuhr. The messianic hope for the future became deflected in a consideration of why Israel, the chosen people, should suffer more than the other nations which had not been chosen. It is this unresolved dilemma of the Old Testament which is answered in the Cross of Jesus. The myth of the Atonement sorts out the problem of the relation between the justice and mercy of God, between the wrath and forgiveness of God. Judgement is not the final word, there is mercy beyond; but the distinctions between good and evil remain. The Cross is a revelation which has chosen the most inexplicable experience to illuminate the truth of history. The full meaning of God and history is revealed in suffering innocence.

One of the reasons why Niebuhr fails to draw the myth of the Parousia into the work can be located here. He could have included in 'general' revelation the feeling of longing for social harmony. It is an inexplicable omission on Niebuhr's part, especially in the light of his constant interpretation of eschatology in social rather than individual terms. Its omission here has probably led Denis McCann's otherwise excellent critique of Niebuhr to underestimate the importance of the myth of the Parousia in his work.[8]

CREATION AND FALL

The bulk of Volume I of *Nature and Destiny* is taken up with an exposition of the myths of Creation and Fall. Without too much attention to the biblical source Niebuhr interprets the myth of Creation as teaching that human beings were created in the image of God, and that they were created creatures. The image of God (which in the original Hebrew includes the bodily form, that is, to look at, human beings have the appearance of God) is interpreted as emphasizing the height of self-transcendence, and creation as creature as emphasizing dependence on the flux of time and nature. It insists that the human person is a unity of nature and spirit. The harmony and balance between the two aspects of human nature represents the goodness of creation, and the inducement to sin is caused through the anxiety which is a concomitant of creatureliness. Sin itself is either overestimating the degree of self-transcendence by failing to accept the limitations of creatureliness, or it is a failing to accept the responsibility of self-transcendence. Niebuhr refers to this as the sin of sensuality, losing the self in the vitalities of nature.

The source of anxiety is the feeling of insecurity caused through the condition of creatureliness.[9] The self pretends not to be limited and finite, and in so doing commits the basic sin of pride. In the Bible pride is defined in both religious and moral terms, in vertical and horizontal directions. The double love command of Jesus corresponds to this double failing of sin. Sin is both rebellion against God, and the cause of social injustice because the pride of the ego immediately subordinates other life. Anxiety is also the precondition of the sin of sensuality, hiding from the freedom of self-transcendence and losing the self in creatureliness.

Anxiety is an internal description of the state of temptation. It is equivalent to the serpent in the myth. To believe in the Devil (Christianity interpreted the serpent as the Devil) means there is a force of evil antecedent to action. The fact that the Devil 'fell' before the first human couple means that the human rebellion against God is not an act of sheer perversity, and that it does not follow inevitably from the situation of finiteness and freedom. Sin is not merely error in overestimating human capacity. The occasion for temptation lies in the two facts together, human greatness and human weakness.

Niebuhr distinguishes three types of pride, the pride of power, knowledge, and virtue. Knowledge always pretends to be more than it is; moral pride makes virtue a vehicle of sin; and the pride of power is most apparent in its collective dimension, and most consistently expressed in the national State. (Prophetic religion began by combating national self-deification.) Niebuhr finds that modern fascist States are more demonic than anything in the ancient world because they express their pride within and against the Christian culture. To explain the objection that this type of collective pride is usually the pride of the powerful, and that people are more sinned against than sinners, or at least appear to be so, Niebuhr develops a concept he calls 'equality of sin, inequality of guilt'. By this he means that although capitalists cannot be considered greater sinners than members of the working class, they are certainly more guilty.

> Capitalists are not greater sinners than poor labourers by any natural depravity. But it is a fact that those who hold great economic and political power are more guilty of pride against God and of injustice against the weak than those who lack power and prestige. (N&D I, p. 240)

The same is true for Gentiles against Jews, and whites against blacks, for example.

Although Niebuhr defines the sin of sensuality he only analyses it in its personal dimension and his writing appears somewhat embarrassed and uncomfortable. Later, he equates the isolationist impulse in the US with the collective dimension of the sin of sensuality.[10]

Niebuhr does not offer a solution to the paradox of original sin which involves the teaching that sin is the natural condition, the inherited and universal condition of the human being, while at the same time holding that humanity is responsible before God for its sin. Niebuhr finds that the truth in the myth which insists on both inevitability and responsibility, on fate and freedom, can best be illustrated by examining alternative explanations for evil. Various attempts to rationalize the myth usually leave some important facet out of the account. The myth is only rational in the sense that it circumscribes the limits of rationality, and it is an expression that a rationally irresolvable contradiction points to a truth that logic cannot contain.

> The final paradox is that the discovery of the inevitability of sin is man's highest assertion of freedom. The fact that the discovery of sin invariably leads to the Pharisaic illusion that such a discovery guarantees sinlessness in subsequent actions is a revelation of the way in which freedom becomes an accomplice of sin. (N&D I, p. 279)

Niebuhr acknowledges that Kierkegaard's explanation of the dialectical relationship between freedom and fate in sin is one of the profoundest in Christian thought.

The myths of Creation and Fall, when interpreted correctly, illustrate errors in both Catholic and Protestant thought regarding 'essential nature' and 'original righteousness'. In Catholic thought the consequence of interpreting the Fall with chronological literalness encouraged the idea that original righteousness was a special supernatural gift which had been added to pure nature or essential nature and which was removed because of Adam's sin, leaving essential nature intact. In radical Protestant thought the balance between the image of God and creatureliness was obscured to the extent that the Fall was thought to have completely removed the image of God from human nature. But once it is recognized that the paradox of image of God and creatureliness necessarily remains a paradox, and sin is located in the will, it becomes clear that since the whole person is involved in the sin, then both the image of God and creatureliness are corrupted but not destroyed. Against Catholic thought it must be stated that essential nature is corrupted, and against Protestant thought it must be stated that the image of God remains, though corrupted.

The myth of Creation indicates that essential nature is composed of two elements. It consists of natural determinations, such as physical and social impulses, sex and race determinations, and describes the character of the creature imbedded in the natural order. It also consists of freedom of spirit over natural processes, and human self-transcendence. Both of these elements of essential nature correspond to original virtues. Natural determinations correspond to the natural law, and freedom over natural processes corresponds to what in Catholic thought are referred to as 'theological virtues', faith, hope, and love. Now because sin is a corruption of both elements of essential nature both the corresponding virtues of original righteousness are unrealizable ideals. This means that the theological virtues and natural law conceptions are never free from the taint of sin. In other words faith, hope, and love are never perfectly expressed in historical life, nor is natural law so clear that unequivocal expression is possible. An uncorrupted natural justice does not exist (against the Catholic teaching) but neither has original justice been completely lost (against radical Protestant teaching).

> The freedom of man sets every standard of justice under higher possibilities and the sin of man perennially insinuates contingent and relative elements into the supposedly absolute standards of human reason. (N&D I, pp. 297–8)

In sum, essential human nature is human nature which exists in a triple harmony of the self with God, the self with the self, and the self with the neighbour. The law of this original perfection is the law of love. It is the claim of essential nature and it is received with a sense of moral obligation.

NOTES

1 Paul Merkley, *Reinhold Niebuhr: A Political Account* (Montreal and London, 1975), p. 139.
2 February 1941 issue of *Christianity and Crisis*; quoted in Merkley, *op. cit.*, p. 151.
3 'Repeal the Neutrality Act', *Christianity and Crisis* (October 1941).
4 'History (God) has overtaken us', *Christianity and Society* 1941 (Winter); in D. B. Robertson (ed.), *Love and Justice: Selections from*

the Shorter Writings of Reinhold Niebuhr (Cleveland and New York, 1967), pp. 262–3.

5 'The coming presidential election', Radical Religion (Fall 1939), in Merkley, op. cit., p. 145.

6 Radical Religion (Spring 1939).

7 There is a list of examples in Gerhard von Rad, Old Testament Theology (London, 1975), I, pp. 136–8.

8 Dennis P. McCann, Christian Realism and Liberation Theology (New York, 1982). Niebuhr's omission is more surprising in view of the point made on p. 45 and the quote there from Moral Man, pp. 60–1.

9 Niebuhr's interpretation of anxiety here closely follows Kierkegaard's analysis of despair in The Sickness Unto Death (1849).

10 The first hint of this is The Irony of American History, p. 112.

7

Theology of Democracy

ATONEMENT

In Volume II of *Nature and Destiny* Niebuhr establishes the fact that the myth of the Atonement is the centre of meaning for life and experience. If any other principle of coherence is postulated, either explicitly or implicitly, it is of necessity a subordinate centre, and the interpretations and expositions, the ethics and life activity, which issue from this proposed centre of meaning are involved in idolatry. It follows from this that Niebuhr's theology is very dependent upon biblical interpretation and his efforts to probe the meaning of the myth involve exposition of the scriptures.

> The bible contains the history . . . in which the whole human enterprise becomes fully conscious of its limits, of its transgressions of those limits, and of the divine answer to its problems. (N&D II, p. 157)

In Volume I the importance of the myth had been underlined:

> The doctrine of atonement and justification [which is the appropriation of the atonement] is the 'stone which the builders rejected' and which must be made 'the head of the corner'. It is an absolutely essential presupposition for the understanding of human nature and human history. It is a doctrine which . . . was subordinated to the 'time–eternity' implications of the doctrine of the Incarnation in patristic Christianity. It was qualified by that same doctrine in

medieval Catholicism, so that Catholicism failed to understand the full seriousness of human sin or the full tragedy of human history. It emerged with elemental force in the Protestant Reformation, to become the central truth of the Christian religion. But it quickly lost its central position, so that modern liberal Protestantism knows less of its meaning or significance than the Middle Ages did. (N&D I, p. 159)

Volume II consists of an extended exposition of the importance and relevance of the myth. Biblical material is harnessed to support this interpretation, and Christian doctrines are reinterpreted in the light of the myth. The whole purpose is to restore the meaning and significance of the myth for liberal Protestantism. The theme is set out early:

> In the New Testament the Atonement is the significant content of the Incarnation. To say that Christ is the 'express image of his person' (Heb 1:3) is to assert that in the epic of this life and death the final mystery of the divine power which bears history is clarified; and, with that clarification, life and history are given their true meaning. (N&D II, p. 57)

Where Niebuhr presents the Atonement as the main theme of the volume, he also uncritically aligns his interpretation with Gustav Aulén's 'classical' categorization of the myth. This dependence means that Niebuhr's theology is also vulnerable to the same criticisms which have been levelled against Aulén's conception of the Atonement.

After the analysis of the myth Niebuhr draws the following conclusions:

> The Christian doctrine of the Atonement, with its paradoxical conception of the relation of the divine mercy to the divine wrath is therefore the final key to this historical interpretation. . . .
>
> The Christian doctrine of the Atonement is not some incomprehensible remnant of superstition, nor yet a completely incomprehensible article of faith. . . .
>
> [I]t is the beginning of wisdom in the sense that it contains symbolically all that the Christian faith maintains about what man ought to do and what he cannot do, about his obligations and final incapacity to fulfil them, about the importance of decisions and achievements in history and about their final insignificance. (N&D II, p. 220)

Just as Volume I began by discussing the classical and biblical views of human nature before embarking on the mythical analysis, so too the second volume discusses the classical and biblical views of human history before introducing the myth of the Atonement. The distinguishing feature is the problem of meaning attached to the historical process. Where the processes of history have no meaning, there a Christ is not expected. Where the processes do possess meaning, there some resolution of the meaning is expected—a Christ is expected. Prophetic religion expects a Christ. It was certain that the end of history would resolve the problems of meaning, and that God would ultimately triumph, but it was not certain how divine mercy was related to divine wrath, and how the mystery of the total human enterprise standing in defiance of God would be resolved. Niebuhr finds that this unsolved problem of the Old Testament is remarkably expressed in an apocalyptic context in 4 Ezra 7:118–120, an extra-canonical apocalypse:

> O thou Adam what hast thou done? For though it was thou that hast sinned, the fall was not thine alone but also ours who are thy descendants. For how does it profit us that the eternal age is promised us whereas we have done the works that bring death? And that there is foretold us an imperishable hope whereas we are so miserably brought to futility. (N&D II, p. 34)

This is an example of how Hebrew prophetism overreaches itself to ask a question for which it possesses no answer.

The answer to the problem is to be found in the myth of the Atonement. Niebuhr traces the basis of the mythical interpretation to the words of Jesus found in the Gospels concerning his own work and messianic understanding. Jesus rejected Hebraic legalism, and nationalistic particularism, and reinterpreted the figure of the Messiah to be a synthesis of the Suffering Servant of Deutero-Isaiah, and the Son of Man figure in apocalyptic literature. However, although Niebuhr insists that Jesus himself brought these two titles together to explain his messianic consciousness, he then argues that Jesus separated them by assigning the concept of the Suffering Servant to the first coming and the concept of the Son of Man to the second coming. Niebuhr does this to explain the complex double affirmation that on the one hand the Kingdom has appeared in the person of Jesus, and on the other hand the Kingdom will come in the future. The separation gives history its meaning, that the law of life—suffering love—will never achieve final triumph in history.

Without disagreeing with Niebuhr's conclusion regarding suffering love, the combination of the servant of YHWH and the apocalyptic Son of Man does not make sense if they are separated again. The point is that the two titles are two descriptions of two types of work combined in the ministry of Jesus. They must be understood as representative figures. In the person of Jesus we have the representative of God and the representative of the human race. In Paul's writings this figure is the Second Adam. The consequences of this will become clear in the critique of Niebuhr in Chapter 10.[1]

The revelation of the Atonement is both wisdom and power. It is a source of knowledge about life and history, but it is also power to shatter and reconstitute the self. Although Niebuhr separates these constituent elements for the sake of analysis their interrelation is too difficult to analyse with precision:

> It is not possible to give a fully logical or exactly chronological account of the relation . . . of the apprehension of truth which is beyond our comprehension to the shattering of the self by a power from beyond ourself. If a man does not know the truth about God . . . he cannot repent of the premature and self-centred completion of his life around a partial and inadequate centre. But it can be . . . argued with equal cogency, that without . . . the shattering of the self-centred self, man is too much his own God to feel the need of, or to have the capacity for, knowing the true God. The invasion of the self from beyond the self is therefore an invasion of both 'wisdom' and 'power', both 'truth' and 'grace'. (N&D II, p. 104)

The myth of the Atonement reveals the paradoxical truth that in Christ it is learnt that God has a resource of mercy beyond his law and judgement, but he can only make this mercy effective by taking upon himself the consequences of his wrath and judgement. 'Wrath' is not an easy concept to grasp. Niebuhr explains it by saying wrath is 'the world in its essential structure reacting against the sinful corruptions of that structure' (N&D II, p. 58). By 'structure' he does not mean something which sociologists could analyse. 'Essential structure' means the sum of all the individuals who possess an 'essential nature' with 'original righteousness'. 'Wrath' is therefore the disintegrating process which is consequent upon the corruption of the triple harmony of self with God, self, and neighbour. The law of life of the essential structure is the law of love. Wrath is the consequence of the defiance of the law of life as love. It is the exercise of justice for the defiance of the law of life.

113

The seriousness of this defiance is so great that only God, in his own freedom, can overcome this defiance. But God can only overcome the defiance by becoming subject to it. In this way the law of life is not abrogated, and the freedom of God over his own law is a demonstration of mercy. The subjection to wrath involves God in human suffering, and the apprehension that this is the situation shatters the self which is defying both essential nature and the law of life, and reconstitutes the self in conformity with the law of life by adding the 'theological virtues'. Thus the Atonement is *wisdom* in that it provides the knowledge that God must suffer, and it is *power* in that this knowledge shatters and reconstitutes the self. The effectiveness of divine mercy over justice could be termed the Holy Spirit.

Powerful and convincing as this description of Niebuhr's is, it still only answers to the sin of pride. He does not explain how the myth of Atonement reconstitutes a self which has been lost in the vitalities of nature. Nor is the social dimension of the Atonement dealt with; it is purely a Protestant conception of the individual and God. It answers to the 'longing for forgiveness' of general revelation but of course since Niebuhr did not include the 'longing for social harmony' in his description of general revelation there is no concept of a provisional answering to that need or longing by referring to a community of social harmony, the Church.

Nevertheless, Niebuhr does acknowledge that the myth of the Atonement presupposes a Christian community for its formulation. The titles 'servant of YHWH' and 'Son of Man' as applied to Jesus are claimed to have originated in Jesus. With the titles 'Son of God' and 'Second Adam', they can only be explained on the basis of reflection about the status and significance of Jesus by the Church.

The myth of the Atonement, whose constituent elements are wisdom and power, is a revelation completed by faith, argues Niebuhr. It is the declaration that an historical event has disclosed the full meaning of history. The title of Jesus which clarifies the historical event as revelatory is 'Son of God':

> The revelation of Christ is not completed until the little Christian community surveys the whole Christian epic, which includes the life and the teachings of Christ, but also and supremely the sacrificial death upon the Cross, understood by Christ as a necessary 'ransom for many'. . . . It is by the contemplation of the whole of this history in terms of expectation and fulfilment that Christian faith arrives at the

confession, 'Surely this was the Son of God'. (N&D II, pp. 54–5)

Since the revelation of ultimate truth occurs in history it provides a principle of coherence for the interpretation of history. Thus, the revelation of Jesus as the Son of God reveals the divine sovereignty over history and releases the knowledge that there are elements in history which point beyond history to the hidden source of life. Second, the revelation has the capacity to clarify obscurities and contradictions in history. Third, it is able to provide a basis for refuting alternative explanations of the meaning of history. The most consistent application of these principles is to be found in *Faith and History*.

The significance of the title 'Second Adam' is derived from reflection on the Atonement by the 'little Christian community'. It is the symbol used to express the truth that Christ is the perfect norm of human nature, the 'perfection of sacrificial love' (N&D II, p. 71) not attainable in history, or 'essential man' (N&D II, p. 80). It is the title which expresses the ethical dimension of the Atonement:

> As the revelation of the paradoxical relation of the divine justice and mercy He discloses the ultimate mystery of the relation of the divine to history. This revelation clarifies the meaning of history; for the judgment of God preserves the distinction of good and evil in history; and the mercy of God finally overcomes the sinful corruption in which man is involved on every level of moral achievement by reason of his false and abortive efforts. Christ as the norm of human nature defines the final perfection of man in history. (N&D II, p. 71)

Niebuhr argues that the Christological doctrines concerning the sinlessness of Christ, and the doctrine of the two natures, that Christ was both fully human and fully divine, can be rescued from philosophical absurdity by redefining them in terms of the ethical dimension of the Atonement. The doctrine of the sinlessness of Christ can be understood in the paradoxical relation of sacrificial love (*agapē*) to mutual love. *Agapē* describes harmony with divine love rather than harmony with other human interests and vitalities, which are only partial and incomplete because of the inclusion of sinful egoism into the calculation of interests. But even though mutual relations have to cope with the intrusion of egoism there is no situation where the ethical norm of Christ does not impinge. There is no point where the conscience can rest easy and not visualize a higher good which coincides with the perfection of *agapē*, the complete surrender of self-interest.

> The perfection of *agape* as symbolized in the Cross can neither be simply reduced to the limits of history, nor yet dismissed as irrelevant because it transcends history. It is the final norm of human nature which has no final norm in history because it is not completely contained in history. (N&D II, p. 78)

The doctrine of the two natures can be understood as an attempt to rationalize the paradox that in Christ the power of God and the goodness of God coincide but the goodness of God is demonstrated by refusal to use self-assertion in the rivalries of history, that is, the refusal to use power.

According to St Paul, Christ as Second Adam restores the innocency of Adam before the Fall and also exceeds that primal perfection. According to Niebuhr this means that life can approach its original innocency only by aspiring towards its unlimited end. What does Niebuhr mean by this?

> History must move from the innocency of Adam to the perfection of Christ, from the harmony of life with life in unfree nature to the perfect love of the Kingdom of God. (N&D II, p. 89)

He sees the Second Adam as a symbol of historical development, the formation of larger, more integrated and cohesive groups.

> There are no limits to be set in history for the achievement of more universal brotherhood, for the development of more perfect and more inclusive mutual relations. (N&D II, p. 89)

Galatians 3:28 describes this limitless goal to which history must aspire:

> There is neither Jew nor Greek, there is neither slave nor free, there is neither male nor female; for you are all one in Christ Jesus.

Race, sex, or class cannot be used to limit the development of 'brotherhood' (*sic*) in history.

It could be argued from this that since we cannot change the colour of our skin, or (in most cases) change our sex, then if a strategy for social change exists which involves the eradication of class, a strategy which does not consider race or sex as limiting factors, then the logic of Niebuhr's argument would suggest a serious engagement with its principles. If classes are defined in relation to the mode of production, and the development of the mode of production draws greater numbers into social units while maintaining the distinctions of class, then a mode of production must be favoured which eliminates class distinctions. In other words the logic of Niebuhr's theology would seem to coincide with Marxist goals for social change and development. Aware of where this argument leads, Niebuhr supplies the limits in aspiring to the limitless goal of history:

> The New Testament never guarantees the historical success of the 'strategy' of the Cross. Jesus warns his disciples against too sanguine historical hope [Lk 10:20]. . . . In that warning we have a telling refutation of the utopian corruptions of Christianity [i.e. Marxism]. . . . The Cross clarifies the possibilities and limits of history and perennially refutes the pathetic illusions of those who usually deny the dimension of history which reaches into Eternity [i.e. Marxists], and in the next dream of achieving an unconditioned perfection in history. . . .
>
> Since this possibility does not exist [i.e. the classless society of the Marxist ideal] it is not even right to insist that every action of the Christian must conform to *agape*, rather than to the norms of relative justice and mutual love by which life is maintained and conflicting interests are arbitrated in history. (N&D II, pp. 91–2)

Thus the Atonement is a myth which reveals wisdom to faith about the meaning and value of history. That is, it says that history is meaningful and it defines the ethical character of that meaning. The symbol of Christ as the Son of God relates to the overarching sovereignty of God over history, and the symbol of Christ as the Second Adam clarifies the ethical dimension of this sovereignty. However,

> in Christ both 'wisdom' and 'power' are available to man; which is to say that not only has the true meaning of life been disclosed but also that resources have been made available to fulfil that meaning. In him the faithful find not only 'truth' but 'grace'. (N&D II, p. 102)

Therefore the Atonement is a myth which becomes a source of power to faith, power to shatter and reconstitute the self. This double aspect of power corresponds to the double aspect of wisdom expressed in the titles Son of God and Second Adam. It is power over humanity and power within humanity, roughly corresponding to the distinctions in orthodox theology between justification and sanctification. Niebuhr calls this double aspect of power 'grace' and finds that its most adequate expression is located in the writings of St Paul.

To illustrate this point Niebuhr embarks on a detailed biblical analysis of Galatians 2:20:

> I have been crucified with Christ; it is no longer I who live, but Christ who lives in me; and the life I now live in the flesh I live by faith in the Son of God, who loved me and gave himself for me.

Niebuhr concludes that sin is destroyed in principle but not in fact. When Paul tells Christians they are sinless and then exhorts them not to sin he means 'self-love is destroyed in principle in your life—see to it that the new principle is actualized'.

The Hellenistic influence in Christianity did not balance its interpretation of the Atonement between wisdom and power. It tended to emphasize the former because the main problem was attempting to understand how the finite is related to the eternal. Power over sin did not receive the same attention. Niebuhr argues that it was St Augustine who first expressed that the primary issue of life and history was the relation of grace to sin rather than the time—eternity problem. Nevertheless, even in Augustine the double aspect of grace as power over and power in humanity is obscured and he failed to appreciate the power and persistence of self-love on every level of achievement. Justification therefore becomes subordinated to sanctification and the Church becomes the locus where the contradiction between the historical and the divine is overcome rather than the locus where the judgement and mercy of God is mediated, and where the contradiction between the historical and the holy is overcome in principle.

This perfectionist tendency of mediaeval Christianity was checked by the Reformation, the 'culmination of the prophetic interpretation of history' (N&D II, p. 153). The full truth of the Atonement was realized because grace was interpreted not primarily as the power of God in humanity, but as the power of God towards humanity as mercy and forgiveness. Grace was not restricted to a power which completes human nature by supplying a wisdom which was beyond the reach of profane reason. Instead grace was thought of as a power beyond all human power and operative only when human powers recognize their own limits. It was a power available to faith apart from any institution.

If the Reformation had access to the full truth of the Atonement, why have these biblical insights been neglected or destroyed? asks Niebuhr. This question is answered by explaining how it came about that the view of life characterized by the Renaissance was more effective than the view of life expressed in the Reformation. One reason Niebuhr gives is the fact that the phenomenal development of human knowledge and capability which has occurred since the mediaeval period seemed to emphasize what was true and to hide what was false in the Renaissance estimate of life. The Renaissance was a unique combination of half the biblical idea (minus the eschatological element) of a meaningful history, the classical confidence in human capacity, and a secularized version of grace as sanctification, coupled with an individual perfectionist urge mediated by Franciscan theologians. Because the spirit of the Renaissance was more effective than the spirit of the Reformation it has resulted in a modern culture which believes that the laws of reason are capable of bringing the vitalities of history within its power and which fails to take seriously the Christian eschatological symbols of judgement. Niebuhr considers that liberal Protestantism is merely an attempt to introduce Christianity into this scheme without offending it, and in that respect it is a betrayal of the spirit and genius of the Reformation and a confirmation of the triumph of the spirit of the Renaissance.

> No alternative perspectives [to the problems of the day] are available because [this triumph] was so complete that it destroyed not only particular interpretations of the Christian religion, but submerged the Christian religion itself as a potent force in modern culture. The Catholic form of the religion became discredited by the fact that all the liberties of modern life and all the achievements of social and political justice were established in defiance of Catholicism's premature identification of its feudal society with the sanctities of the Kingdom of God. The Reformation form of the religion was not so much discredited as simply lost. (N&D II, p. 189)

In order to understand further reasons why the insights of the Reformation have been lost in modern culture Niebuhr analyses the relevant aspects of both Luther and Calvin. Luther's confusion is caused by the highly personal and interior concept of sanctification which obscures the social dimension of justification and therefore

119

fails to prompt a sense of obligation in ever-widening circles of life. Luther's theology is explicitly defeatist in the social sphere and the Christian is under no obligation to change the social structures to improve social harmony. In fact, Luther's social morality is 'perverse':

> He places a perfectionist private ethic in juxtaposition to a realistic . . . official ethic. He demands the state maintain order without too scrupulous a regard for justice; yet asks suffering and non-resistant love of the individual without allowing him to participate in the claims and counter claims which constitute the stuff of social justice. (N&D II, p. 201)

Calvin's weakness lies in his bibliolatry, the extracting of eternal laws from the Bible without regard to their original social setting and their meaning within that setting. For Calvin, grace becomes a rigorous obedience to the law as found in the Bible, which is used as an indiscriminate source book of moral and social answers to the contemporary problems. Thus one side of the Reformation considered the social problem insoluble and left the social realm to sort it out for itself, and the other side of the Reformation solved the problem too simply by insisting on biblical standards in a world far removed from the Bible.

It is surprising that Niebuhr does not mention Weber's thesis about the Protestant work ethic in this context, especially since that was one of the main themes of his first book. This would have been appropriate if Niebuhr had also mentioned that Calvin's theology of sanctification or double justification was a reaction against Luther's unilateral accentuation of justification which could find no value in 'works' of social justice. For Calvin justification and sanctification are equal graces issuing from the same Christ. This means that the works of the justified are no longer viewed by God as if they were works before justification or apart from it. The works of the justified are acceptable because they are performed by gifts of the Spirit, but they are not acceptable in themselves. Calvin's theology of sanctification could have led to an increased sense of social obligation, but combined with the doctrine of the predestination of the elect in the end it only invited further introspection about membership of the elect.

'The Reformation', concludes Niebuhr, 'has discovered the final truth about life and history' (N&D II, p. 218), but it has failed to relate this insight to the whole range of human experience. The final truth consists of a series of dialectical affirmations which constitute the myth of the Atonement. It asserts,

> that the Christian is both sinner and righteous, that history fulfils and negates the Kingdom of God; that grace is continuous with, and in contradiction to, nature; that Christ is what we ought to be and also what we cannot be; that the power of God is in us in judgment and mercy. (N&D II, p. 211)

It is these affirmations 'which must be applied to the experiences of life from top to bottom' (N&D II, p. 211).

The next section of *Nature and Destiny* is a demonstration of how the truths contained in the myth of the Atonement can be applied to questions of social justice. Since Niebuhr also wrote a practical application of these theological principles entitled *The Children of Light and the Children of Darkness* (1945) this theme will be dealt with before the eschatological section of *Nature and Destiny*. This latter theme will be incorporated into the discussion of *Faith and History* which attempts to relate eschatology more coherently to the mythical pattern.

TEST OF TOLERANCE

At the beginning of the previous chapter it was mentioned that major world events had influenced Niebuhr's theology. The class war in Europe had led to the rise and triumph of fascism, and it was clear to him that the Communist judgement of capitalist society would not materialize. Right-wing forces were winning control of states, democratically at first, and then by waging war. In America a different method of harnessing the power of the State in support of capitalism had been developed and the methods and the measure of its success had impressed Niebuhr. He had left the Socialist Party and counselled that the primary duty of capitalist society in the present crisis was to defeat the enemies of those who advocated democratic control of State power. The New Deal, it has been previously noted, was not informed by a central organizing philosophy. Things were tried out. If they worked they were kept, if they did not work they were scrapped, and if they offended people in high places the Supreme Court ruled them unconstitutional. Sometimes policies countered each other's effectiveness. Niebuhr sensed that this stumbling towards justice was preferable to those forces which sought to abolish democratic control of the State, and that a philosophy was required which could substantiate the American approach to these practical difficulties of social organization. On the premise that human beings are by nature religious, and if this is not acknowledged it can result in fanaticisms, it was important that the underlying philosophy should be informed by a religion which could steer human activity away from fanatical solutions to the problems of social justice.

> The truth, as it is contained in the Christian revelation, includes the recognition that it is neither possible for man to know the truth fully nor to avoid the error of pretending that he does. (N&D II, p. 225)

It follows that if Niebuhr is to propose that the resources of the Christian religion contain valid insights into human nature and history which must be realized by those who play leading roles in social organization, then excuses have to be made as to why Christians throughout the centuries have often given the impression that they are extremely prone to fanaticism. In *Nature and Destiny* he puts historic Christianity to the test of the liberal virtue of tolerance. In practice he has to explain why both Catholic and Reformation Christianity were intolerant. The location of Catholic intolerance is found to be its peculiar ideas of grace which ultimately led towards perfectionism, claiming possession of unconditional truth. One might have expected more toleration among the Reformers since, according to Niebuhr, they had discovered the final truth about life and history, but because the final truth contains the recognition that the final truth itself cannot be known, there is an escape route to explain their intolerance. Certainly Luther fails the test of toleration because of his recommendations that peasants should be killed even though they had appealed to his theology to support their social grievances. Niebuhr argues that the source of modern tolerance belongs to the secular spirit of the Renaissance and derives from its optimistic naturalism that life does have meaning and does not face a terrible judgement at the end.

Despite the fact, according to Niebuhr, that the only form of historic Christianity which has shown any degree of tolerance is the 'heretical' liberal Protestantism which he had spent a lifetime criticizing, he rejects Marxism because of the fanaticism its theory encourages. There are no excuses for this 'religion':

> All truth but its own is tainted with the 'ideological' taint of

interest. But obviously the pretension of any class or nation, of any culture or civilization, that it alone has escaped from the finiteness of human knowing, and the corruption of interest and passion, is merely another form of the taint of pride which confuses all quests for the truth. It is a secularized version of the pretension of complete sanctification. The fruit of fanaticism is the natural consequence of this claim. (N&D II, p. 251)

Stalinist practice is regarded as the inevitable fruit of Marxist theory. However, if Frederick Engels can be regarded as a contributor to Marxist theory then his chapter 'Morality and law. Eternal truths' in *Anti-Dühring* clearly illustrates that Stalinist practice is not derived from this strand of Marxist theory. He wrote:

In all probability we are but little beyond the beginning of human history, and the generations which will put *us* right are likely to be far more numerous than those whose knowledge we are in a position to correct. . . .

If mankind ever reached the stage at which it could only work with eternal truths, with conclusions which possess sovereign validity and have an unconditional claim to truth, it would then have reached the point where the infinity of the intellectual world both in its actuality and in its potentiality had been exhausted, and this would mean that the famous miracle of the infinite series which has been counted would have been performed.[2]

In short Engels pours contempt on any form of utopianism.

THE ATONEMENT AS MODEL OF SOCIAL ORDER

During one of the sessions of the Gifford Lectures the Luftwaffe were bombing the naval dockyard at Leith. The sound of exploding bombs punctuating Niebuhr's rhythmic oration added a sombre poignancy and urgency to his words. Social life had to maintain a precarious balance between tyranny and anarchy. There were two examples of totalitarian tyranny, the Nazi regime and the Communist regime, and one example of anarchy, *laissez-faire* capitalism. To maintain a precarious balance it was necessary to insist that two principles of social order should be acknowledged, the organization of power and the balance of power. Social life should be a combination of these two principles in correct proportions. The question is: What form of social organization balances these two principles most effectively? Faced with the three intolerable examples Niebuhr concluded that the form of society which the New Deal was creating offered the best choice.

But it was more than just a simple matter of rational choice. Western civilization was facing a judgement because of its injustices. Just as it had been helpless to avoid this judgement, so too its achievements had been reached through more than conscious design:

> The complexity of the technical, rational and prophetic-religious factors which contributed to the rise of modern democracies, illustrates the complex and intimate involvement of all these factors in the whole historical process. The interweaving of these various strands in the total fabric of historical development refutes both vitalists and rationalists, who would interpret the social process either as merely a chaos of vital forces or as a simple progressive triumph of reason over force. (N&D II, p. 274)

Niebuhr is making the simple equation that the form of Western democracies best reflects the truths revealed in the myth of the Atonement. Niebuhr expresses this as follows:

> No possible refinement of social forces and political harmonies can eliminate the potential contradiction to brotherhood which is implicit in the two political instruments of brotherhood—the organization of power and the balance of power. This paradoxical situation in the realm of the social life is analogous to the Christian conception of the paradox of history as discerned in other realms of life. (N&D II, p. 268)

Although 'prophetic elements in Christianity have contributed to the rise of modern democratic societies' (N&D II, p. 274), Niebuhr has to agree that its contribution has 'seldom stated the full truth of its twofold approach to the political order in such a way that it would give guidance in the complexities of political and social life' (N&D II, p. 278), with the result that 'history had to stumble by tortuous process upon the proper techniques for avoiding both anarchy and tyranny' (N&D II, p. 278). Therefore because the liberal democratic tradition embodies the 'principle of resistance to government within the principle of government itself' (N&D II, p. 278), it embodies within itself a form of structural contrition.

The evolution of Western democracies in the world, and Niebuhr's pluralist conception of the interventionist State regulating a competing balance of private capitals as the form of society which best reflects the truth in the myth of the Atonement, leads to the conclusion that the Kingdom of God is growing. In view of Niebuhr's previous attacks on liberal Protestantism for its complacent attitude towards the growth of the Kingdom it seems odd that he should now insist on this essential truth at the very moment of history when Nazi bombs were threatening the existence of civilization. What must be remembered, Niebuhr asserts, is that each advance creates a new peril: 'History moves towards the realization of the Kingdom, but yet the judgment of God is upon every new realization' (N&D II, p. 296).

PROPHETIC RELIGION AND LIBERAL DEMOCRACY

The final section of *Nature and Destiny* is a discussion of the myth of the Parousia (the Second Coming of Christ), and the myths associated with it. It was mentioned earlier that Niebuhr did not bring the knowledge these myths reveal about human nature into organic relation with the rest of the work. They are attached to Volume II like an appendix. In the next two important books Niebuhr published he completes and corrects aspects of Volume II. *The Children of Light and the Children of Darkness* (1944) is a deeper practical analysis of the issues dealt with relating the myth of the Atonement to the Western form of society, and *Faith and History* analyses the four primary myths of prophetic religion in relation to history with greater importance given to the eschatological content.

Children develops the conclusion of *Nature and Destiny* that Western civilization has produced a form of social organization which most approximates to the truths revealed in the myth of the Atonement. Competing interest groups and private capitals continually place checks upon self-interest, and the interventionist State regulates the competition preventing its disintegration into anarchy. At the same time the competition checks the development of the organizing centre and prevents it from evolving into a tyranny. The book also reflects the prevailing mood of the period. The Allied victory seemed certain and Britain and America were planning global strategies for peace. Both John Maynard Keynes and Harry Dexter White had planned an economic institution to regulate international trade and to provide liquidity. The 'Keynes Plan' and the

'White Plan' had been published in the spring of 1943, and they became the basis of the Bretton Woods negotiations in the summer of 1944. Niebuhr was providing a religious version of these hopes for stabilizing global society. In short, he was trying to provide a religious philosophy for the mixed economy.

> If democracy is to survive, it must find a more adequate cultural basis than the philosophy which has informed the building of the bourgeois world. (CLCD, p. 12)

Niebuhr divides political strategies into two types. There are those people who do not understand the power of self-interest, and those who do understand the power of self-interest and possess the skill to harness it for their own ends. The former are called 'children of light' and the latter 'children of darkness'. The bases of both the liberal and Marxist creeds are formed by children of light; in both there is an unwarranted optimism and innocence regarding human nature. Adam Smith, John Locke, Thomas Paine and Jeremy Bentham are hauled in as witnesses for the charge against the liberal creed, and Karl Marx and 'Marxists' are included as children of light because:

> their provisional cynicism does not save them from the usual stupidity, nor from the fate, of other stupid children of light. That fate is to have their creed become the vehicle and the instrument of the children of darkness. (CLCD, p. 29)

Some children of light have seen their ideals, especially on the relation between the national and international community, adopted and used by the children of darkness, the Nazis. Nietzsche, Fichte, Rousseau, Hegel and Herder are placed in this category.

If the stupid children of light are to become as wise as the children of darkness they must learn how to devise a political philosophy which will allow sufficient freedom for human creativity to develop, and sufficient order to prevent the destructive elements in human nature from stimulating anarchy. This means appreciating the twin principles of order and balance in the realms of the economy, politics, and the international community.

In the case of the economy it means a central regulatory body, the State, policing a competition of private capitals:

> The intricacies of modern commerce and industry could not have developed if the medieval moral and political controls had been maintained; and even now when we know that all

economic life must submit to moral discipline and political restraint, we must be careful to preserve whatever self-regulating forces exist in the economic process. If we do not, the task of control becomes too stupendous and the organs of control achieve proportions which endanger our liberty. (CLCD, p. 56)

The same principle applies on the property question. During the 1930s when Niebuhr thought that Marxism was the instrument of divine judgement, he supported the idea of the social ownership of property, and argued that individual ownership of the means of production was anachronistic. Now that it had been revealed, on further analysis, that the form of Western democracy best approximates the truth in the myth of the Atonement, centre and balance must apply here:

> The social ownership of the power and wealth derived from unified process is certainly more plausible than the effort to maintain its individual character in defiance of inexorable historical developments. Yet it may be wise for the community to sacrifice something to efficiency for the sake of preserving a greater balance of forces and avoiding undue centralization of power. . . . The property issue must, in other words, be continually solved within the framework of the democratic process . . . [T]he political process requires the best possible distribution of power for the sake of justice, and the best possible management of this equilibrium for the sake of order. (CLCD, pp. 81–3)

The same principle applies on the question of class. In *Nature and Destiny* Niebuhr argued that social class should not be a limiting factor in the creation of wider spheres of 'brotherhood', and then added that the attempt to organize a form of society which sought to eliminate class distinctions should be prevented because of the insinuation of egoism into the process. In other words the abolition of social class should not be a goal of political and economic activity. In *Children* further evidence is supplied to support the idea that the abolition of class differences should not be an achievement of social progress:

> Every modern democratic society has been prompted, both by its natural necessities and by the voting power of the workers, to redress economic inequalities through the use of political

power. This process has invalidated the Marxist thesis that the state is merely the executive committee of the possessing classes. (CLCD, p. 74)

It follows from this that if the State is a neutral organizing principle with regard to class then civil society is characterized by a competition between the classes for economic and political power.

The one requirement is that there be some equilibrium between class forces; and the other is that the equilibrium should not become static, but be subject to the shifts of power which conform to the development of the economic and social situation. (CLCD, p. 102)

Once the function of the State is considered to be divorced from the process of accumulation of capital, and once the question of class is divorced from the structural exploitation of the production of surplus value, then it can be argued that the liberal democratic form of society provides a sound basis for the gradual achievement of social justice. When the theory that the practice of liberal democracy is an indication of divine grace is put forward, then the essence of Niebuhr's earlier estimation of Marxism is undermined. Nevertheless Niebuhr is careful to stress the point that democratic society is only an approximation of social order, the best form available given the nature of sin.

To make a democratic society the end of human existence is a less vicious version of the Nazi creed. It is less vicious because it is prevented from becoming completely idolatrous. The creed is nevertheless dangerous because no society, not even a democratic one, is great enough or good enough to make itself the final end of human existence. (CLCD, p. 92)

This warning is directed at America where:

the bourgeois mind has not yet faced the ultimate issues, nor been confronted with the inadequacy of its own credos. This is why the secularization of culture still seems an adequate answer in America both for the ultimate questions about the meaning of life and the immediate problem of the unity and harmony of our society. (CLCD, p. 93)

Niebuhr realizes that pre-war isolationism is no longer a real option for America because the war has transformed a potential hegemony into actuality. He therefore brings to the surface a theme which first

128

occupied him in the 1920s, American foreign policy and the international community.

> If America achieves maturity, the primary mark of it must be the willingness to assume continuing responsibility in the world community of nations. We must seek to maintain a critical attitude to our own power impulses; and our self criticism must be informed by the humble realization of the fact that the possession of great power is a temptation to injustice for any nation. (CLCD, p. 125)

The crisis of the age is caused by the fact that modern technology has created a potential world community but there are no political instruments to organize the community. The task of the future is to prevent the power which integrates the world community from becoming tyrannical. Such a power will require the checks and balances of a democratic order. Because there is a potential or latent world community the world is fated to pass through a period where corrupt forms of universalism must be defeated. The Nazi effort marks the first attempt to create a world system. The Communist threat will mark the second, but he does not mention that threat in this context. His Cold War theology is a later development. However, because Niebuhr has a concept of the State as a neutral structure, and because he does not see the primary relation between the accumulation of capital and the advancing technological achievement, and because he rejects the labour theory of value, and because he thinks in terms of autonomous nation-states, he is not able to consider the possibility that the universal community will eventually be created by a particular class which controls a particular economic system.[3] For Niebuhr the creation of a world community is the task of the more powerful autonomous nation-states, and what is important is that they realize the Christian religion possesses resources for assisting with the building of such a community:

> It will be a long while before modern idealists will recognize that the profundities of the Christian faith, which they have disavowed, are indispensable resources for the historic tasks [the building of a world community] which lie before us. . . . From the standpoint of such a faith it is possible to deal with the ultimate social problem of human history: the creation of community in world dimensions. (CLCD, p. 127)

This theme of the concept of a world community is also the subject

129

of a number of articles written between 1942 and 1944.[4] The problem with forming a world community is that it is extremely difficult to form an organizing centre to control the equilibrium of powers, and without an organizing centre the equilibrium would be displaced for anarchy with the probability of another war. It is obvious to Niebuhr that there must be an organizing centre and that it should be composed of some sort of harmony between the major powers. In 1942 he therefore considers that the alliance with Russia is a 'great gain' if it could continue beyond the war because this would prevent a 'pure Anglo-Saxon imperialism'. Restricting the organizing centre to one such power would probably end in a new tyranny.

In a 1943 article he again stresses that there must be a group of nations to form an organizing centre capable of setting up instruments of justice in the world community. It is also important, he argues, for a close European unity, with perfect cultural autonomy, but each nation should not possess absolute independence in the political and economic spheres.

In a 1944 article on the question of European unity, when the Allied victory was certain, Niebuhr argued that excessive punishment of the guilty nation would detract from the more important task of reconstituting community:

> The final health of Germany depends upon the creation of a healthy Continent, just as a healthy Continent also requires an ultimately healthy and sane Germany, and as a tolerably healthy world community requires a decently reorganized European continent.[5]

He thought that if Europe were partitioned into spheres of influence it would soon lead to another war.

Inevitably the American role in the formation of the world community was dealt with. In 1943 he noted that America's 'coming of age' coincided with a period of world history in which the creation of the world community had assumed primary importance.[6] It is the most powerful nation on earth, he wrote, but it has the 'least experience in the complexities of international relations'. Niebuhr feared that because security was not threatened in the same way as it was with the other powers there would be a temptation to evade international responsibility. The war had taught that a balance of power between nations was insufficient to maintain peace, and that Europe was too weak to maintain order in the total world situation. Since it is important for the world to discover adequate instruments for preventing further anarchy, America must step into the vacuum. When America does assume this responsibility the profounder insights of the Christian faith will be required since 'it is not possible to build a community without the manipulation of power and it is not possible to use power and remain completely "pure" '.

The religious context for Niebuhr's conception for an organizing power is clarified in the article: 'Anglo-Saxon destiny and responsibility' (1943). It was written in response to a speech by Churchill at Harvard. As the title suggests it is ostensibly about co-operation between Britain and the United States in stabilizing the post-war world. But during the course of the article Britain tends to disappear from Niebuhr's considerations.

> Only those who have no sense of the profundities of history could deny that various nations and classes, various social groups and races are at various times placed in such a position that a special measure of the divine mission in history falls upon them. In that sense God has chosen us in this fateful period of world history.

It could be that one reason for God's choice is that the political forms of these nations, and the moral and political ideals are 'less incompatible with international justice than any other previous power in history'. On the other hand it must be realized that no nation is ever good enough for its responsibilities. First of all it must be acknowledged that when a nation achieves hegemonic status it is the gift of God's grace that has made this possible:

> The grace that determines the lives of men and nations is manifest in all the special circumstances, favours, and fortunes of geography and climate, of history and fate that lead to eminence despite the weakness and sinfulness of the beneficiary of such eminence.

If 'grace' is obscured, then the 'sense of destiny' becomes purely the 'vehicle of pride'. Therefore although the democratic traditions of the Anglo-Saxon world are actually the potential basis of a just world order, 'in God's eyes' they are not just. Contrite recognition of national sin is required to apprehend 'grace' in national life.

The Anglo-Saxon democratic form has been chosen for a particular task. If it fails in this task it will bring judgement upon itself and the world. There must be a sense of humility and responsibility to 'come to terms' with Russia and China. It is necessary to perceive what is good in the new Russian order, especially their values of equal justice. But at the same time it is important that Russian tyranny is recognized as 'a false answer to our own problems of social justice'.

NOTES

1 For a more comprehensive presentation of this point see Oscar Cullmann, *The Christology of the New Testament* (London, 1963), pp. 79ff.
2 Frederick Engels, *Herr Eugen Dühring's Revolution in Science [Anti-Dühring]* (London, Martin Lawrence Ltd., no date), pp. 100–1.
3 In the work of the sociologist Immanuel Wallerstein it is argued that the genius of capitalism lies in the fact that it is a system which prevents political control from interfering with the process of creating a world community. No nation-state is powerful enough to take control of the process and it is because the system prevents the creation of empire that it is moving towards the creation of a world community. Previous world economic systems have been taken over by the hegemonic power of the day with the result that the system implodes. There are references to Wallerstein's work in Chapters 9 and 10.
4 A selection of these articles includes:
'Plans for world reorganization', *Christianity and Crisis* (19 October 1942); 'The United Nations and world organization', *Christianity and Crisis* (25 January 1943); 'American power and world responsibility', *Christianity and Crisis* (5 April 1943); 'Anglo-Saxon destiny and responsibility', *Christianity and Crisis* (4 October 1943); 'The basis of world order', *The Nation* (21 October 1944).
5 'The German problem', *Christianity and Crisis* (10 January 1944) **3**, 2–4.
6 'American power and world responsibility', *op. cit.*

8

Theology for the Nations

How is it possible for a historian to claim that Niebuhr 'provided a historical basis and rationale for the tone, the outlook, the unsaid and often unconscious assumptions'[1] of the American people in the first years of the Cold War when Niebuhr himself had implied in 1946 that America was a nation of 'semipagan arrogance'[2] which called itself Christian? How could it be that a theologian whose writings had inspired students to raise a red flag on the Union Theological Seminary flagpole on 1 May 1934 should appear on the cover of the 25th anniversary issue of *Time* magazine, and be labelled as 'the official Establishment theologian'?[3] How could a man who had once said that academics were 'supported by generous crumbs which fall from the rich man's table' and were full of self-deception 'derived from a special kind of detachment from the inertia and brutality of impulsive life'[4] be considered as a serious candidate for the summit of the Establishment, the president of Yale University?

Niebuhr thrived in contradictions like these.

During the second half of the 1940s Niebuhr had reached the pinnacle of his powers and his success. Since his theology was conditioned by world events it is first necessary briefly to summarize those events which influenced his theology of this period.

THE COLD WAR

In June 1941 the State Department debated the Nazi invasion of the Soviet Union. They issued an announcement condemning atheism and Stalin's intolerable dictatorship, but agreed that Hitler was a greater threat and that Stalin should be helped. Harry S. Truman, Democratic Senator from Missouri, went on record as saying:

> If we see that Germany is winning we should help Russia and if Russia is winning we ought to help Germany and that way let them kill as many as possible, although I don't want to see Hitler victorious under any circumstances.[5]

Washington officials, when they looked into the future, feared for another depression unless world markets were opened to absorb American goods. Anything less would lead to further government intervention in the economy. The Assistant Secretary of State, Dean Acheson, had said that the capitalist system was essentially an international system and that if it was unable to function internationally then it would break down completely. The US required an open world market after the war. It was argued that the cause of the war in the first place had been the existence of closed economic blocs. During the war industrial output had risen by 90 per cent. It was the war itself which had cured the Depression, not the New Deal. In 1944 the Bretton Woods conference had established the existence of the supranational institutions, the International Monetary Fund (IMF) and the World Bank.

The requirements of an open world market conflicted with Britain's hold on the closed market of the Empire. This was prised open in return for a $3.8 billion loan to assist the economic recovery of the UK. The US wanted an open Europe, but Stalin wanted a buffer zone against the West for security and to exploit for the rebuilding of the Soviet economy. Churchill complicated relations between the US and the Soviets by agreeing a secret deal with Stalin, swapping Eastern Europe for Greece, an important strategic point for British trade with the Empire. Churchill warned Stalin to speak tactfully to Roosevelt about it and not to use such phrases as 'dividing into spheres' because that might shock the Americans.

In the 1945 meeting of the Big Three at Yalta there was a furious row over what to do with Poland. Stalin appeared to get his way. Two weeks after the conference there were US protests about Stalin's treatment of Rumania. Churchill was silent on this issue—he had assurances about Greece.

Then Roosevelt died, and Truman stepped in, determined to get tough with the Russians.

The conflict was basically over two methods of security. For the US a peaceful world meant an open system of trading. For the

Soviet Union security meant isolating itself from the anarchy of capitalism and the inevitable wars which trail in its wake. The war had claimed the lives of 20 million Russians, destroyed 1,700 towns, 70,000 villages, and left 25 million people homeless. Six hundred thousand had starved to death in the siege of Leningrad. By contrast the US had lost 300,000 servicemen.[6] It is difficult for nations to understand each other when there is such inequality of suffering.

The two powers also disagreed over the fate of Germany. During the period 1943–5 Roosevelt had first considered destroying the nation, and then, after a change of mind, allowing it to industrialize under strict control. Stalin was more consistent. He favoured transferring German industry to Russia. This would kill off the nation as a future threat and offer some degree of compensation for the heavy Russian losses. The Potsdam Conference separated Germany economically, and the US would hold on to the industrial heartland and rebuild the German economy.

There was some vacillation too on the question of Russian assistance with the war against Japan. This issue was settled by 6 August when one atomic bomb killed 80,000 people in Hiroshima. This was almost as many killed as in the massive bombing raid on Tokyo earlier in the year. Japan surrendered after another bomb landed on Nagasaki three days later. In the same month Secretary of State James F. Byrnes explained how America would build a peaceful world. His speech concluded with: 'to the extent that we are able to manage our domestic affairs successfully, we shall win converts to our creed in every land'.[7]

In 1946 Stalin renewed the pledge to Marxist-Leninism. He argued that capitalism would lead to yet another war and that the Soviet people were to make sure that capitalist forces no longer posed a threat to the Soviet Union. Churchill responded to this at Fulton, Missouri on 5 March with the 'iron curtain' speech. He explained that it was God's will that the US should have atomic bombs rather than the Communists and the Fascists. These bombs had given the world a breathing space to prepare for peace. Churchill wanted an Anglo-American unity to provide unity in Europe in which 'no nation should be permanently outcast!' To the Soviets, this was a direct challenge to their power. Stalin disapproved of Churchill's theory that those who spoke the English language should rule the world. In the end the Soviets refused to join the World Bank and the IMF.

In the summer of 1946 the German problem intensified. Byrnes proposed a treaty unifying Germany and guaranteeing its demilitarization. However, this conflicted with Russia's changed plans concerning reparations. Instead of moving German industry to Russia they had decided to operate the German factories using cheap labour and sending the products to Russia.

On the nuclear issue Bernard Baruch, an American delegate to the new UN Atomic Energy Commission, made a speech in which he suggested that there should be international control of all raw materials, and countries should not be able to use the veto—it should be a simple majority decision. This was unacceptable to the Russians because it would mean external control and inspection within the Soviet Union. Their response was to suggest that America scrap its existing weapons and then talks could begin. America refused, and there were no talks.

An indication as to how rapidly events were moving can be gauged by the sacking of Henry Wallace.[8] Wallace insisted in a speech in New York that there must be an open door for trade throughout the world. This included the Soviet Union. America and Russia should compete on a friendly basis and gradually the two nations would become more alike. Unfortunately he was twelve months too late—it was now September 1946.

Truman declared the Cold War had commenced on 12 March 1947. He presented the 'Truman Doctrine' to Congress and asked for a global commitment against Communism. The impetus for this dramatic context was the British support for government forces against the National Liberation Front in Greece and Turkey. The UK claimed they had run out of the money necessary to support the fight against the Tito-backed NLF. On hearing the news Truman appealed to Congress for $400 million. It was explained that the threat was not civil war in Greece. It was instead a stage in the advance of Russian Communism aiming to capture control of the Middle East, South Asia, and Africa, and with the ultimate aim of capturing Germany and then Europe.

A few days prior to the announcement of the 'Truman Doctrine' the President had warned about the expansion of State controlled (command) economies. Unless businessmen could operate in the world market place properly, he warned, it would be back to the 1930s in America and more State intervention. Freedom of speech, freedom of worship, and freedom of enterprise were all interrelated, he claimed. Without the latter the first two would disappear.

The economic side of the 'Truman Doctrine' eventually became embodied in the Marshall Plan. It was assumed that the US must lead in restoring the economic fortunes of Europe. The Plan provided convertibility of local currencies into dollars. Its aim was to stimulate private investors to rebuild Europe. There were a number of advantages for America of this 'New Deal' in Europe. It held back the threat of nationalization and socialism, it maintained demand for American exports, and it preserved European and American control of oil supplies from the Middle East. It also tied in with the plan of rejuvenating the German economy. The Secretary of State appointed a policy planning staff under the direction of George Kennan.

Reinhold Niebuhr was invited to attend some of these sessions. According to the 'revisionist' historian Walter LaFeber, he was the leading exponent of the ideological side of the 'Truman Doctrine'. Niebuhr's article 'For peace we must risk war' (*Life* XXV, 30 September 1948) expressed, said LaFeber, the views which 'underlay the foreign policy planks of both parties'.[9]

STATE THEOLOGIAN

Neither American socialism nor pacifism provided an adequate forum for debate and action in response to Hitler's foreign policy. In 1940 Niebuhr was instrumental in founding the Union for Democratic Action (UDA). Its members were mainly New York socialists who had left the Socialist Party on account of its isolationist policy. No party member was allowed to join, and conservatives and Communists were also excluded. Niebuhr would not allow Communists to enter because they were taking orders direct from Moscow. After the Nazi–Soviet Pact in August 1939 orders were sent out from headquarters saying that anti-fascist behaviour must cease. This hypocrisy was more than Niebuhr could bear.

The UDA was a group of intellectuals and labour leaders and it was chaired, as usual, by Niebuhr. Its main activity was to push the interventionist line. The moral scruples of socialists and pacifists were no longer a luxury to indulge in, or hide behind. Hitler had to be defeated and the US should take all action short of war to ensure that he was defeated. In 1943 Niebuhr and his group appealed for the relaxation of the immigration laws. Hitler was trying to exterminate the Jewish race, cried Niebuhr, and it was important that European Jews should be allowed to escape from Europe and enter the US with the minimum amount of fuss.

Niebuhr also helped a group called American Friends of German Freedom. It was started by the German socialist Karl Frank and it was set up to help refugees escape from Germany. Niebuhr's contacts with the German underground and the State Department proved useful.[10]

After the war he was invited to join a fifteen-member mission sponsored by the State and War Departments to remove Nazis from educational establishments in the American occupied zone and to find suitable replacements. Some of his writings were translated into German as part of the 'Reorientation Program in Occupied Territories'. While he was in Germany he learnt that German socialists and Christian Democrats were appealing for American military and economic support if they were to avoid having another totalitarian regime imposed on them. In the light of this experience Niebuhr saw no hope in Wallace's conciliatory policy. 'The Russians are not', he said, 'and will not be, satisfied with any system of eastern European defences but are seeking to extend their power over the whole of Europe.'[11] *Time*, *Life*, and the *Reader's Digest* magazines published Niebuhr's articles preparing for the Cold War. One *Life* article carried the subtitle: 'A distinguished theologian declares America must prevent the conquest of Germany and Western Europe by the unscrupulous Soviet tyranny'.[12]

In November 1946 Niebuhr addressed the CIO convention in Atlantic City on 'Labor's stake in the fight for Europe'. His performance won over union officials Walter Reuther and James Carey, and with this increased popularity in the labour movement his invitations for the formation of a new group met with a favourable response. This group became known as the Americans for Democratic Action. It replaced the UDA and pushed the anti-Communist line to exclude 'sympathizers with Communism' from its membership. But as this group became closely associated with the Democratic Party Niebuhr's involvement waned, and he applied his political energies to working for the Liberal Party in New York State.

He was a firm supporter of Truman's appeal to Congress over the $400 million aid to Greece and Turkey, and he was already pressing for loans to boost the European economy prior to the publication of the Marshall Aid programme. In 1949 he was invited to join George Kennan's policy planning staff. He was also elected as a member of the American delegation to the fourth conference of UNESCO in Paris during the same year. One month later Secretary of State Dean

Acheson invited him to a Washington conference on plans to strengthen the non-Communist world without impairing the UN.

GOD'S SCORNFUL LAUGHTER

Despite a hectic schedule, somehow Niebuhr managed to find time to write *Faith and History*. It represents a deeper reflection on the significance of the war and its immediate aftermath in the light of the theology of history developed in *Nature and Destiny*. What has become clear to Niebuhr in this period is the fact that there are two levels of sin corresponding to the two dimensions of harmony in the ethic of Jesus. The love command involves love of God with the whole being and love of neighbour as the self. Sin is rebellion against God, and the failure to love the neighbour. In collective existence this means the opposition of the entire human enterprise to the will of God, and the collective struggles of group with group. This double aspect of sin is expressed in a 1946 article for *Christianity and Crisis*: 'The conflict between nations and nations and between nations and God'. In the Bible the prophets, particularly Amos, declare that God's judgement falls upon all nations for their sins. Israel does not receive any special protection because of election. On the contrary, because of election the judgement will be much more severe.

> Nothing gives Biblical faith a greater consistency than this subordination of the struggle between good and evil men to the more significant struggle between all men and God in 'whose sight no man living is justified'.[13]

This is not an abstract point of theology for Niebuhr. It forms the basis of his political theory regarding the Allies' attitude towards the defeated Germany.

> The war has punished the victors also. But no one would quarrel at the justice of that fact, since they are also guilty of the evils we are seeking to overcome.[14]

God has judged all the nations because all have sinned and unless leniency is shown to Germany the sin will be compounded and the judgement will be even more severe.

In the eschatological section of *Nature and Destiny* Niebuhr wrote:

Modern technical civilization is bringing all civilizations and cultures, all empires and nations into closer juxtaposition to each other. The fact that this greater intimacy and contiguity prompt tragic world wars rather than some simple and easy interpenetration of cultures, must dissuade us from regarding a 'universal culture' or a 'world government' as the natural and inevitable *telos* which will give meaning to the whole historical process. (N&D II, p. 325)

In other words the whole historical process which is creating greater intimacy and contiguity of people has no meaning in itself except that, in terms of Christian eschatology, it is still the expression of the 'struggle between all men and God', and the proof of that, for Niebuhr, is the fact that a breakdown in part of the system, either through natural catastrophe or human agency, possesses a greater effect involving more people than previous breakdowns in simpler systems. Two experiences, for Niebuhr, illustrate that conflict between nations is a symptom of the total process remaining in opposition to God. The atomic experiments on the Bikini atoll 'prove that the Bible is still right and that the contest of greatest significance is not between good and bad nations, but between all nations and God'.[15] The second experience is the conflict between the two types of security, the two types of political and economic systems, sought after the war.

Perhaps the vicious circle of mutual distrust between us will work itself out to the final chapter of another universal conflict. Such a conflict would give a new kind of vivid historical proof of the fact that the conflict between nations and God is more significant than the conflict between good and bad nations.[16]

Given this growth of interdependence, which is still an expression of the human struggle against God:

it is obvious that the technical interdependence of the modern world places us under the obligation of elaborating political instruments which will make such new intimacy and inter-dependence sufferable. (N&D II, p. 325)

If it is possible to fashion political instruments which are capable of anticipating divine judgement then harmony can be increased and conflict avoided

for a very wise statesmanship does manage to insinuate some

vestige of the divine judgment into human judgments. The Christian faith . . . in so far as it can insinuate something of this ultimate perspective into the competing and contradictory judgments of nations . . . introduces some leaven of pity, mercy and forbearance into the conflicts of men and nations.[17]

It is in this context that Niebuhr introduces the symbol of the Antichrist. This symbol expresses the truth that '[t]he most explicit denial of the norm of history must be expected in the most ultimate development of history' (N&D II, p. 327). The Antichrist, which is a symbol that history is a struggle between all nations and God, indicates that the ultimate development of historical interdependence which can be considered 'good' in so far as it is the creation of wider communities, contains 'a new peril of evil on every new level of the good' (N&D II, p. 327). Niebuhr is saying that although historical development through technical achievement leads to greater interdependence, and although, because of the sin of all against God, this greater interdependence will become an ultimate expression of the human sin against God, human activity should not involve contending against interdependence, trying to prevent greater cohesion amongst the peoples of the world. It should be making what is inevitable, tolerable. There is no escape from the responsibility of working towards a more tolerable harmony, but there is always the knowledge, because of the human rebellion against God, that more tolerable harmonies may, in the end, become more explicit forms of that rebellion. But even the explicitness of the evil is not immediately apparent to the world:

> Closely related to this idea of the final evil at the end of history, is the general anticipation of evils in the course of history, which believers will understand but by which the world will be taken unawares. (N&D II, p. 327)

But there is neither moral progress nor moral regression, human beings are neither getting better nor worse.

> The processes of growth in history are so obvious that the modern error of confusing growth with progress [i.e. moral progress] may be regarded as an equally inevitable mistake. . . . It is obvious that history does not solve the basic problems of human existence but reveals them on progressively new levels. The belief that man could solve his problem either by an escape from history or by the historical process itself is a mistake which is partly prompted by the most

141

universal of all 'ideological' taints: the pride, not of particular men and cultures, but of man as man. (N&D II, p. 331)

Faith and History begins where Volume II of *Nature and Destiny* ends. Niebuhr claims that the various explanations for the catastrophic war the world has just experienced are inadequate if they do not take Christian eschatological symbols seriously. In one section he attacks those who want to think of the war as some kind of moral hiccup compared to the vast expanse of human development which lies before the human species. Such an appeal to future millennia is not reassuring for Niebuhr because:

> history contains the development from partial and limited to total wars; and the evolution of means of combat from spears to atomic bombs. To be sure historical development contains creative movements as well as progress in means of destruction. But the fact that history contains such developments as progress in the lethal efficacy of our means of destruction and the increasing consistency of tyrannical governments must prove the vanity of our hope in historical development as such. The prospect of the extension of history into untold millennia must sharpen rather than assuage man's anxiety about himself and his history. (FH, p. 12)[18]

The war, the symbol that the nations rebel against God, is perfectly captured for Niebuhr in Psalm 2:4: 'He that sitteth in the heavens shall laugh: the Lord shall have them in derision'. However, despite the fact that Niebuhr repeats the significance of the symbol of the Antichrist—'ultimately the drama consists of God's contest with all men' (FH, p. 30), and 'ultimately this rebellion of man against God is overcome by divine power' (FH, p. 31), and 'nations are never free of the taint of rebellion against God' (FH, p. 31), and finally 'the New Testament faith anticipates that man's defiance of God will reach the highest proportions at the end of history (FH, p. 31)—he is now concerned to make the point that 'history is a realm of endless possibilities of renewal and rebirth' (FH, p. 31). *Faith and History* is a theological reflection on the post-war experience of the rebuilding and restructuring of the world economy and the containment of Communism.

REVERSAL OF COMTE

In Niebuhr's first book he established the importance of religion to be that of providing an ultra-rational framework for understanding life and experience. In the next twenty years he argued that the primary myths of biblical religion provided an adequate framework, and his major writings are attempts to substantiate this claim. In *Faith and History* he offers further clarification of his method.

Human life is bounded by mystery, argues Niebuhr. But in a secular and scientific age the significance of this realm of mystery has been discredited because of the impressive successes of science. Its ability to chart the observable structures and coherences of nature has led to the assumption that ultimate problems of existence will yield to rational enquiry. Niebuhr accepts that Auguste Comte's description of the progress of culture from theological to philosophical to scientific knowledge is a correct portrayal of the general movement in the history of culture. However, Comte and modern culture have reached the dubious conclusion that the final form of expression is the profoundest expression. The idea that theology is a fumbling for the truth which philosophy clarifies through application of the rational method, and that the ultimate conclusion of this rational technique is the birth of science which traces the world's coherences empirically, is an irrational supposition if it does not acknowledge the possibility that this is a reversible system.

The movement from primitive religion to modern science is an understandable phenomenon. It is obvious that the developing power of human reason should seek to bring the 'little islands of meaning'[19] of primitive religion into some system of coherence and intelligibility. Likewise it is understandable for these rational systems to become subject to empirical verification or falsification. Niebuhr notes that the scientific method performs two tasks. Its usual function is to fill in the details 'in the picture previously outlined'. But 'sometimes the analysis of detailed coherences, empirically observed, changes the picture of the whole'. It is interesting to observe that these two functions of science, the 'filling in' of the previously outlined picture, and the 'changing the picture of the whole' are both developed in Thomas Kuhn's *The Structure of Scientific Revolutions*. Kuhn describes the bulk of scientific work as a 'mopping-up' process with the intention of filling in details within a given paradigm.

Normal scientific research is directed to the articulation of those phenomena and theories that the paradigm already supplies. [20]

When a number of contradictory results appear which cannot be explained by the paradigm a crisis develops which is only resolved through a 'paradigm shift'. The interesting feature of Kuhn's description of the mechanics of a paradigm shift is that during the crisis period recourse must be had to both 'philosophy' and 'faith'.

> Confronted with anomaly or with crisis, scientists take a different attitude towards existing paradigms, and the nature of their research changes accordingly. The proliferation of competing articulations . . . *the recourse to philosophy and to debate over fundamentals*, all these are symptoms of a transition from normal to extraordinary research.

> The man who embraces a new paradigm at an early stage must often do so in defiance of the evidence provided by problem solving. He must, that is, have *faith* that the new paradigm will succeed with the many large problems that confront it, knowing only that the older paradigm has failed with a few. A decision of that kind can only be made on faith. [21] [My emphasis]

The point that Kuhn is making is that scientific progress is not a linear progression following a rational sequence of prescribed rules. At some stage there must be a reaching out into a 'penumbra of mystery'. This observation illustrates the point Niebuhr was trying to make when he argued for a reversal of Comte's characterization of the development of modern culture. For him, modern culture was facing a paradigm crisis. The prevailing philosophical and social scientific paradigms had failed both to predict, and to offer a suitable analysis of, the tremendous dislocations of a world war and the consequent tensions of conflicting ideologies after the war. Only by reaching into the 'penumbra of mystery' could an adequate framework be found to situate modern experience. Niebuhr proposed that the primary myths of biblical religion were capable of situating the height and depth of experience in a framework of meaning. The failure of modern explanations suggests

> that there must be a movement from science to philosophy to counteract the movement from philosophy to science. In the same manner when philosophy approaches the ultimate issues of life and finds itself incapable of overcoming the ultimate

144

ambiguities of human existence, it is forced to recognize the realm of mystery as both the fulfilment and negation of the realm of meaning and to acknowledge the function of faith as both the fulfilment and the negation of reason. (FH, p. 60)

It is important to stress the fact that Niebuhr is not attacking the empirical or the social sciences.[22] He is merely pointing out that they cannot perform the function of religion in social life.

Ideally there should be a constant commerce between the specific truths, revealed by the various historical disciplines, and the final truth about man and history as known from the standpoint of the Christian faith. In such a commerce the Christian truth is enriched by the specific insights which are contributed by every discipline of culture. . . . The social and historical sciences may give constantly more accurate accounts of cause and effect in the wide field of human relations. But without relation to the Christian truth they finally generate structures of meaning which obscure the profounder perplexities of life, offer some plan of social enlightenment as a way of redemption from evil and lose the individual in the integrity of his spirit to the patterns of cause and effect which they are able to trace. (FH, pp. 189–190)

Once Niebuhr has posited the primary biblical mythology as the principle of coherence the paradigm 'may be tested' (FH, p. 196) by carrying out rational analyses and by observing life and knowledge. He sometimes expresses this 'testing' as 'correlation'. For example, the positive apologetic task

consists in correlating the truth, apprehended by faith and repentance, to truths about life and history, gained generally in experience. Such a correlation validates the truth of faith in so far as it proves to be a source and a centre of an interpretation of life, more adequate than alternative interpretations, because it comprehends all of life's antinomies and contradictions into a system of meaning and is conducive to a renewal of life. (FH, p. 187)

Perhaps the passage which best sums up Niebuhr's approach to theology should be presented in full:

[A] limited rational validation of the truth of the Gospel is possible. It consists of a negative and a positive approach to the relation of the truth of the gospel to other forms of truth;

145

and of the goodness of perfect love to historic forms of virtue. Negatively the Gospel must and can be validated by exploring the limits of historic forms of wisdom and virtue. Positively it is validated when the truth of faith is correlated with all truths which may be known by scientific and philosophical disciplines and proves itself a resource for coordinating them into a deeper and wider system of coherence. (FH, p. 172)[23]

TESTING THE PARADIGM

Faith and History is an experiment which tests the relevance of the myths of Creation, Fall, Atonement, and Parousia, as principles of historical interpretation. There are a number of significant differences between this book and *Nature and Destiny*. In *Nature and Destiny* the myths of Creation and Fall were analysed from the point of view of the light they shed on the human being as an isolated individual. In *Faith and History* these two myths are immediately placed in a social context by locating them in relation to the Sinaitic covenant instead of in the personal religious experience as in *Nature and Destiny*. Also there are two significant additions to the exposition of the Atonement. First the details of the Passion narratives in the gospels are analysed from the perspective of an interpretation of the Pauline theory of the Atonement, and second, for the first time in his theology, Niebuhr analyses the resurrection of Jesus.

The book is carefully structured. The first chapter is a prophetic lamentation on the plight of modern civilization, having just emerged from a world war, and now plunged into an international form of the class war—the Cold War. The second chapter introduces the four primary myths, the analysis of which forms the basis of the work. The myth of Creation is then studied for its insight into the problem of time and history, and this is followed by an analysis of the mystery at the end of existence (Parousia). The Fall is examined as an overestimation of power, wisdom and virtue. The myth of the Atonement is discussed following two chapters which explicate the 'mythical method' of analysis. The theology is then brought to bear on the political situation, and the book concludes with a section on the significance of the Christian Church.

The problem of time and eternity had been dealt with in *Nature and Destiny* in relation to the myth of the Parousia. This symbol, and the subordinate symbols of the Last Judgement and the General Resurrection, are attempts to relate the eternal to the historical. There is a tendency in Christianity, observes Niebuhr, to reduce the ultimate vindication of God to a point in history. Such a tendency has resulted in the concept of the millennial age. Niebuhr is referring here to an idea which is found in some apocalyptic writings, and particularly in the book of Revelation, that there will be some sort of transitional period where God reigns on earth but the final consummation has not occurred. In Niebuhr's words it is an age where 'history is supposedly fulfilled despite the persisting conditions of finiteness' (N&D II, p. 299). The symbols should be taken seriously but not literally. Even the wisest tadpole could not explain literally the experience of a future existence hopping through the air.

He concludes that there are two dimensions of the eternity/time relationship. Eternity stands both over time and at the end of time. To say it stands over time is to say that the eternal is the ground and source of the temporal. To clarify what he means by this Niebuhr compares human memory and foresight with God's consciousness. Just as the human mind can comprehend simultaneously a number of moments of history, so the whole of time is present to God in his memory and foresight.

To say that eternity stands at the end of time is to say that the temporal process cannot be conceived without a *finis*, without an end to the existence of matter. However, what is eternal cannot have a *finis*.[24]

Niebuhr's purpose in discussing the relationship between eternity and time is to show that these two perspectives result in two perspectives on the meaning of history. He argues that some historical events gain their significance without a necessary relation to the sequence of historical events. He gives the example of martyrdom to indicate that events can have eternal value without relation to the historical context. Niebuhr calls such events 'tangents of the eternal' revealed in time. From another perspective, however, it is impossible to make a 'final' judgement on a historical event because all the causes and all the consequences of an event cannot be known. The effort to reach such a vantage point to form a judgement of history illustrates the second dimension of the relationship between eternity and time. Besides possessing tangents of the eternal history is also a total process which can only be understood from the vantage point of a 'final judgement'. The fact that the total process results in a final judgement is an indication that the total process of history, despite the redemption, is opposed to God.

In *Faith and History* the eternity/time/history problem is analysed in relation to the myth of Creation, and he compares the biblical view of the problem with the dominant trends in both the classical world and the modern world. The classical view of the relationship between eternity and time is that time is a corruption of the eternal changeless form. Nevertheless, it is related to the eternal, although it is a corrupt image. The modern view dispenses with the concept of an eternal changeless realm and finds time self-explanatory. The myth of Creation indicates that time is neither a corruption of the changeless form, nor is it self-explanatory. It is related to the changeless in that the changeless is revealed in time. It is related to the modern view in the sense that time does have meaning and forward momentum. But the idea of creation *ex nihilo*[25] prevents the concept of time from being thought of as self-explanatory. Niebuhr admits that this concept does not form part of all the creation narratives and ideas found in the Bible, but in mature prophetic religion (Deutero-Isaiah) the concept is implied.

Niebuhr also allows for the fact that the myth of Creation did not anticipate the emergence of the 'novel' in time. It is modern culture which has achieved this insight. Unfortunately he does not explain what he means by 'novel' and therefore the whole discussion is unsatisfactory. He attempts to show that the myth of Creation *ex nihilo* compensates for its failure to anticipate the 'novel' by now safeguarding the discovery of modern culture from its own logic:

> Though the idea of creation is not in conflict with any scientific account of natural causation, which accurately describes the relation of an antecedent cause to a subsequent event, yet without the idea the antecedent cause tends falsely to become the sufficient cause of the subsequent event. This logic, when consistent, would exclude precisely the emergence of the novel in time, which it has been the achievement of modern culture to discern. (FH, p. 54)

Without a definition of 'novel' the argument becomes meaningless.

The relationship between the eternal realm and time illustrates the relationship between time and history, and consequently the meaning of history. In the classical world, argues Niebuhr, there is an unqualified identification of history with time. There is no concept of history pointing towards fulfilment. Fulfilment is only possible through emancipation from the cycle of natural-historical recurrences, and results in a negative attitude towards the realm of history. By contrast the modern view finds meaning in history, but it equates historical growth with redemption from evil, and the problem of meaning is solved too simply. As in *Nature and Destiny* the Christian conception of history is expressed in eschatological mythology. Only in these myths is it possible to find a principle of interpretation which does justice to the fact that the human being possesses transcendent freedom over the structures of history but is also involved in the flux of history and time.

Niebuhr does go some way towards defining what he means by 'transcendent freedom'. Human memory of the past, and desire and ambition for the future, give rise to structures which have a much longer lifespan than anything found in the natural world. This is an example of human freedom over time. In addition, human freedom is displayed in the fact that historical changes occur much more rapidly than change through the natural mutations of nature.

In short, the myth of Creation serves to prevent a false view of history, which in turn prevents a false view of historical evil. The myth of the Parousia is capable of providing for a meaningful history while at the same time incorporating the threat to patterns of meaning occasioned by the human rebellion against God.

Niebuhr's discussion of the Fall in relation to history is mainly confined to the sin of pride. It will be remembered from the discussion of sin in *Nature and Destiny* that he divided sin into the sin of pride and the sin of sensuality, one form overestimating human self-transcendence, the other overestimating involvement in the flux of nature. Again in the collective dimension the predominant sin appears to be pride. He does not consider the collective dimension of sensuality, although he does identify a form of thought which underestimates human transcendent freedom. The example he gives of this is social Darwinism.

It is on the basis of sin as overestimation of freedom that Niebuhr characterizes the world situation. It is not so much a conflict of two concepts of security as a conflict between two 'creeds', each one imagining that it can become the master of historical destiny. The conflict

> has already produced an historical situation which cannot be encompassed in the philosophy of history of either creed . . . [E]ach is armed with a social philosophy which obscures the partial and particular character of its objective. (FH, p. 95)

Sin is not only an overestimation of the power of human freedom, it is also an overestimation of the virtue of human freedom. This temptation results in a culture identifying its own scheme of redemption as the centre of the total human destiny. The Cold War is also a conflict between two national messianisms:

> The virulence and truculence which flow from the Russian illusions are important reminders of the fact that secular civilizations do not escape religious idolatries by a formal disavowal of religion. . . .
>
> The concept of the 'American Dream' according to which America is a kind of second chosen nation, ordained to save democracy after the effete nations of Europe proved themselves incapable of the task, is a milder form of such nationalistic messianism. (FH, p. 131)

The myth of the Atonement is analysed as wisdom, power, and virtue, covering much the same ground as in *Nature and Destiny*, but, as mentioned earlier, there are two significant additions. Niebuhr refers to some of the details in the synoptic Passion narratives to illustrate their revelatory character. Also, for the first time in his theology, he deals with the resurrection of Jesus.

The features of the Passion narratives which he singles out for discussion are the deaths of the two criminals, and the nature of the two 'oligarchies', the Roman and the Jewish. The significance of the disciples, the women, the betrayal, the denial, the dereliction of Jesus, the centurion's faith, the rending of the temple veil, etc., are not considered in this context. The Roman system of jurisprudence and the Jewish religious legalism are illustrations that principles of values are often imposing façades covering anxious selves, anxious for prestige and security. Worldly power, expressed in the historical majesty of Roman dominance, is revealed to be more anxious and insecure than it pretends, and likewise the 'eternal verities' of the Jewish religion are equally exposed as a façade of prestige and security. The wisdom of the Jews, the power of the Romans, and the virtue of both, are exposed in their relativity and partiality in the details of the story.

Niebuhr's treatment of the resurrection is slightly ambiguous. It has been noted that the resurrection of Jesus has not featured as a theme in his theology, not even in *Nature and Destiny*. In that book, the only discussion of resurrection was the General Resurrection in the eschatological section. The reason for this omission is quite simple, he explained to Norman Kemp-Smith, a Scot who had heard the Giffords. 'I have not the slightest interest in the empty tomb or physical resurrection', he said.[26] But a major theologian could hardly be expected to avoid the topic, and Niebuhr is finally forced to deal with it in *Faith and History*.

Initially Niebuhr links the resurrection to his concept of the Atonement as the revelation of God's mercy over his justice, the centre of which is the cross.

> [T]o see the whole mystery of God's mercy disclosed is to know that the crucified Lord had triumphed over death. . . . It is the revelatory depth of the fact which is the primary concern of faith. (FH, pp. 166, 167)

The problem with this interpretation, especially in the context of the Passion narratives, is that the cross itself was not a revelation of triumph for the disciples. They either betrayed Jesus, or denied him, or fled in fear from the scene. The only recognition of the cross as revelatory is the centurion's confession of faith. If the cross was not a revelation of triumph for the disciples in the story, then how did it come to be regarded as a triumph? There is no indication in the narratives that the centurion's confession marks the beginning of the Christian Church. Obviously, for the disciples who ran away, to believe in the revelatory significance of the cross requires a miracle. But the miracle is not the resurrection of Jesus, the miracle is the fact that the disciples believed in the resurrection:

> Belief in the resurrection is itself a miracle of a different order, and a miracle without which the church could not have come into existence or could not continue to exist. It is the miracle of recognizing the triumph of God's sovereignty in what seemed to be very ambiguous facts of history. (FH, p. 167)

Therefore the resurrection of Jesus can be said to be the miracle that a group of people who ran away from the cross because they failed to understand its significance actually came to believe that what they were running away from was of revelatory significance. The Church

> is thus not grounded upon a slowly dawning consciousness of the true significance of Christ. It is founded in the miracle of the recognition of the true Christ in the resurrection. (FH, p. 167)

Now if the resurrection of Jesus cannot be separated from the faith of believers because it is *literally* the faith of believers, then what Niebuhr is saying is that the miracle on which the Church was founded was the miracle that some people who ran away from an event later found that what they ran away from possessed revelatory significance. The resurrection narratives which specifically refer to the resurrection of Jesus from the dead and which picture the disciples as still slow to believe, fearful, or even doubting are dismissed by Niebuhr:

> The effort to certify this triumph through specific historical details may well be regarded as an expression of a scepticism which runs through the whole history of Christianity. (FH, p. 167)

This means that the disciples, having experienced a miracle of coming to believe in the revelatory significance of the cross, composed stories about the resurrection of Jesus because they were sceptical of the miracle of coming to believe in the resurrection of Jesus. When the logical implications of Niebuhr's theology of the resurrection are investigated, it is not difficult to understand why Niebuhr's theology has previously disregarded this theme.

But whatever the difficulties Niebuhr encountered in drawing the resurrection of Jesus into his theology, the real significance of the Christ event is in the pattern it establishes to assist with the interrelation of reality:

> The climax of the crucifixion and resurrection thus becomes not merely the culmination of the whole series of revelations but the pattern of all subsequent confrontations between God and man. They must contain the crucifixion of self-abandonment and the resurrection of self-recovery. (FH, p. 168)

Another way of saying the same thing is to promise a new beginning 'in the life of any man, nation, or culture which recognizes the depth and persistence of man's defiance of God. Where such self knowledge is achieved . . . the hope of new life is possible' (FH, p. 158).

This brings Niebuhr to a third form of characterizing the contemporary situation. He has considered the overestimation of both power and virtue. Now he considers the type of political knowledge which informs modern culture. He classifies secular paradigms as either idolatrous or atheistic, and their ultimate consequences are either complacency or despair in their approach to political problems. An idolatrous paradigm is one which exalts a relative or partial achievement related to a particular tribe, nation, or culture, into the place of God, by making it the source, centre and end of the meaning of life. Complacency is the result of believing that the historical process is itself capable of solving all the problems of existence, and despair is what accompanies the realization that the historical process does not lead to ethical improvement. The contemporary situation is a conflict between two forms of complacency, the 'new and more fanatic' complacency of Marxism, and the complacency of liberal culture in America

> which still bears some semblance to the stability of previous centuries. The opulence of American life and the dominant position of American power in the world, create the illusion of a social stability which the total world situation belies . . . [T]he abyss of meaninglessness is avoided by the confidence that a critical analysis of all historic political and moral positions will gradually establish the universal truth. (FH, p. 183)

THEOLOGY FOR THE COLD WAR

The anarchy of international relations which culminated in the world war is a clear indication that if future conflicts of this magnitude are to be avoided some form of global community must be established. The problem is that any centre of power which seeks to order this community will inevitably regard itself as an absolute power. Nevertheless, the attempt must be made to establish community on a global scale. Faced with this paradoxical situation Niebuhr considers what resources are available in historic forms of Christianity for the building of wider communities. As in *Nature and Destiny* Niebuhr considers the record of Lutherism, Calvinism, and Catholicism. From these three examples he draws the conclusion:

> They prove that just as sin is the corruption of man's creative freedom so also the ultimate form of sin is a corruption of man's quest for redemption. (FH, p. 233)

Thus the attempt to order the world from a particular organizing centre will express itself as a power of world redemption.

Niebuhr then studies the methods of sectarian Christianity for enlarging the community. These sects are divided into 'soft' utopians and 'hard' utopians. The former try to convert tyrants by not resisting them, and the latter usually create a fighting group which believes itself to be the perfect embodiment of perfect justice and/or perfect love. Within the confines of the Christian faith the perils of these fighting sects are limited. However, with the advent of Marxism, argues Niebuhr, all the errors of Calvinism, Catholicism, and the 'hard' utopians are amalgamated into a force which claimed to be 'the final triumph over evil in history' (FH, p. 239). Marxism is therefore depicted as a type of Antichrist. It is even possible to conclude, in view of the hysterical tone of Niebuhr's anti-Communism, that he regarded it as *the* Antichrist. It is also important to note that he does not distinguish between Marxism, Marxist-Leninism, Stalinism, and Russian Communism. Marxism and Communism are interchangeable terms. The hysterical tone can be illustrated by selecting examples from three paragraphs from *Faith and History* (pp. 240–1). 'Orthodox Marxism' is a 'fanatic fury'; 'orthodox Communism' is a 'self-righteous fury' and a 'real peril'. The 'fanaticism of this new religion' has 'rent' Western society, and created a 'fantastic religious situation'. It has 'messianic pretensions'; it is a 'desperate hope' and 'faith'; it introduces 'new evils'. It is a 'new fanaticism', and the 'perversion of a profound truth'.

It is an understanding of the biblical eschatological symbols which prevents acceptance of false centres of meaning because in these symbols there is a sense of the divine fulfilment beyond provisional meanings. But if biblical faith is to be worth anything it 'must be fruitful of genuine renewals of life and history in both the individual and collective existence of man' (FH, p. 244). The question to be answered is: What light does the myth of the Atonement shed on the fate of civilizations and cultures? In Niebuhr's first book Spengler's descriptions of the rise and fall of civilizations had been a source of fascination. In *Faith and History* (and *Nature and Destiny*) he finds Arnold Toynbee's view more perceptive because it combined Christian elements with Spengler's classicism. Toynbee refers to 'creative' and 'oppressive' periods in the life of a ruling oligarchy. Niebuhr transposes Toynbee's moralistic interpretation of this phenomenon by suggesting that these two periods are reflections of 'grace' and 'judgement'. The myth of the Atonement illustrates truths about collective life by indicating how the creative elements can be harnessed.

When a civilization or culture, nation or empire, harnesses its creative elements, it is an example of grace. When destructive elements overcome creative elements it is an example of judgement. A period of creativity in the life of a culture or a civilization occurs when the ruling oligarchy 'exhibits . . . [a] genuine concern for life beyond its borders', and possesses 'a creative interest in the welfare of the community' (FH, pp. 251–2), and also when its own interests coincide with the total interests of the community. When this occurs there is a visible expression of 'grace'. Creative grace is the historic coincidence between the will-to-power and the requirement for a wider community which that will-to-power serves. Niebuhr then gives an example of this collective concept of grace. The rise of the bourgeois class is an example of the 'grace' of God because 'the profits it claimed for its services did not completely annul the benefits it bestowed upon the modern community by the extension of the community's technical power' (FH, p. 253). The oppressive period of judgement is a period of 'decay'.

> An analysis of the historic process of this decay will bring us closer to the secret of the possibilities of both 'death through life' and of 'new life through death' in the destiny of civilization. It is this alternative which constitutes the relevance of the biblical concept of the renewal of life through the death of the old self, for the collective experience of mankind. (FH, p. 253)

The ruling classes of nations face the alternative of 'dying because they try too desperately to live, or of achieving a new life by dying to the self' (FH, p. 254). This alternative is offered when new forces of history challenge their power and prestige. They are forced into conflict, into a life or death struggle, into mortal combat. The emergence of these new forces is an inevitable execution of divine judgement because of their sin.

The difference between the conflict here and the conflict in *Reflections* is that now Niebuhr is talking about renewal and rebirth, whereas before he was talking about salvaging what was of value from a dying social order. The stress on renewal and rebirth coincides with an attempt to be more specific about the resurrection of Jesus, and to see renewal and rebirth as a reflection of the 'general resurrection' at the end of history. Furthermore the concept of creativity coinciding with will-to-power and the needs of the wider community suggests that what is involved here is a theology not only of the Cold War, but also a theology which will form the basis for American political activity in the global arena. It is no coincidence that Niebuhr's theology of resurrection, rebirth and renewal coincides with the Marshall Plan and the establishing of the American hegemony in the political, economic, and military spheres.

NOTES

1 Walter LaFeber, *America, Russia, and the Cold War 1945–1975* (New York, 1976), p. 48.
2 *Love and Justice*, p. 163.
3 Richard Rovere, *The American Establishment* (New York, 1962), p. 13.
4 *Reflections*, p. 11.
5 LaFeber, *op. cit.*, p. 6.
6 Figures quoted from: Peter King, *Modern World Affairs* (London, 1984), p. 23. A slightly different set of figures in Daniel Chirot, *Social Change in the Twentieth Century* (New York, 1977), p. 116, lists 460,000 US military deaths.
7 LaFeber, *op. cit.*, p. 27.
8 Henry A. Wallace, former Vice-President, broke with the Truman administration and ran as presidential candidate of the Progressive Party in 1948.
9 LaFeber, *op. cit.*, p. 79.
10 Niebuhr's contacts with Bonhoeffer are well documented in Eberhard Bethge, *Dietrich Bonhoeffer: A Biography* (London, 1970); his part in bringing Tillich from Germany is recorded in Richard Fox, *Reinhold Niebuhr: A Biography* (New York, 1985).
11 Fox, *op. cit.*, p. 229.
12 Ibid.
13 *Love and Justice*, p. 162.
14 Ibid., p. 228.
15 Ibid., p. 165.
16 Ibid.
17 Ibid.
18 A good example of the type of thinking Niebuhr is attacking here is to be found in the writings of the French Jesuit Pierre Teilhard de Chardin. In a curious amalgam of biology, palaeontology, geology, physics, chemistry, astronomy, and Christianity, Teilhard was drawn into a number of absurdities. He became ecstatic at the thought of war, totalitarian regimes, and the atom bomb. The historical process which Niebuhr is referring to is termed 'totalization' by Teilhard, and the force of totalization is termed 'amorization'. The greater complexity and interconnectedness of life, which Niebuhr sees as ultimately a rebellion against God, in Teilhard is a mirror of the evolutionary process from simple atoms to complex, from simple molecules to complex, from simple life forms to complex, from simple social structures to complex, and so on. Placed in this vast context of totalization, wars and totalitarian regimes are steps on the evolutionary way of progress:

We need only recall those moments in time of war when, wrested out of ourselves by the force of a collective passion, we have a sense of rising to a higher level of existence. (*Future of Man*, Collins/Fontana, 1973, p. 22)

Seen in this light [i.e. totalization] the modern totalitarian regimes are neither heresies nor biological regressions: they are in line with the essential trend of cosmic movement. (*Future of Man*, p. 48)

This meant that for Teilhard 'the present war' (i.e. 1939—45) was 'a crisis of birth almost disproportionately small in relation to the vastness of what it is destined to bring forth' (*Future of Man*, p. 121). Although in the 1930s Teilhard could look forward to more wars as signs of evolutionary progress of the human race by the time the atom bomb exploded he thought it signalled the end of war. Teilhard was in ecstasy:

For the first time in history, through the non-fortuitous conjunction of a world crisis and an unprecedented advance in means of communication, a planned scientific experiment employing units of a hundred or a thousand men had been successfully completed. In three years a technical achievement had been realized which might not have been accomplished in a century of isolated efforts. Thus the greatest of man's scientific triumphs happens also to be the one in which the largest number of brains were enabled to join together in a single organism . . . for the purpose of research. (*Future of Man*, p. 149)

Atomic bombs 'herald the birth into the world of a Mankind both inwardly and outwardly pacified. They proclaim the coming of the *Spirit of the Earth*' (*Future of Man*, p. 152).

These comments written in 1946 at the start of the Cold War could have remained a historical curiosity were it not for the fact that Teilhard's evolutionary Christianity is still influential. A leading exponent of South American liberation theology, Juan Luis Segundo, acknowledges the inspiration of Teilhard.

The evolutionary outlook is *the key* [my emphasis] to Christianity. In other words the whole Christian message—and particularly the relationship between sin and redemption—should be viewed from that angle of vision. (*Evolution and Guilt*, p. 59)

Karl Rahner, a theologian whose works influenced the Second Vatican Council, has also developed an evolutionary Christology. Rahner dissociates his work in this area from Teilhard's but it still implies that the increasing complexity and interdependence of social relationships is an essential feature of the evolutionary thrust of life, and that as social relations increase in complexity the cosmos is able to increase in self-consciousness. The end result of this Christology is a hymn to the core countries of the capitalist world-system.

The history of the West can be regarded (without falling into

Communist utopianism) . . . [as] that epoch towards which the past life of humanity has been striving.

The development of Western civilization is all part of the process of God's self-communication 'thereby permitting the world to discover itself. This new period is one whose ultimate reason is to be found in the faith of Christianity.' It is 'the first really all-human period'. This means that 'man does not need to let everyone be submerged in a sterile equality when he does not wish anyone to feel worse off than anyone else' (*Theological Investigations* 5, pp. 190–1).

19 All quotes from *Faith and History*, pp. 57–61.
20 Thomas S. Kuhn, *The Structure of Scientific Revolutions* (Chicago, 1970), p. 24.
21 Ibid., pp. 91 and 158.
22 Richard Fox is under the impression that *Faith and History* is a 'superficial put-down of the social sciences' (*op. cit.*, p. 237), but that is because he has not analysed the book himself, he has merely listened to the original critics who failed to understand the main argument and the importance of the book in Niebuhr's corpus.
23 In my copy of *Faith and History* the first sentence of the quote reads: 'A limited rational validation of the truth is *im*possible'. However, it is clear from the context that this is a misprint.
24 In *Nature and Destiny* Niebuhr interprets the *end* as *finis* and *telos* in relation to the eschatological myths of the Last Judgement and the General Resurrection. These two myths form 'a part of the vindication of God in the return of Christ' (N&D II, p. 300). The significance of the judgement is that it is Christ who is the judge of history, that historical distinction between good and evil in history forms the basis of the judgement, and that the judgement is the 'end' of history. This idea, the Final Judgement, is an indication that history does not provide its own redeemer. It is this latter shade of meaning which illustrates the distinction between *finis* and *telos*. The psychological fear of death, Niebuhr argues, is a compound of both the fear of judgement and the fear of extinction. Death as extinction can be conceived only by the human species which has freedom over nature, and death as judgement is a threat to those who falsely make themselves the centre of life's meaning. It is prompted by the awareness of both human sin and human creativity. Thus judgement is the religious dimension of the 'end' as *finis*. The 'end' as *telos* is expressed in the biblical myth of the resurrection of the dead, implying that eternity fulfils, rather than annuls, the rich varieties of the temporal process. It is a mythical affirmation of what is rationally inconceivable—that eternity will embody the finite.
25 Creation *ex nihilo*, i.e. 'out of nothing', originally became part of Christian doctrine to refute Gnostic tendencies where God was seen as struggling against intractable evil material.
26 Fox, *op. cit.*, p. 215.

9

Theology for America

Niebuhr's experiences in the State Department, his lifelong interest in American foreign policy, and his theology of history, were combined to produce *The Irony of American History* (1952). It stands in the same relation to *Faith and History* as *Children of Light* to *Nature and Destiny*. It is a secular application of the more abstract theological principles developed in the earlier work. It is a book about the American role in the renewal of civilization after the catastrophic judgement of war. There are two threats to this renewal which must be countered. The first threat is the spread of Communism, and the second threat is the attitude of America. It must avoid the twin perils of isolationism or imperialism. The rise of America to hegemonic status is by virtue of 'grace', and it should accept this responsibility with contrition and humility. *Irony* is a prophetic oracle against the nation to ensure that America's interests are coincidental with global interests so that America will remain under grace rather than face judgement. It is an exercise in the combination of dollars and grace.

SUPER-POWER THEOLOGY

The issue is simple:

Everybody understands the obvious meaning of the world struggle in which we are engaged. We are defending freedom against tyranny and are trying to preserve justice against a

159

system which has, demonically, distilled injustice and cruelty out of its original promise of a higher justice. (IAH, p. 1)

The 'original promise of higher justice' constituted the judgement of the bourgeois world, but since it has overstepped its limits, Communism itself is to be judged, and the careful execution of American power and responsibility in the community of nations is to be the method of its judgement. The hysterical anti-Communism which marred *Faith and History* is carried over into this book. Communism is a religion of 'satanic dimension', a 'noxious creed', a 'monstrous evil', a 'mania', and a 'noxious virulence of unparalleled proportions'.

By portraying a political movement which seeks to gain State control of the national economies in such vivid religious imagery, Niebuhr clearly sees American foreign policy as a global redemptive mission. This fact leads to a discussion of national messianism. After covering the formative messianic ideas about the purpose of 'God's New Israel' he concludes that it has resulted in a type of messianism which does not seek mastery of the human race. Instead America believes itself to be cast in the role of tutor to the nations in its pilgrimage to perfection. Therefore American national messianic dreams are not usually corrupted by a lust for power although they are certainly corrupted by moral pride. Niebuhr points out that Russia, Britain, Germany, and Italy have all expressed forms of national messianism. America, Niebuhr argues, has had a redemptive role thrust upon it without particularly seeking it. Accidents of history have combined to create a nation which wields more power than any previous historical power. The world is now faced with a situation in which the responsible use of this power has become a condition of survival of 'the free world'.

It is not surprising that the communist elite should be filled with fury when they behold the unfolding of this power, marked by their 'logic' for self destruction through its 'inner contradictions'. (IAH, p. 64)

Since the purpose of the redemptive mission is the containment of Communism, and eventually the defeat of Communism, the internal struggle between bourgeois ideology and Marxism and the consequent removal of Marxism as a political threat will be relevant to the future patterns of world development. Niebuhr characterizes the approach to political and economic questions in domestic life as pragmatic. The American pragmatic approach is an ironic success because its policies contradict the social creed of a commercial civilization. American society has managed to establish a degree of justice which has prevented the Marxist threat in both its 'mild' and 'virulent' forms. Niebuhr gives three reasons for this defeat of Marxism. First, the wealth of natural resources, and second, the development of technical efficiency both contributed to mitigate the severity of the social struggle. Third, America managed to achieve a balance of power in its organization of social forces. This success led Niebuhr to reappraise elements of truth in classical economics. It is obvious, he argues, that some form of free market is essential for the survival of democracy. On the other hand the tendency to over-estimate the self-regulating forces of the free market should be avoided.

The balance of power was achieved in American politics because the labour movement was governed by pragmatism rather than political ambition. Niebuhr sees the American experience as proving that the State is not merely the instrument of the privileged classes. Despite the fact that the business community ideologically attacked (Niebuhr does not mention private armies) the labour movement it nevertheless accepted organized labour. The balance of power was also achieved through the fluidity of the class structure ('a gift of providence', p. 89) which is in turn the consequence of an expanding economy.

By these means America has developed social policies which are wiser than its social creed, and it has discovered a middle way between those who want to plan and those who want to remove all restraints. It is the wisdom of democracy itself and the triumph of common sense. Essentially the whole section is a belated appraisal of the New Deal.

The task of repeating this success on a global scale is much more difficult according to Niebuhr because 'the class war, which was orginally designed for industrial society and aborted there, has become the dominant pattern of international relations' (IAH, p. 95). The problem is compounded because the poor of the non-industrial nations have embraced the revolutionary religion of Communism. He selects four reasons to account for Communist influence in Asia. The primary cause is that the first encounter of the agrarian nations with Western technical society was exploitative. The second cause is the inherent poverty of these nations and the Communist propaganda blaming Western society for this poverty. Another reason for the appeal of Communism is its unified culture. Its worldview combines science, religion, and politics in one package. Western cultural imports are, by contrast, contradictory. For example, there is the contradiction between the Christian faith and scientific knowledge, and there is the reluctance of the Christian religion to identify with any political force.

In addition to the problem of poverty in these areas, there is also the problem of illiteracy. Democracy requires intelligent participation, and a spiritual heritage. These nations find it far easier to move from feudal collectivism to the collective Communist structure. Furthermore the indigenous religions offer no 'spiritual resistance to the demonic dynamism of the Communist movement' (IAH, p. 109).

All these facts lead Niebuhr to the conclusion that the Communist 'tyranny' will spread throughout the world for many decades to come. It will grow despite American military power to prevent its growth. But Niebuhr is quick to add: 'We will not, of course, fail to take the strategic military measures which are possible and necessary to arrest its growth' (IAH, p. 110).

Given the reality of the world situation, how should America exercise its hegemonic power? How can it eliminate Communism without destroying civilization in the process? To provide the basis of a political strategy Niebuhr draws on his analysis of sin in *Nature and Destiny* and applies it to the collective dimension:

> There is no nice line to be drawn between a normal expression of human creativity and the sloth which refuses to assume the responsibilities of human freedom or the pride which overestimates man's individual or collective power. (IAH, p. 112)

These categories correspond to Niebuhr's analysis of sin as pride and sensuality applied to the collective dimension of the American nation. Collective pride and sensuality is imperialism and isolationism. America needs to reorientate the whole structure of its idealism if it is to inform its political strategy in the community of nations. It must understand the three aspects of the Atonement Niebuhr analysed in *Nature and Destiny* and *Faith and History*: virtue, wisdom, and power, and the dangers arising from their corruption.

'American idealism' must learn to accept the limits of virtue and human strivings, the fragmentariness of wisdom, and the precariousness of power. The two problems faced by American idealism are the nation's inordinate power, and the complexity of the international situation. The first aspect embodies perils to genuine community because power generates fears and resentments, and the second aspect tempts the nation into impatient solutions in the slow and contradictory processes of history. Unless the philosophical support for this new role of America in world politics is adequate, it 'could bring calamity upon ourselves and the world' (IAH, p. 115). The threat of judgement is never far from the scene in Niebuhr.

> A nation with an inordinate degree of political power is doubly tempted to exceed the bounds of historical possibilities if it is informed by an idealism which does not understand the limits of man's wisdom and volition in history. (IAH, p. 123)

This is precisely what Niebuhr's theology of the Atonement does understand.

He attempts to provide a framework for foreign policy which is deeper and higher than the nation's ideals, and one that will provide a dimension from the standpoint of which the vanity of human ambition and achievement is discernible. This can only be grasped by faith because

> everything that is related in terms of simple rational coherence with the ideals of a culture or a nation will prove in the end to be a simple justification of its most cherished values. (IAH, p. 129)

But is the detection of irony a true reflection of the situation or has it emerged as such because it lies at the basis of the interpretation of the Atonement? The ironic element which lies at the heart of the Christian interpretation of history is derived primarily from the knowledge that the total human enterprise is under the judgement of God, a God who laughs derisively at human pretensions but who shows mercy when pride is transformed into contrition. There is both ironic failure and ironic success. Niebuhr finds examples of both in the contemporary American experience. The ironic success is that America has achieved hegemonic status without seeking it, and the ironic failure is the fact that although America is the most powerful historical force its wider ambitions are continually thwarted.

The final problem Niebuhr addresses is: How far is it possible for human collectives, since they cannot collectively repent, to reflect the pattern of the Atonement in their collective history? The question facing America is to determine

> whether the necessary exercise of its virtue in meeting

ruthlessness and the impressive nature of its power will blind it
to the ambiguity of all human virtues and competencies; or
whether even the nation might have some residual awareness
of the larger meanings of the drama of human existence
beyond and above the immediate urgencies. (IAH, pp. 145–6)

That is, has America a greater role in history than simply combating
the 'monstrous evil' of Communism, or will it expend all its energies
in this direction and then fail like other nations which have been
historical executors of God's judgement?

Niebuhr's concern in *Irony* is that the world should enter a
creative period, a period under grace rather than under judgement.
Since the reality of the situation is a world in which the US is the
dominant power the world must be organized in such a way that the
interests of the American nation coincide with global interests. Such
a world would be under grace rather than judgement. The US must
work towards destabilizing isolationist elements wherever they
occur in the world. That is, economic nationalism must be
countered wherever possible. However, the US must avoid the
collective sins of pride and sensuality. It must not overstep its power
and become imperialistic; it must not absolve itself of its responsibilities to the world community and return to a pre-war type of
isolationism.

This preoccupation with the hegemonic role of the US was also
the subject of three more books published in the 1950s and the
1960s, but before one of these is considered, his next book, *The Self
and the Dramas of History*, must receive some attention.

THEOLOGICAL 'SYSTEM'

On 15 February 1952 Niebuhr suffered a stroke which left him
partially paralysed down his left side. This severely curtailed his
heavy schedule and brought on a depression. But in 1953 he began
work on what he called his *magnum opus*, his 'system'. His doctor
gave him permission to tap on his typewriter for two hours a day.[1]

The Self and the Dramas of History (1954) is a comprehensive
statement of Niebuhr's theological method and purpose. It is an
attempt to systematize his approach to theology. It could be recommended as the best introduction to his thought except for the fact
that its unity tends to be marred by his persistent fanatical anti-
Communism. There is also a eulogy on Winston Churchill which,

regardless of the opinion one might have of this man, is oddly out of place in what proved to be Niebuhr's final theological book. It might have been expected that detachment from immediate affairs would have prevented digressions of this nature so often found in previous works.

The basic theme of the book is the fundamental theme that meaning and experience in life require an 'ultra-rational' framework of coherence. Only the framework provided by the primary biblical myths is sufficient to incorporate the full height of human self-transcendence and the full depth of guilt, evil and sin, and broad enough to impart meaning to the full sweep of historical destiny, the total human enterprise. The primary myths function as a kind of database into which Niebuhr's latest reading is fed in and categorized.

In this book Niebuhr does offer further clarification of some terms and themes which have featured in his work. For example, he identifies five elements of self-transcendence. In addition to memory and foresight and imagination he includes will and conscience and he defines what he means by these terms. The will is the result of the self's transcendence of the complex of impulses and desires. The organization of the will requires a rational analysis of the ends in view, but consistency of will is not an intellectual achievement, it is an achievement of the self because there is no power to compel consistency. The conscience is defined as the self's capacity to judge short- and long-range purposes. It is the self judging its actions and attitudes in which a sense of obligation in contrast to inclination is expressed. It possesses both an individual and a social dimension.

Another term which Niebuhr referred to quite frequently in his works is 'community'. It is defined as

> that association of individuals which has coalesced through forces of history, operating upon the cohesive forces given in nature such as geographic contiguity and racial kinship. . . . They are historical entities who have reacted to unique historical events. Their memory of these events is one of the basic forces of community. They express their consciousness of their uniqueness by their devotion to heroes. (SDH, p. 51)

The national community has become the community of the most inclusive loyalty because of its control of the State's coercive power. In some cases it is necessary to enlarge community beyond national boundaries in the interests of security:

The supra-national integrations have the best chance of success in Western Europe where unity above the level of the national community has become the necessity of survival for those nations which bear the treasures of civilization against the perils of totalitarianism. (SDH, p. 51)

Every community is composed of both organism and artefact. Organism refers to the community which has grown unconsciously, without coercion. Artefact by contrast is the community where integration has been consciously contrived.

In *Self and Dramas* there is the same insistence on the Atonement as *the* principle of coherence. In a comparison with modern existentialism and modern mysticisms Niebuhr strongly asserts the rational, almost empirical validity, of the Christian paradigm:

If we *test* these three alternative solutions for the self's search for the ultimate by the two tests of consistency of coherence with other truth, and by conformity with established facts subject to empirical tests it will soon become apparent that religions which tend to the exaltation of finite values and centres are most easily ruled out. (SDH, p. 79)

Niebuhr uses this observation as a point of departure for the rationale of the mythical method.

During the course of this discussion Niebuhr is more specific about the role of the Church and the function of dogma in guarding the truths of revelation expressed in myth. In order to prevent this mythical heritage from degenerating into private caprice it was necessary to establish the firm authority of the covenant community, the Christian Church, which would attempt to reach a consensus on the interpretation of the revelation. It expressed its authority by promulgating dogmas which were intended to safeguard the revelation from private interpretation. 'Dogma represents the consensus of the covenant community' (SDH, p. 106). Dogmatic formulations mark the contours of interpretation.

It will be remembered that in *Faith and History* Niebuhr's theology of the resurrection of Jesus bore strong resemblance to Bultmann's, the idea that Jesus was risen in the faith of believers. In *Self and Dramas* he distances himself from Bultmann's attitudes towards biblical myths. Bultmann has failed to make a sufficiently sharp distinction between pre-scientific and permanent myth.

Permanent myths are those which describe some meaning or

reality, which is not subject to exact analysis but can nevertheless be verified in experience. The experience which verifies it is usually in the realm of history. (SDH, p. 110)

In *Self and Dramas* Niebuhr becomes even more lyrical about the free market than he was in *Irony*. A free economy 'has released energies for production which no moral or political control' (SDH, pp. 215–16) could have achieved. It has 'harnessed' self-interest rather than suppressed it, and created a system of mutual services through a competition of interests.

Another significant change of tone is to be found in Niebuhr's assertion that possibilities of evil are dependent upon the extension of some 'good'. In earlier works he was always swift to assert that eschatological symbols are embarrassing when taken literally. But now Niebuhr actually uses contemporary facts of experience to support his interpretation:

> The antinomies of history are not caused by the inertia of nature against the freedom of the spirit. They are therefore not overcome by man's gradual triumph over nature. They grow with that triumph so that the most explicit evil, the 'anti-Christ', appears just at the end of history. One need hardly analyse our current perplexities and the perils of tyranny and atomic destruction to prove that this incredible hope [the Parousia] for the end of history is more in accord with actual experience than the alternative hopes which have beguiled, and then disappointed past generations. (SDH, p. 256)[2]

The contradiction that positive validation of a symbol means appealing to facts which indicate a move towards the literal destruction of meaning, life, history, and nature, while at the same time insisting that the symbol cannot be understood to possess a literal dimension, is a theme which shows some further development in *The Structure of Nations and Empires* (1959).

SUPERPOWER HISTORY

Niebuhr's first book on history was the history of America; his second was the history of the world. At the end of the 1950s, Niebuhr published the history of civilization. A grand venture required a grand title, and it was subtitled: 'A study of the recurring patterns and problems of the political order in relation to the unique problems of the Nuclear Age'. According to Richard Fox, T. S. Eliot at Faber and Faber had urged the American editor, L. H. Brague, to go for something simpler like 'Nations and Empires'.[3]

The long fascination which Niebuhr had for first Spengler's, and later Toynbee's, efforts to write the history of civilization, coupled with his interest in the possibility of forming a world community under the auspices of the US conception of democracy, prompted him to turn his hand to a similar venture. However, his stroke had impaired his ability to work: he soon became exhausted and for much of the time he was severely depressed. He wrote to the historian Arthur Schlesinger Jr for help. 'I don't feel I have enough historical knowledge for the chapter', he confessed.[4]

Niebuhr felt that if permanent patterns existed in the anatomy of community which could be discerned in such diverse communities as the tribe, the city-state, and the ancient and modern empires, then the detection of these patterns should be of assistance to the hegemonic role of America in its bid to shape a world according to its wishes. It was an extension of his earlier theology of America which argued that the myth of the Atonement revealed that modern democracies like the American model were most in accord with the law of life, that they had grown through 'common grace' or providence, and that the truth of the Atonement, when followed, would guide the collective realm towards creative activity rather than oppressive activity, thus avoiding the sin of pride (imperialism) or the sin of sensuality (isolationism). The ostensible aim of the book was

> to describe the historical constants and variables in the dominion of nations and empires in order to put the struggle between two nations, both with power of imperial proportions, in its proper setting. (SNE, pp. 8–9)

But in addition to assisting the exercise of US hegemony, it was also necessary to gain an important historical perspective on Communism.

> One of the most pressing problems facing the democratic nations is the formulation of policies which are favourable to the gradual disintegration of the Soviet Empire. (SNE, p. 252)

The study was also intended to gain further knowledge into the nature of the 'autonomous nation' in its relation to super-national communities, and to acquire a deeper knowledge into the nature of State legitimation. America's problem is that it wields imperial power, but it is informed by an anti-imperialist ideology (p. 12). It roars like a lion, but in its own image it is as meek as a lamb.

The basic method of study is to investigate the various collectives which have appeared in the history of the world in relation to what the myth of Creation reveals about human nature in the collective dimension. That is, just as the human individual is both an image of God and a creature, possessing transcendent freedom yet involved in the flux of nature, so too the structure of the human collective consists of both 'dominion', the product of transcendent freedom, and 'community', the product of involvement in the flux of nature. Dominion represents the vertical dimension of cohesion inherent in central authority, and community represents the horizontal, organic dimension of collective life. 'Dominion' and 'community' are equivalent to 'artefact' and 'organism' in *Self and Dramas*. Nations and empires are studied for the light they shed on how they balanced rational and organic factors in the establishing of cohesive societies.

However, the whole thesis is informed by a simple idea that autonomous nations grew as a result of defiance of the universalistic temporal claims of the mediaeval church, and modern nations are described as either 'autonomous' or 'victims of the Communist empire' (SNE, p. 181). The most interesting (and most persuasive) sociology of the composition of the modern world is that of Immanuel Wallerstein and the 'World-System Analysis' school.[5] Their working model is based on the idea that States are created institutions which reflect the needs of class forces operating in the world economy. They do not emerge as isolated, autonomous, entities which then engage in relationships with other States. They arise within the framework of an inter-State system performing a function within a world-economy. This system constitutes a set of constraints which limit individual State machineries in their ability to make decisions. Niebuhr's work in the early 1930s shows evidence that his thinking could have developed along these lines, but in the end he abandoned this monistic model in favour of pluralism, and the only Marxist element which remained in his thought was to do with the necessity of some State ownership of the forces of production.

The sociological inadequacy of Niebuhr's model becomes apparent for example when he investigates the factors which will assist the formation of foreign policy. Instead of analysing how foreign policy decisions are produced and gauging their effects by analysing a whole series of observable factors, he presents a historical study of how foreign policy decisions originate in the liberal tradition. He goes back to the French Revolution, then studies liberal nationalism, then the English tradition, and finally a brief survey of US foreign policy.

Its inadequacy is also apparent when he identifies the 'perennial' historical forces. There are two patterns which remain fixed. The first is 'the integral and autonomous nation' (SNE, p. 198). Niebuhr concludes that the idea of the autonomous nation has achieved universal acceptance. In fact this pattern of autonomous nationality is so universal 'it will finally prove a great hazard to the communist imperialism' (p. 198). The second fixed pattern is the pattern of alliance and co-operation between nations. Included in this category is 'the increasing economic penetration of weak nations by strong ones' (p. 199), and the operation of large companies which find it difficult to function within the political limits imposed by a previous age. The fact that these two 'patterns' contradict each other is not discerned by Niebuhr.

When he turns his attention to the Soviet Union, instead of studying its attempt to run an economy and create a buffer zone based upon the principle of State ownership of the means of production as a step in the direction of greater equality, he begins by describing it as 'a despotic and imperialist political system based upon implausible utopian illusions' (SNE, p. 217).

Finally, there exists in Niebuhr's work a contradiction which cannot be smoothed over by appealing to paradox. Niebuhr writes of the world community as an 'impossible possibility'. There are creative forces at human disposal capable of forming a world community. But because of original sin the possibility of evil exists at every creative level of achievement. Thus the world community is an ideal to be aimed at, but unrealizable. However, the destructive forces of evil are far more capable of destroying not only the hope of a world community, but life on the planet. If the destructive capacity is real does this not imply, on the basis of Niebuhr's theology, that the creative capacity must be real, and that it can only be real if somewhere along the line embarrassing literalism in interpreting the Parousia creeps in? Niebuhr is aware of this threat to earlier theological positions. On the arms race, he writes:

> The dimension is novel because, for the first time, the balance between the creative and destructive possibilities of the mastery over natural forces would seem to have been destroyed. The destructive possibilities are certainly more apparent and more imminent.

Furthermore, modern technical advances have set man's progress in techniques in a new light. Progress in this field is accomplished, as previously, through human agency, but it outruns human desires so that historical developments become more and more analogous to natural forces. (SNE, pp. 267–8)

This dilemma in Niebuhr's theology highlights a previous contradiction which had remained unnoticed because it remained undeveloped. He argued that in the prophetic interpretation it is axiomatic that the total human enterprise remains in opposition to God. On the other hand he interpreted the myth of the Antichrist as revealing that evil is always parasitic upon the good, it is always the corruption of some good, and that creative forces are always superior to destructive forces. It is of course impossible to imagine a situation where some good exists on a higher level than the evil of the Antichrist but still remains in opposition to God. Niebuhr's solution is to reverse the equation by suggesting, in a sense, that good is 'parasitic' on evil:

> The one remaining hope is that the recognition by both sides of being involved in the common fate of the nuclear dilemma may create the first strands of community which could be enlarged by various forms of mutuality. (SNE, p. 266)

Although *Nations and Empires* is more of a historical curiosity than a contribution to our understanding of the contemporary world it does raise interesting questions regarding the mythical method and sociological paradigms for characterizing the real world. The way Niebuhr dealt with the nuclear problem indicates that he is still operating within his theological framework. It is a theological framework which provides the sociological framework. Once a sociological paradigm is capable of supplanting the model Niebuhr used for social analysis, does this invalidate Niebuhr's theological method? Or does it simply mean that his interpretation of the myths requires updating? If there is to be a constant commerce between prophetic religion and the various disciplines as Niebuhr maintained, how is it possible to relate the basic paradigm of the World-System school to the mythical method? To answer these questions with the depth they require is beyond the scope of this book. These and other questions will be looked at briefly in Chapter 10, but for now it is enough to note that they are a sample of the intriguing questions arising out of Niebuhr's theology.

The critics disliked *Nations and Empires*, and after this book and its muted reception his literary output waned. He retired from teaching part-time at Union in 1960, although he did teach a course at Harvard during 1961 along with a political scientist, Paul Sigmund. The book of these lectures was published in 1969 as *The Democratic Experience*. Its theme was the problem of establishing democratic governments in Africa and South America. In 1963 he published another joint venture, with Alan Heimert, *A Nation So Conceived*. This slim volume repeated some of the arguments of *Irony*.

In 1965 he published a book of three essays, *Man's Nature and His Communities*. An interesting feature of this work is the autobiographical preface and the revelation that much of his theology has been a joint venture with his wife Ursula. Niebuhr's illness had restricted his pulpit performances, and church attendance as a member of the congregation had become boring for him. He began to understand the value of the more elaborate liturgy of the Catholic Church. In this preface he confesses that he has discovered new virtues in both Catholic and Jewish traditions. At this point he acknowledges Ursula's influence. From 1940 Ursula had taught Biblical Studies to classes containing Protestants, Catholics, and Jews at Barnard College, New York. Her teaching experiences and general theological knowledge were responsible for 'modifying [Niebuhr's] various forms of provincialism and homiletic polemics'. In his old age Niebuhr had become conscious of 'the spiritual and intellectual debt' he owed his wife. Her influence was such that he could write

> I know she is responsible for much of my present viewpoint and that it would be difficult for either of us to mark any opinion expressed in these pages as the unique outlook of one or the other. (MNC, p. 19)

Although he published the book in his own name, it was in effect a work of 'joint authorship'.

The three communities under consideration in these essays are the world community, the American community, and the religious community. The long essay on the world community contains an historical survey of classical, biblical, and Christian political and social thought. This leads into a discussion of the emergence of the Western democracies and the existence of the Cold War conflict between the American and Soviet hegemonies. The conclusion is similar to the one in *Nations and Empires* where Niebuhr considers that new dimensions of community arise out of threats to existence.

[T]he interests of the community of mankind are obliquely served by the concern of both contestants for their own survival. This universal community—the dream of Hebraic Messianism and Stoic universalism, the concern of idealists from Augustine and Dante to the French utopians—although not sufficiently organised to become the concern of practical statecraft, is brought into historical calculations and indirect concerns. (MNC, p. 62)

The contribution of the nuclear threat to the creation of the global community is considered to be 'the final ironic culmination of the dreams of the ages' and a 'final revelation of the incongruity of human existence' (MNC, p. 62).

The second essay primarily concerns racial prejudice and the civil rights movement in America. Niebuhr concludes that the problem will last for at least a century. The third essay makes the point that religious communities often tolerate social injustice, and social improvement is not usually the direct inspiration of the Christian community. Expressed in theological language, improvement in social conditions is often the product of 'common grace' rather than 'saving grace'.

Man's Nature and His Communities was Niebuhr's last book. However, he continued to write articles for various magazines and journals, notably editorials on the Vietnam war.[6]

Niebuhr's final years have been beautifully narrated by Richard Fox. He died quietly and peacefully at home on Tuesday evening, 1 June 1971.

NOTES

1   Richard Fox, *Reinhold Niebuhr: A Biography* (New York, 1985), p. 261.
2   Further reflections on this theme are to be found in 'Christ the hope of the world: what has history to say?' *Religion in Life* (Summer 1954). In this article Niebuhr explains why he is reluctant to press the argument:

>   We are living in an age in which the modern substitute for Christian eschatology, which was once so plausible, has become more fantastic than the Christian hope of the parousia of Christ. . . .
>   While the present seems a very strategic era in which to restore all parts of the New Testament faith which had become discredited and obscured, we need only to analyse the needs of our generation to recognize that it is not particularly redemptive to

approach a disillusioned generation with a proud 'I told you so' and a fanciful picture of the end of history, *or at least a picture which will seem fanciful to our generation*. [My emphasis]

3 Fox, *op. cit.*, p. 269.
4 Ibid., p. 268
5 Among the most important works of Immanuel Wallerstein are: *The Modern World-System* (New York, 1974); *The Modern World-System II* (New York, 1980); *The Capitalist World Economy* (Cambridge, 1979); *Historical Capitalism* (London, 1983); *The Politics of the World Economy* (Cambridge, 1984; see p. 33 of that book for the growth of the State system).
6 A survey of Niebuhr's changing attitudes towards the Vietnam war can be found in Ronald Stone, *Reinhold Niebuhr: Prophet to Politicians* (Nashville, 1972), pp. 191ff.

10

The Test of a Method

The one constant feature of Niebuhr's work is the theme that all knowledge must be situated ultimately in an ultra-rational framework. As his work developed he insisted that the primary myths of biblical religion, Creation, Fall, Atonement, and Parousia, provided the substance for this ultra-rational framework. The myths in the first instance expressed the experience of a community. The myths of Creation, Fall, and ultimate redemption were situated in the Jewish community. The myths of redemption were situated in the Christian community in relation to the Jewish myths. Thus Atonement and Parousia became a more explicit expression of the inchoate sense of redemption in the Jewish tradition. The myths were products of experience in community but they received their power then, and continue to exercise power now, because they relate to the deepest experience of human nature. This illumination of the deepest experience of human nature is termed faith, and faith is the response to 'special' revelation.

The four primary myths act as principles of interpretation of life and experience and they cannot be conflated or isolated. That is, the interpretation of each one depends on the interpretation of the other three. Some critics of Niebuhr have argued that anthropology is the fundamental key for interpreting his work, thus raising the myth of Creation to a primary interpretative status. Others have classified his work as neo-orthodox, which throws the balance in favour of the eschatological mythology. Others have placed the centre in Christology, thus elevating the myth of the Atonement to primary status. The correct approach is to observe that Niebuhr held all four

175

myths in a creative tension, but the Atonement provides the key to interpretation of all the myths.

The question arises: Why should these four myths be chosen out of all the myths in existence? Niebuhr's theology is itself an attempt to justify the choice. The interpretation which Niebuhr gives to these myths can be either positively or negatively validated. Positive validation consists of correlation with the various disciplines of modern knowledge. He insists that there must be a constant commerce between the truth as revealed in this mythology and the truths obtained in other fields of knowledge. The myths are tested by correlation with other knowledge. However, Niebuhr is always careful to assert that there can be no rational proof for faith. The truths of faith cannot be proved empirically, but they can be empirically tested.

Negative validation consists in the demonstration that all alternative mythologies or systems of knowledge contain vital flaws, misunderstandings, and errors, when they are brought into relation with the primary biblical mythology. Since Niebuhr holds the view that all knowledge is ultimately situated in an ultra-rational framework, one of his usual moves when faced with a system of knowledge is to project the logic of the system into the metaphysical and then to compare this projection with the biblical mythology. This exercise often involves an oversimplification of the system in question, and it is not difficult for people with knowledge in these areas to criticize the representation of the area.

Just as the mythology originated in community, so the existence of a community is an essential prerequisite for its preservation. It is necessary for the mythology to preserve its public character and it must not become subject to private caprice. Therefore a Church exists which preserves the mythology and its interpretation, and the principles of access to the mythology are codified in dogma. Dogma is one step towards rationalizing the mythology, and it consists of a series of rationally absurd statements which nevertheless set the parameters for interpretation of the mythology. Examples of rationally absurd statements which preserve the meaning of the mythology are the insistence that God is both three persons and one person, that Jesus is both human and divine, and so on.

The Atonement is the key to interpretation because of the way in which it expresses the paradoxical relationship between grace and sin, mercy and judgement. The myth of the Atonement reveals the pattern which is stamped on the historical process. The one certain element in this pattern is its uncertainty. The total process of history is under the judgement of God, but within that process there are moments of mercy and grace, which Niebuhr refers to as 'tangents of the eternal'. The prophetic role of the Church is to exhort strategies and policies which conform with what is known about the operations of grace and avoid what would lead to judgement. When centres of collective activity conform with grace they are creative, when they oppose grace they are oppressive.

SEARCH FOR THE CENTRE

Given the simplicity of Niebuhr's theological project and the relationship between this theology and the political philosophy which it informed, it is surprising that critics fail to appreciate what Niebuhr was trying to achieve. It was Paul Tillich, a colleague of Niebuhr's for twenty years at Union, who first narrowed the basis of Niebuhr's thought to the primary myths of Creation, Fall, Atonement, and Parousia.[1] But although he could see that Niebuhr's thought centred on this mythology, Tillich attempted to demonstrate in public what he had been attempting in private for many years—trying to convince Niebuhr that his own approach was more fundamental. For Tillich, the basic theological question is not about the activity of God in history and the human opposition to this divine activity. Instead Tillich argues that the basic theological question is the question of the being of God, and by that he means the whole question of being, the whole question of existing. Tillich describes this as a movement from epistemology to ontology. The ontological question is: What is being? Tillich pinpoints Niebuhr's basic theological premiss, and rejects it. Niebuhr responded to this attack by simply suggesting that the point at issue was the old question of the debate and conflict between philosophy and theology, reason and faith. Tillich considered that every theological assertion presupposed an ontological assertion about the nature of being. Niebuhr rejected this as a subordination of theology to philosophy and he negatively validated his own method by illustrating how Tillich's theology was inadequate because it fused Creation and Fall, upsetting the creative balance which must be maintained between the myths.[2]

Despite the fact that Tillich correctly located the centre of Niebuhr's theology, critics have not used this insight with any consistency. Many have probably been sidetracked by Paul Lehmann's discussion in the same volume as Tillich's, and, it must

177

be hastily added, by Niebuhr's response which seemed to condone Lehmann's interpretation.[3] Lehmann attempts to gather Niebuhr's thought around the myths of Incarnation and Atonement, the branch of Christian theology known as Christology. According to Lehmann, Niebuhr once remarked that his theology was nothing more than an analysis of the truth about *Christus pro nobis* and *Christus in nobis*, Christ 'for us, on our behalf' and Christ 'in us'. The Christological fulcrum is not obvious, remarks Lehmann, but Niebuhr's own key has 'provided a fresh and rewarding discovery of an intrinsic unity. Christology is the leitmotiv of Reinhold Niebuhr's theology.' Having established Christology as the basis of Niebuhr's thought, Lehmann has to explain why there is no Christology in Niebuhr's work before 1937 and *Beyond Tragedy*. He concludes that the Christology is 'concealed', but *Beyond Tragedy* marks the turning point because the biblical view is explicitly affirmed and the significance of the Cross is asserted. Up to *Beyond Tragedy* the Christological theme is *Christus in nobis*. It is only with the switch to *Christus pro nobis* that the Christological centre becomes apparent. According to Lehmann the central concern of *Nature and Destiny* and *Faith and History* is to show how the Cross expresses the transcendental reality of Christ (*pro nobis*) and the transforming power of Christ (*in nobis*) in human nature and destiny, which is to say that the central concern of both works is an exposition of the Atonement and its anthropological corollary, justification by faith. Lehmann therefore concludes that Niebuhr has returned via the *Christus pro nobis* to the *Christus in nobis*. He puts it this way:

> Starting from the *Christus in nobis*, Niebuhr discovers the *Christus pro nobis*. Then he insists that the *Christus pro nobis* can be correctly stated only with reference to the *Christus in nobis*.

Lehmann then wonders why no one else has thought of this among Niebuhr's critics. Why has this Christological key not been discovered? The answer is that there is 'a particular oversight in the movement of ideas from the *Christus in nobis* to the *Christus pro nobis* and back again'. This oversight is Niebuhr's failure to develop a trinitarian Christology. In the last analysis it is binitarian because the Holy Spirit is missing. In short, Lehmann subordinates Niebuhr's theological method to an interpretation of Christology. His analysis fails to understand the importance of the creative balance which must exist between all the primary myths and fails to explain why Niebuhr's thought appealed to practising Jews.[4]

Douglas J. Hall (a pupil of Niebuhr's) sees Niebuhr as a modern Luther translating the *theologia crucis* into contemporary contextual terms in the face of an American civilization which is governed by a *theologia gloriae* and which demands that religion provides 'the spiritual, attitudinal undergirding that is essential to the psychic maintenance of the American Dream'.[5] Hall compares Niebuhr to Moltmann, a more recent exponent of the tradition, who believes that *theologia crucis* is not a single chapter in theology but the key signature for all theology. In Niebuhr, Hall argues, the logic of the Cross 'informs every major statement'. Hall avoids use of the term 'myth', preferring 'paradigm' instead. 'The Cross of Jesus Christ is the paradigmatic centre of this whole mode of thought . . . and of course it is more than merely paradigmatic.' A more adequate basis for evaluating Niebuhr's work is necessary than that which can be provided by intellectual piety.

It has been demonstrated earlier that the myth of the Atonement is the key to interpreting the primary biblical mythology of prophetic religion. Ernest Dibble in *Young Prophet Niebuhr* correctly notes the importance of this myth but he does not attempt to analyse Niebuhr's work on the basis of this knowledge. He only refers to the myth in a loosely structured section dealing with a few randomly chosen myths. Dibble is merely listing symbols and he makes no attempt to indicate how they are interrelated in Niebuhr's work. The Atonement fits into Dibble's thesis like an optional extra.

A similar failure to distinguish between primary and subordinate symbols is found in an essay by Robert E. Fitch.[6] He notes the importance of the chapter 'As deceivers, yet true' in *Beyond Tragedy* where Niebuhr presents a concise formulation of his mythical method. Fitch lists the symbols but omits Christ as the Second Adam and Son of God, and he omits the Parousia and the attendant myths. In his list of symbols found elsewhere in Niebuhr's work, the 'Parousia' fits between 'the peeling of an onion' and a 'cedar of Lebanon', the 'Antichrist' sits between 'Woodrow Wilson' and 'a cake and its icing', and the 'Last judgement', which completes the list, follows 'an envious beauty and her rival'. While psychoanalysis of this list might illuminate the dark recesses of the critic's mind, the essay reveals nothing of Niebuhr's mind.

The most perceptive attempt to analyse Niebuhr's epistemology is to be found in Dennis P. McCann's *Christian Realism and Liberation Theology*. He picks up three-quarters of Tillich's observation about the mythological base by showing how Niebuhr's method can be reduced to an analysis of Creation, Fall, and Atonement. However, McCann's failure to locate the importance of the Parousia and attendant myths leads to some distortion in the presentation of Niebuhr's theology.

THREE CRITIQUES

Some criticisms of Niebuhr's work are the consequence of his superficial treatment of a position in order to slot that position into his classificatory scheme of biblical mythology. For the most part these critics are sniping at various facets of his theology. But there are three criticisms which strike at the heart of his theology, and it is interesting to see how his theological method copes with these attacks. Niebuhr's theology has been accused of being firmly rooted in patriarchal ideology, his ethics have not been considered Christian ethics, and his theology has been labelled as a 'theology of the establishment'.

In *Sex, Sin, and Grace*, Judith Plaskow makes the point that Niebuhr's doctrines of sin and grace focus upon aspects of human experience which are more likely to be associated with the experience of men rather than women. Since Niebuhr claims to be speaking about the human situation, this one-sided theology needs to be informed by the experience of women. The net result is that Niebuhr's theology is unwittingly supporting a patriarchal society. More specifically Plaskow makes the point that although Niebuhr has defined sin as both sensuality and pride, in his subsequent analyses he loses sight of the former and concentrates too much on the latter. He fails to expand on the sin which is associated with the human flight from freedom. According to Plaskow this is predominantly woman's sin, the failure to have a self and to take on the responsibility of becoming one. Her self is dissipated tending to her husband, caring for her children, and in keeping the house clean and tidy. By arguing that self-assertion is sinful and applying this universally, Niebuhr is supporting the patriarchal order of society. Furthermore, when Niebuhr does mention the sin of sensuality he undervalues human creatureliness. The experience of pregnancy and motherhood is at once an experience of enrichment and injury, an experience of both dependence and affirmation of the human condition, a unique and dramatic experience of human existence as both nature and spirit, of transcendence through the vitalities of nature.[7]

Similarly, Niebuhr's presentation of grace does not answer to the experience of women. The sacrificial love revealed in the Cross of Christ only answers to the sin of pride. Niebuhr does not develop a theology of grace which corresponds with the sin of sensuality. Plaskow locates the source of this problem in Niebuhr's failure to provide a description of sanctifying grace which in turn is the consequence of the lack of an ecclesiology, a doctrine of the Church as a community of grace. The concept of grace as shattering an already shattered self is not a realistic proposition. It is only relevant to a self that readily asserts itself. Again, argues Plaskow, it is a theology which merely reinforces patriarchy. Niebuhr's theology fits into an environment which has been shaped by centuries of male arrogance.

Plaskow's critique of Niebuhr's concept of grace is more damaging than the critique of his concept of sin. In the latter it is a failure of emphasis, in the former a failure of omission. Here Niebuhr's interpretation of the Atonement is brought into question. It will be seen later that this omission is related to Niebuhr's weakness in his theology of the resurrection of Jesus.

A second critique of Niebuhr's work challenges the assumption that he has developed a Christian ethic. Stanley Hauerwas, in clearing a space for his own approach to Christian ethics, has felt it necessary to resist Niebuhr's approach to the subject. Hauerwas argues that Niebuhr continued the most important theological and social presuppositions of the Social Gospel movement. Like them, 'he never questioned that Christianity has a peculiar relationship to democracy'.[8] For Niebuhr and the Social Gospel movement the subject of Christian ethics was America. Despite the fact that many associated Niebuhr with the neo-orthodoxy of Bultmann, Barth and Brunner, he continued to be a liberal theologian. He never shared Barth's theological rejection of liberalism. Hauerwas, having linked Bultmann with neo-orthodoxy, then compares him with Niebuhr in the same paragraph. Both Bultmann and Niebuhr continued liberal theology's presupposition that theology must be grounded in anthropology.

It is Hauerwas's contention that if theologians are to contribute to reflection on the moral life 'they will do so exactly to the extent they can capture the significance of the church for determining the nature and content of Christian ethical reflection'. This is because

Christian beliefs about God, Jesus, sin, the nature of human existence, and salvation are intelligible only if they are seen

181

against the background of the church—that is, a body of people who stand apart from the 'world' because of the peculiar task of worshipping a God whom the world knows not. This is a point as much forgotten by Christian theologians as by secular philosophers, since the temptation is to make Christianity another 'system of belief'.[9]

The proof that Niebuhr's ethic is not Christian is located in the fact that many of Niebuhr's contemporaries were attracted to his account of the human condition without sharing his theological convictions. If ethics were properly Christian it would be impossible to accept them without becoming a member of the Church and sharing Christian beliefs. Niebuhr attempted to demonstrate the intelligibility of theological language through its power to illuminate the human condition. Those who accepted Niebuhr's social theory were not making a mistake because he never clarified the relationship between ethics and theology.

However, Niebuhr thought of the Church as the Body of Christ, as a community of grace, as the leaven in the social fabric, a concept which was developed by the Catholic Church at the Second Vatican Council. Hauerwas's conception of Christian ethics would have been strongly criticized by Niebuhr, picturing church communities as little 'islands of neutrality'. Niebuhr's Christian ethic called for the US to support Britain in its fight against Hitler. Where would Hauerwas's Christian ethic have stood in this crisis? Hauerwas writes:

> Those who are violent must be resisted, but resisted on our terms, because not to resist is to abandon them to sin and injustice. Such resistance may appear to the world as foolish and ineffective for it may involve something so small as refusing to pay a telephone tax to support a war.[10]

A third critique of Niebuhr's theology tries to answer the question about his identity as the 'Establishment theologian'. It has been mentioned earlier that Niebuhr figures prominently in a textbook of the Cold War by the 'revisionist' historian Walter LaFeber. According to LaFeber:

> Niebuhr's work . . . provided a historical basis and rationale for the tone, the outlook, the unsaid, and often unconscious assumptions of these years.[11]

By 1952 Morton White was writing in the *New Republic* that

Niebuhr's views formed 'part of the canon of a new generation of American liberals and the spiritual guide of those who are now revisiting conservatism'.[12] However, LaFeber did notice a change of tone in Niebuhr's work around this time. Niebuhr was against extending the Cold War. A combination of factors such as the Russian atomic bomb, McCarthyism, the Truman administration's dedication to remoulding Europe, and the fear that a Republican administration might commit the ultimate transgression, led to a softening of his position. But by the early 1970s these fine nuances of opinion and policy were too opaque to be noticed from the perspective of liberation theology. In an argument conducted in the pages of *Christianity and Crisis* (1973) the Latin American liberation theologian Rubem A. Alves considered that Niebuhr's Christian realism was nothing more than American ideology decked in religious symbols.

Dennis P. McCann in *Christian Realism and Liberation Theology* questions whether this 'ideological drift' in Niebuhr's work is a natural corollary of Niebuhr's theology or whether it is a case of misunderstanding his paradoxical vision and the misapplication of his principles. McCann notes that in the Cold War Niebuhr appealed to policy makers for humility and restraint, but by the early 1960s he was recommending a new activism in seeking to extend democracy to the Third World, and in this the principles of Christian realism seemed indistinguishable from American moral idealism.

McCann locates the fundamental problem as the relationship between Niebuhr's theological anthropology and his theology of history. Niebuhr tries to relate anthropology to history by a process of metaphorical extension. This means that concepts which are used to define the self can be used to define society as a whole. McCann accepts that these concepts might be psychologically illuminating, but they are less adequate as a framework for social theory. Anthropological insights can be used as a guide for politicians and social activists but they cannot be used to construct a model of 'national character'. Such a concept obscures processes of social conflict.

Niebuhr's theology was successful for a while in America because it did produce 'a public discourse that allowed some kind of popular participation in foreign policy decisions'[13] but it became part of that reality and it was unable to provide for later developments. McCann wonders whether or not it would have been possible for Niebuhr, if he had not been ill, to provide a perspective on the Vietnam problem without dismantling his theological framework. McCann concludes that Niebuhr's anthropological model is based on the successful urban American of his day and that is why the emphasis is on self-restraint and self-criticism. But this self is not the only personality type. Those who are oppressed tend to be submissive, and to advocate self-restraint and self-criticism for the oppressed is nonsensical. McCann therefore arrives at similar conclusions in the consideration of class relations to Plaskow's conclusions in consideration of gender. McCann argues that the theological framework does not need dismantling because the anthropological insight of sin as sensuality could be developed.

McCann also exposes both strength and weakness in Niebuhr's position by comparing it with liberation theology, particularly that of the Peruvian Catholic priest Gustavo Gutiérrez. The Christian confession of faith that God acts in history is interpreted by the two theologians differently. McCann *thinks* that Niebuhr says 'God acts in a hidden manner through human agents who have opened their hearts to him in repentance, humility, and faith'.[14]

By contrast Gutiérrez does not consider that God is hidden. He is directly manifest in the struggles of the oppressed. The paradigm of God's historical activity is the Exodus showing that God espouses the cause of oppressed peoples. The meaning is hidden only for those who fail to act in solidarity with the oppressed. From the point of view of liberation theology Christian realism's ahistorical anthropology means that the biblical narratives are read for wisdom and not for the hope they proclaim for the oppressed in history. The myths of Creation and Fall are not read in terms of the Exodus paradigm as they are in Gutiérrez. They are not seen as initiating history in Gutiérrez's sense. The weakness of Christian realism is its ahistorical approach, but its strength, according to McCann, is that it is more open to biblical criticism than Gutiérrez's use of the Exodus paradigm. Niebuhr might well have pointed out that the Exodus myth cannot be seen in isolation from the military possession of the land. God might have rescued oppressed people from Egypt but what can be made of Samuel's instruction to Saul?

> Now go and smite Amalek and utterly destroy all that they have; do not spare them, but kill both man and woman, infant and suckling, ox and sheep, camel and ass. (1 Sam 15:3)

McCann's point that Niebuhr's analysis of post-war America hides the class conflict within society cannot be faulted. By 1955 the New Deal era was considered to be the development of the social and economic strategies which *perfected* justice in the dynamics of a technical society by equalizing power in both the economic and the political sphere. (SDH, p. 178; my emphasis)

Niebuhr even managed to call people 'consumers' (SNE, p. 254) by 1959! However, Niebuhr's theology of collective destiny cannot be entirely described as 'metaphorical extension' of individual characteristics. There is a section in *Faith and History* where he asks the question whether such extension is possible and helpful.[15] But Niebuhr's main understanding of collective destiny is derived from his theology of the Parousia and attendant myths, conveniently ignored by McCann in his description of Niebuhr's mythical method. Niebuhr argued that historical patterns are not woven by those who sought consciously to weave them. Eschatological mythology illuminates truths about collective destiny quite apart from any metaphorical extension. The fact that it was democracy which survived the Depression and the war is a clear indication that democracy enjoys God's favour. It is a system which possesses structural contrition, and it is capable of both harnessing and checking self-interest. This being the case, it seems obvious to Niebuhr that to work towards the extension of democracy throughout the world is to work in accordance with the will of God ensuring a creative period for the world, a world under grace rather than judgement. Since America is the hegemonic power America's role is clearly mapped out. The fact that Niebuhr's thought moves in this collective dimension apart from metaphorical extension is a fact overlooked by McCann. This also answers McCann's mistake about the locus of God's historical activity. 'God acts in a hidden manner' means that God acts in history regardless of those who feel they are weaving historical destiny. Those who have opened their hearts in repentance, humility and faith are those who can see what is hidden to the rest.

NIEBUHR AND THE NEW RIGHT

It often happens in public life that support from one quarter is more dangerous than criticism from another quarter. Such is the case with Michael Novak's call for a reappraisal of Niebuhr. In his book *The Spirit of Democratic Capitalism* Novak aligns himself with a movement which is generally known as the New Right. This tendency emerged in the late 1970s as a response to what it considered to be the weakness of conventional pluralism. Political parties vying with each other for votes by bribing the electorate, and the involvement of too many interest groups influencing State activity, are seen as causing an overburdened heavily bureaucratized State structure. The New Right seek to redress the balance by concentrating on the needs of the individual citizen. The movement has adopted the neo-classical economics of people like J. M. Clark, F. Y. Edgeworth, I. Fisher, A. Marshall, V. Pareto, L. Walras, and K. Wicksell. It is against excessive State growth and seeks to limit State budgets.

Seen from the world-system perspective developed by Immanuel Wallerstein, the New Right would be an ideology to support the nature of the present phase of the capitalist world-system. Command economies, and extensive State involvement in the economy, could have been considered necessary once to support the system when the contradictions of capitalism took on a blatant form almost to the point of collapse, but now states lack the required flexibility to deal with capital's capricious nature. In fact, the latest phase of the world economy is revealing that command economies are roughly equivalent to large holding companies unable to compete effectively in the world system. The New Right provides the ideology in the West for the break-up of State involvement. In the Communist bloc, the same phenomenon is known as 'perestroika'.[16]

Given that the function of the New Right is to provide an ideology for the latest phase of capitalism, it has to be powerful enough to justify the increasing inequalities in the world-system between the core nations and the nations of the periphery, and within core states between the rich and the poor. For this reason some in the New Right feel that religious respectability will help to smooth over the contradictions. It is in this context that Novak's call for a reappraisal of Niebuhr should be understood.

Niebuhr is needed again, to penetrate the utopianism, perfectionism and moralistic passions sweeping through our highly educated and religious classes as they did when Niebuhr first wrote. Niebuhr is needed because so many uncritically accept the oppressed of the Third World as a messianic force, attribute Third World poverty to US exploitation, discount the military threat to the West by an armed force greater than Hitler's, and resume again the attacks of the 1930s on

186

'concentrations of economic power' in the multinational corporations.[17]

Novak implies that the movement in Niebuhr's thought mirrors his own development, and Niebuhr would be, if he were alive now, a supporter of 'democratic capitalism'. Novak's presentation of Niebuhr is fair—he does not make the claim that Niebuhr had already moved so far to the right. The question is: Does Niebuhr's theology offer support for Novak's worldview?

In the early 1930s Niebuhr's theology of the Atonement in the collective dimension taught that it was better for a dying social order to yield to the force of judgement in history. Yielding was equivalent to repenting and repenting would ensure mercy, and mercy would ensure that the virtues of the dying social order would not be eliminated. When the threatened judgement did not materialize from this direction, and the West survived Depression and war, Niebuhr argued that the particular form of Western society which had emerged without the conscious design of individuals or groups was an example of 'grace'. The centre of power and the balance of power which must exist in all collectives was more perfectly attuned to social justice than in any alternative social order. The central authority of the State regulating a competition of private capitals and interest groups possessed structural contrition within the system. On the basis of this theology it is difficult to imagine how Niebuhr could have thought of the New Right as anything other than the latest example of 'hubris'. If, on the other hand, Novak's ideas are mainly to do with the necessary repairs in order to maintain US hegemony, and the continued function of the capitalist system, then they do not contradict Niebuhr's later theology.

MARX AND THE BIBLE

The criticisms of Niebuhr's work by McCann and Plaskow raise two important questions regarding his theology. First there is the question of the value of a social analysis of a capitalist system which completely rejects Marxist social philosophy. Second, there is the question of the value of the 'mythical method' without a deeper analysis of the biblical source of the mythology. These two questions are not unrelated because together they raise a third: Is it possible for Marxist social analysis to contribute anything towards an understanding of the biblical mythology employed by Niebuhr?

Strictly speaking Niebuhr did not reject Marxism; he never really embraced it in the first instance. The most that can be said is that for a time he held the view that the social ownership of the means of production was more conducive to social justice than to continue its private ownership. This idea expressed itself in Niebuhr's work as nothing more radical than Clause Four of the British Labour Party constitution. His total repudiation of Marxism was supposedly on pragmatic grounds. The Russian experiment proved it did not work, and the experience of America during the Depression proved that social justice could be obtained apart from Marxist prescriptions. The problem with this line of argument is that Niebuhr should have rejected Christianity on the same grounds. Niebuhr himself had documented examples of the tyranny of Christianity. His mythical method was a search for the pure biblical mythology because all historic realizations of the mythology were corruptions of the truth in the mythology. Also, the achievement of a tolerable level of social justice in industrial society had small reason to be thankful for Christianity. A study of nineteenth-century labour struggles in Britain, for example, provides gloomy reading for Christians. There were a few individuals and small groups of socialist Christians who survive with honour, but for the most part the Christian establishment took the side of capital and land against labour. The working classes were, by and large, on their own.

But Niebuhr was not consistent, he did not reject Christianity. Furthermore he did not repudiate Marxism because of errors in social analysis. He claimed this as a reason but he never produced any analyses of the Marxist concept of the tendency of the rate of profit to fall, he did not question the morality of a system based on the appropriation of surplus value, and he did not question the Marxist concept of alienation. He rejected Marxism because he regarded it as a Christian heresy. It was a false religion, a secularized Christian or Jewish apocalypse. Second, his interpretation of grace showed that Western democracy was a social order which reflected the truth in the myth of the Atonement better than any other form of social order. Third, as a force of judgement Marxism had over-stepped its allotted function and was now being judged in turn by Western democracy. In short, he rejected Marxism because of Stalinism but he did not reject Christianity despite a whole catalogue of instances of tyranny in the name of the religion, its general lack of tolerance exemplified by its disintegration into countless sects, or its encouragement of anarchy through its naïve view of human nature (in its liberal Protestant form).

This raises the question: Would it be possible to derive a theory of the Atonement which was capable of incorporating truths about human nature which have been revealed by a Marxist analysis of social reality? If there is to be a constant commerce between the social sciences and prophetic religion such a task should always be on the agenda.

It was mentioned earlier that Niebuhr accepted Aulén's typology of Atonement theories (p. 111). Aulén's thesis that the 'classic' type of Atonement theory was predominant in the Bible, the early Church fathers, and Luther, but had since fallen into decline, has been influential.[18] It has been considered that the theory successfully combined elements of what used to be known as the objective and subjective Atonement theories. However, on close analysis, Aulén's claims for the classic type reveal that it is not a distinctive type, it has merely selected one particular eschatological symbol—the divine cosmic victory over the demonic—and brought it into relation with the Christ event.[19] The positive value in Aulén's thesis is to show that Atonement theories must harmonize with eschatological mythology.

Since Niebuhr accepted the classic type as a description of his own Atonement theory, and since it has been shown there are weaknesses in Niebuhr's understanding of the Atonement, what of the Atonement types rejected by Aulén? Aulén classified these as the Anselmian type and the Abelardian type, or the Latin type and the Subjective type. The former is based on the thesis by St Anselm of Canterbury in *Cur Deus Homo?* which asks the question: Why did God become man? The essence of the argument is that the merits of Christ's death were transferred to the human race because Christ was sinless and did not deserve to die a criminal's death on the cross. Christ was substituted for the rest of humanity. He acted as our representative. The latter type is derived from a younger contemporary of Anselm, Peter Abelard. He emphasizes Christ as the great Teacher who arouses responsive love in men and women. The Latin type became associated with mediaeval Catholicism, and the Subjective type with liberal Protestantism.

A modern revival of the Latin type of Atonement theory is to be found in *Jesus the Christ* by the German Catholic theologian Walter Kasper. Kasper maintains that any idea of the Atonement is inadequate if it does not deal seriously with Marx's understanding of humanity as a complex of social relationships. Anselm's theory achieves a new relevance because of the concept of social solidarity in which it is grounded. The idea of Christ as representative can be understood much more easily than any interpretation of Christianity provided by bourgeois individualism. Kasper's approach is an interesting alternative to Niebuhr's Atonement theory because Niebuhr's theory is used to invalidate Marxist social analysis, whereas Kasper's takes the Marxist concept of social reality as its starting point.

A more consistent attempt than Aulén's to relate the mythology of the Atonement with the eschatological mythology is exemplified in the work of Wolfhart Pannenberg. The most interesting feature of this theory of substitutionary Atonement is the continuing positive role of Israel, the chosen people.

> When one understands the universal human significance of the Jewish Law as the explicit formulation of the universally valid relation between deed and its consequences, as one form of the legal structure of the social life which is realized everywhere in different ways, then the Jewish people actually represent humanity in general in its rejection of Jesus as a blasphemer in the name of the law.[20]

Pannenberg also emphasizes the stark horror of the death of Jesus. He died 'excluded from the nearness of the God in whose nearness he had known himself to be in a unique way'.[21] This death signifies the horror of the separation of human life from divine life. The utter dereliction of the death is a symbol of the lostness of the human race. It follows from this that the verdict that Jesus must die is a verdict which issues from the lostness of the human race, and it follows from this that the ultimate symbol of the lostness of the human race is the rejection of the gospel. It also follows that if the Jewish people represent humanity in the rejection of Jesus and the rejection of Jesus is a symbol of the lostness of humanity, then the Jewish people are a symbol of the lostness of humanity. Their election to reject the gospel is the divine method of redeeming humanity, incorporating the principle of rejection into the redeeming activity. This type of theology turns the attention on the Jewish people, for the prophets taught that God could be known through the fortunes of historical Israel, whether they are escaping from Egypt, conquering the land, imposing an empire, being carried off into exile, and so on. The question has to be faced whether the Holocaust and the reconstitution of the state of Israel still fall within this sacramental or symbolic character of the divine activity. There is a passage in the Gospel of Luke which hints of a return to Jerusalem after an extensive period of Gentile domination.[22] It is one of the eschatological symbols.

Also, there is nothing in this theology which is antithetical to Paul's conception of the role of Israel in the Epistle to the Romans.[23] According to Paul the two earthly realities of the Church and Israel reveal that the Atonement is a process of transformation of humanity into the likeness of the Risen Lord, a transformation of humanity under Adam, mediated by Israel, into humanity under Christ, mediated by the Church. The Catholic dogma of the Assumption of the Blessed Virgin Mary supports this interpretation of the Atonement confirming the ultimate destiny of Israel and the Church and humanity. The symbol of Christ as the Second Adam is primarily a symbol of the transforming power of God and the first response is one of wonder at the magnitude of the vast redemptive process at work in the world. The gospel message is: Repent and believe this good news about the divine activity most perfectly realized in the Risen Lord. In Niebuhr the symbol of the Second Adam represents the ethical impossible possibility from the human point of view. In Paul's theology the Second Adam is a confirmation of the ultimate destiny of humanity. The philosophical consequence of this symbol is that for the Christian no definition of the human species can be considered adequate if it does not include the Risen Christ in the definition.

Finally, although Niebuhr did identify his theology of the Atonement with the classic type, his theory is more perfectly harmonized than Aulén's with biblical eschatology. Niebuhr avoided any description of the redemption which smoothed over the fact that the total historical process remains in opposition to God. The most explicit biblical statement of this concept which Niebuhr used is to be found in the central and pivotal section of the book of Revelation.[24] To bring out in full the implications of Niebuhr's theory requires an extensive exegesis of this section. The basic principle of interpretation is that the eschatology of apocalyptic literature is generally composed of a recapitulation of primordial mythology. This combination of ancient motifs and symbols from apocalypses such as the book of Daniel is used as a symbolical portrayal of the time of the end, the recapitulation of the sixth day of creation in a fallen world (666?). It is, in effect, a primitive form of the mythical method in that the early audience searched this wisdom for any points of contact or correlation with present reality. They wondered if the Roman Empire were the embodiment of this ultimate form of human development and expansion. It was seen earlier how the logic of Niebuhr's eschatology continually brought him face to face with this question of the end. Would it be a continuation of Niebuhr's method to seek positive validation in this interpretation of eschatological symbolism by testing for correlations with modern social scientific paradigms of the world system?

These intriguing questions are raised as a direct result of Niebuhr's methodology. This is the measure of his stature as a Christian thinker. Given a more positive understanding of the resurrection of Jesus, a deeper awareness of biblical exegesis, and a careful examination of the disciplines of the social sciences, it is possible to build on the theological foundations laid by Reinhold Niebuhr.

NOTES

1 Paul Tillich, 'Reinhold Niebuhr's doctrine of knowledge' in Charles W. Kegley and Robert W. Bretall (eds), *Reinhold Niebuhr: His Religious, Social, and Political Thought* (New York, 1956), pp. 35–44.
2 Reinhold Niebuhr, 'Biblical thought and ontological speculation in Tillich's theology' in Charles W. Kegley and Robert W. Bretall (eds), *The Theology of Paul Tillich* (New York, 1952).
3 Paul Lehmann in Kegley and Bretall, op. cit. (1956), pp. 251–80, and Niebuhr's reply, pp. 438–9.
4 A mark of the respect which the Jewish community had for Niebuhr can be gauged by the fact that Rabbi Abraham I. Heschel helped to officiate at the funeral.
5 A paper delivered at the conference: 'Reinhold Niebuhr reconsidered', King's College, London, 19–21 September 1984.
6 Robert E. Fitch, 'Reinhold Niebuhr's philosophy of history,' in Kegley and Bretall, *op. cit.* (1956), pp. 291–310.
7 For another example in support of Plaskow see the superficial interpretation of D.H. Lawrence in *Nature and Destiny* I, p. 253.
8 Stanley Hauerwas, *Against the Nations* (Minneapolis, 1985), pp. 31f.
9 Ibid., p. 42.
10 Stanley Hauerwas, *The Peaceable Kingdom* (London, 1984), p. 106.
11 Walter LaFeber, *America, Russia, and the Cold War 1945–1975* (New York, 1976), p. 48.
12 Quoted from ibid., p. 136.
13 Dennis P. McCann, *Christian Realism and Liberation Theology* (New York, 1982), p. 126.
14 Ibid., p. 200.
15 See *Faith and History*, pp. 244ff.
16 This view has been expressed recently in articles in *Pravda* and *Sotsialisticheskaya Industriya*, as reported in the *Financial Times* (6 December 1988), p. 1.

17 Michael Novak, *The Spirit of Democratic Capitalism* (New York, 1982), p. 332.
18 John Macquarrie praised Aulén in *Principles of Christian Theology* (London, 1966), p. 286.

> In recent years the classic view of atonement has been rescued from oblivion and its merits brilliantly vindicated by Gustaf Aulén. It seems to me to offer the most promising basis for a contemporary statement of the work of Christ.

19 The best criticism of Aulén's *Christus Victor* is by Gordon Rupp, *Christologies and Cultures: Towards a Typology of Religious Worldviews* (New York, 1974), partly because he provides a better method of classifying Atonement theories.
20 Wolfhart Pannenberg, *Jesus, God and Man* (London, 1970), pp. 262–3.
21 Ibid.
22 Luke 21:23–24, referring to the fall of Jerusalem (AD 70), writes:

> For great distress shall be upon the earth and wrath upon this people; they will fall by the edge of the sword, and be led captive among all nations; and Jerusalem will be trodden down by the Gentiles, until the times of the Gentiles are fulfilled. (RSV)

While this is not a positive reference to a Jewish return to possession of Jerusalem it is emphatically implied in the context. It must not be supposed that the writer is a clairvoyant receiving visions of the distant future; he is simply setting the theology in the received tradition of Jewish apocalyptic literature. The idea that repossession of the land, and in particular Jerusalem, would herald the dawn of the messianic age belongs primarily to the prophetic element in Jewish apocalyptic. The end of Gentile domination of the city is an eschatological sign for the world. There is a continuing debate about the origins of apocalyptic literature in Judaism between a setting in the type of groups which produced Wisdom literature, and those who produced the prophetic books of the Bible. One of the differences between prophetic literature and apocalyptic literature is to do with the history of Israel—in prophecy Israel is in sharper focus, while apocalyptic concentrates on the Gentile nations' rebellion against God. Just as the Exodus and Creation are linked in late Jewish prophecy, so too the return from exile and the messianic consummation are brought together. A good example is to be found in the book of Zechariah.

23 In 'Paul and the salvation of Israel: a perspective on Romans 9–11', *Catholic Biblical Quarterly* (July 1988) **5**, no. 3, 456–469, Mary Ann Getty substantiates the view that 'Paul is broadening his understanding of Israel to include the Gentiles, not attacking the fundamentals of Israel's theology', and she lists the literature related to this 'revolution' in Pauline studies.
24 The mythical representation of the total human enterprise in opposition to God is found in Revelation 13, and this is set within a section which links the myth of the Atonement with the Parousia. It is the central pivotal section running from 11:15 to 14:20. It would seem a

193

sensible thing to expect theologians who tackle the myth of the Atonement in relation to eschatology to refer to this section and to take some sort of positive attitude towards it. The general tendency among biblical exegetes is to lock up its interpretation with the Roman Empire and develop a few ahistorical platitudes about its modern relevance.

DEMCO